POLTERGEIST PARALLELS AND CONTAGION

REVISED EDITION*

Also by the Author

Ghost Hunter: True Life Encounters from the North East
In Search of Ghosts: Real Hauntings from around Britain
The South Shields Poltergeist
Ghost Taverns
Ghost Taverns of the North East
Haunted Newcastle
Paranormal North East
The Supernatural North
Haunted Durham
Ghosts at Christmas
Haunted Berwick
Haunted Northumberland
Haunted Tyneside
The Haunting of Willington Mill
Paranormal County Durham
Haunted Carlisle
Newcastle East Through Time
Haunted Wearside

This book is dedicated to the poltergeist, whatever you are, wherever you come from.

POLTERGEIST PARALLELS AND CONTAGION

REVISED EDITION*

Darren W. Ritson

*The first edition was titled Contagion:
In the Shadow of The South Shields Poltergeist

www.whitecrowbooks.com

Poltergeist Parallels and Contagion

Copyright © 2014, 2021 by Darren W. Ritson. All rights reserved.

Published in the United States of America and the United Kingdom by
White Crow Books, an imprint of White Crow Productions Ltd.

The right of Darren W. Ritson to be identified as the author of this work has been asserted by him in accordance with the Copyright, Design and Patents act 1988.

No part of this book may be reproduced, copied or used in any form or manner whatsoever without written permission, except in the case of brief quotations in reviews and critical articles.

For information, contact White Crow Productions Ltd.
by e-mail: info@whitecrowbooks.com

Cover Design by Astrid@Astridpaints.com
Interior design by Velin@Perseus-Design.com

ISBN: Paperback: 978-1-78677-177-3
ISBN: eBook: 978-1-78677-178-0

Non-Fiction / Body, Mind & Spirit / Parapsychology / Afterlife & Reincarnation

www.whitecrowbooks.com

'If one shared the belief of Miss Stewart, Virginia Campbell's teacher, that the poltergeist is an "obscure ailment", one might almost think that it is also contagious.'

~ **William G. Roll**, Author, *The Poltergeist*

'It is common for the poltergeist to follow its primary victims, who, as I have pointed out before, are probably causing the disturbances to begin with. But on rare occasions a poltergeist will also infest neighboring houses. Few poltergeist investigators are aware of this fact. Such events cannot be explained by the theory that the poltergeist focus is himself producing the effects. They indicate that the poltergeist is a much more complex phenomenon than many parapsychologists would have us believe.'

~ **D. Scott Rogo**, Author, *The Poltergeist Experience*

'Are Poltergeists contagious like diseases?'

~ **Maurice Grosse**, *Psychical Researcher And Investigator Of The Enfield Poltergeist*

'I had mentioned that some strange things started happening to Maurice Grosse, such as the episodes of his car engine, and the lost diamond ring – could the syndrome be contagious?'

~ **Guy Lyon Playfair**, Author, *This House is Haunted: An Investigation of the Enfield Poltergeist*

'Where responsiveness leaves and contagion takes over is not always clear, but the evidence is that poltergeists do have an element of contagion attached to them. Those involved find that they 'take a little home with them' after working in poltergeist infested houses.'

~ **John and Anne Spencer**, Co-authors, *The Poltergeist Phenomenon*

'Poltergeist phenomena can also behave like a virus, following the agent from house to house'.

~ **Dr Barry E. Taff**, AUTHOR, *Aliens Above: Ghosts Below*

'When we enter the world of poltergeist infestation, we shouldn't be too surprised to find evidence of contagion. We may not understand the mechanism, but it happens nonetheless'.

~ **Michael J. Hallowell**, CO-AUTHOR, *The South Shields Poltergeist*

'In effect, it could be said that the 'poltergeist syndrome' is actually highly contagious'.

~ **John Fraser**, AUTHOR, *Poltergeist! A New Investigation into Destructive Haunting*

PRAISE FOR *POLTERGEIST PARALLELS AND CONTAGION*

'The role of the serious independent paranormal investigator such as Darren W. Ritson is often overlooked and overshadowed by the lurid stories which regularly appear in the press and on social media. Such stories serve only to massage the ego of the investigators but contribute very little to extending our knowledge of people's experiences. In *Poltergeist Parallels and Contagion*, Darren W. Ritson is once again to be complimented on his diligence and the significant contribution he has made; sadly, both of which are now a rare thing amongst his fellow investigators'.

~ **Steven T. Parsons**, Author of *Ghostology: The Art of the Ghost Hunter*

'Read Nandor Fodor and William Roll to get the 'Poltergeists 101' perspective and learn the current 'politically-correct' hypotheses and models. Then read *Poltergeist Parallels and Contagion* to be faced with the undeniable realisation that poltergeists are much more inscrutable than we have ever been led to believe. They are intelligent, capricious, vengeful, plotting, tricksterish, and perhaps most disturbing, contagious. *Poltergeist Parallels and Contagion* may be the most important book written about poltergeists so far this century. Darren W. Ritson makes observations and connections that others have overlooked or ignored. The questions asked herein have potential solutions that may have a profound impact on our understanding of the poltergeist phenomenon and, more so, the nature of the very universe we live in'.

~ **Randy Liebeck**, Parapsychological Field Investigator, Media Consultant & Lecturer on Psychical Phenomena.

'This is a fascinating yet disturbing book. Ritson puts forward a cogent argument in relation to poltergeist cases actually being 'contagious' and provides evidence from cases he has personally investigated. He also cites examples of poltergeist contagion from case studies in the UK and overseas. It is unsettling, thoughtful, and well-written. I will certainly recommend it to my parapsychology students for reading and discussion'.

~ **Professor Nick Neave**, Lecturer in Parapsychology, Northumbria University.

'A most interesting book, one that challenges the readers with a novel and disturbing hypothesis deduced from direct personal experience with poltergeist activity'.

~ **Alan Murdie**, Former Head of the Spontaneous Cases Committee for the Society for Psychical Research

'An important contribution to our understanding of poltergeist phenomena'.

~ **Peter A. McCue, Ph.D.**

CONTENTS

ACKNOWLEDGEMENTS..XIII
AUTHOR'S NOTE...XV
FIRST EDITION FOREWORD...XVII
FOREWORD...XXIII
INTRODUCTION..1

PART ONE: POST SOUTH SHIELDS 5
   1. DEFINING MOMENTS 7
   2. PRINCIPLES OF CONTAGION..11
   3. SHADOWS 19
   4. INVESTIGATION AT JARROW 23
   5. POLTERGEIST PARALLELS 29
   6. THE HOUSE ON PALLISTER STREET 57
   7. CATALYST 61
   8. THE HAUNTED LOOM 71
   9. CONTAGION – LOCK STREET FRIENDS & FAMILY 77
   10. OUR CONTAGION..79
   11. TIME AND TIME AGAIN..87

12. I'M SICK OF THE BASTARD!..97
13. ECHOES OF LOCK STREET 109
14. THE INCUBUS – SUCCUBUS PROSPECT 123
15. MAYHEM IN MIDDLESBROUGH 139

PART TWO: FORWARD THINKING: PROBING THE POLTERGEIST... 149

16. STANDBY – THE POLTERGEIST POWER SOURCE?.................... 151
17. MY NAME IS LEGION, FOR WE ARE MANY 157
18. THE ENFIELD CASE, AND 'OUR' CASE PARALLELS 161
19. TEXTUAL INNUENDOES..173
20. CONTAGION: THE DESIRE TO SURVIVE.................................179
21. HISTORIC CONTAGION 187
22. A UNIVERSAL POLTERGEIST? 223
23. A FINAL THOUGHT..229

ABOUT THE AUTHOR 235
BIBLIOGRAPHY 237
INDEX 241

ACKNOWLEDGEMENTS

Enormous gratitude must go to Peter A. McCue Ph.D., for providing the new edition foreword, for proofreading the updated manuscript, and for his help during the final stages of preparation. To the late Colin Wilson, for kindly agreeing to write the first edition foreword for this book, and for his welcome advice and encouragement; to the late Guy Lyon Playfair, B.A. for supplying certain material and anecdotal accounts for inclusion in this work; to Alan Murdie and Steven T. Parsons of the Society for Psychical Research Spontaneous Cases Committee for their advice and input via many telephone conversations and discussions during the updating of this work. Thanks go to Paul Adams, for his friendship, guidance and advice in all matters concerning Harry Price; to American psychical researcher Randy Liebeck, for information in relation to the contagion events of both the Midwestern USA case (Minnesota), and the San Pedro Poltergeist case. Further thanks must go to Barry E. Taff Ph.D., for his kindness, and for allowing relevant text from his work to be reproduced; to Peter Johnson, secretary of the Society for Psychical Research for also allowing certain journal extracts to be reproduced herein; to Malcolm Robinson for sharing his 'contagion' event, and for allowing certain passages in his book, *Paranormal Case Files Vol One* to be reproduced. Thanks go to Darren Olley and Lesley Cottrell, for co-operating and generously supplying information regarding their experiences; to Derek* and Mandy* tenants of the house in Pallister Street for graciously allowing the researchers into their home to carry out the investigation. Doreen*, for sharing her personal account; thanks go to Drew Bartley, for his assistance in investigating the Newcastle poltergeist case; To Gemma O'Connor (née Gorner), for allowing us in to investigate her haunted flat in Newcastle, and of course thanks to Jo Risolino, Liz Mills, and Rosie Holliday (née Earl) for their co-operation during the investigation. To Paul Rook for sharing his experience regarding the tilting glass. Thanks to Freda* and Arnold Longthorne*, for their courage and co-operation; Kelly Barton* and Les McFallen*, for describing to Michael J. Hallowell their bizarre encounters; to Mark Winter for his kind assistance during the investigation at Newcastle and at Pallister Street in Jarrow; Minnie*, who was gracious enough to invite Michael to her home and share with him her disturbing experiences. To Paul McDonald, Curator of Newcastle Keep, for his kind support; Steven Taylor, for introducing the researchers to a number of new cases, which are detailed in this book; Stuart and Lauren Smith, for allowing Michael into their home to investigate the case of the Boldon Colliery poltergeist; To Tony* and Linda*, for giving the researchers the opportunity to investigate the strange phenomena at their home in Middlesbrough. To Victoria Nesbitt, her family and colleagues, for their co-operation during the investigation into the craft shop at Blyth – and, finally, I would like to thank my long-time friend and fellow researcher Michael J. Hallowell for accompanying me on this amazing journey into the unknown.

AUTHOR'S NOTE

Ironically, during the years 2020 and 2021, when one of the world's deadliest and infectious viral outbreaks in living history (Covid 19, Coronavirus) was relentlessly sweeping its way across the planet, sadly killing hundreds of thousands of people, at the same time making millions more seriously and gravely ill, Darren W. Ritson was at home, alone – in compulsory isolation and lockdown – working his way through *Contagion: In The Shadow of The South Shields Poltergeist* which was first published in 2014. The revised and updated manuscript is what you now hold in your hands under the new title, *Poltergeist Parallels and Contagion*. Although in 2014, Darren W. Ritson and Michael J. Hallowell shared the by-line for *Contagion*, you will notice that this version is under the name of Darren W. Ritson. This decision was made by both Darren and Michael in 2020 leading up to its re-naming and its re-publication and it is a decision that both Darren W. Ritson and Michael J. Hallowell are more than happy with.

As with the third edition of *The South Shields Poltergeist*, Michael J. Hallowell requested that his name be removed from the by-line for personal reasons, leaving Darren W. Ritson to *continue* to move onwards and upwards in relation to taking *both* works forward, and to continue to actively promote the research that we both carried out. Both Michael and I feel that we came up with some interesting and thought-provoking theories and ideas that must be carried forward – and, as it turns out, we are not alone in thinking this. It has therefore been the intention of Darren W. Ritson to update, refine, and add to the work. One chapter has been removed, whilst another chapter (Historic Contagion) has been added. A new edition foreword by Peter McCue Ph.D., sits alongside the late Colin Wilson's original first edition foreword, which remains in place as a tribute to him. This book was essentially written by *two* authors, with only the *one* taking it forward. Therefore, it stands to reason that I have left in Michael's name and his valuable contribution within these pages – after all, the first edition was a joint effort. Overall, the book text has been largely refreshed to suit the relevant and current situation, along with quoted material being *slightly* edited for presentational purposes only, although its meaning has not been changed. To avoid excess referencing within the main body of the text, sourced references to both books and journals can be found in the Bibliography.

The events related in this book are entirely true. However the names of some witnesses have been changed to protect their anonymity. Pseudonyms have been marked with an asterisk thus * at their first appearance.

Darren W. Ritson,
March 2020

FIRST EDITION FOREWORD

It was over forty years ago, back in 1969, that I wrote a chapter called 'The World of Spirits' in my book *The Occult*. In the years since then, I have probably unlearned as much as I have learned about the nature of the poltergeist, and even now would hesitate to say I understood it. But I would still say that the present book is as sound an introduction as any in existence.

The two researchers, Darren and Michael, are from Tyneside in the north east of England. It happened in the home of a young couple, Marc* and Marianne,* living in Lock Street, who had a son called Robert.* On one occasion, the entity dragged a chest of drawers out of Robert's bedroom on to the landing; on another, it hung his rocking horse by its reins from the ceiling. A large toy rabbit was found in a chair with a box-cutter blade in its hand. Obviously, the poltergeist wanted to create fear, and it succeeded. Ritson and Hallowell's book about the case, *The South Shields Poltergeist*, is not recommended for nervous readers late at night.

One of the basic questions that every psychical investigator faces is where the entity is getting its energy. In the 19th century, when many such cases were recorded, there seemed to be little doubt: it was from the fear of the victims involved. In a famous case in the Rue des Noyers in Paris, when the 'ghost' smashed all the windows and threw objects around, a medium (spirit-communicator) got it to admit that its energy came from the 'electrical nature' of a maidservant, who was providing it. The girl was apparently unaware of this; 'She was the most frightened of all', said the ghost.

This is an extremely interesting answer, since the investigators succeeded in ending the Lock Street haunting by getting the victims to switch off all electrical appliances at night. In the first part of the 20th century, most investigators concluded that poltergeist energy was sexual in nature, having noted how often there was a pubescent adolescent – labelled 'the focus' – in the haunted house. And the high esteem in which Freud was held in those days meant that the unconscious mind of the 'focus' tended to get blamed for the manifestations. It was a view that I also held when I wrote my book, The Occult. What changed my mind was when, in August 1980, I drove to Pontefract, in Yorkshire, to look into a poltergeist haunting that had started in 1966. Phillip, the son of the house, had just reached adolescence when pools of water began to appear on the kitchen floor. (Poltergeist phenomena often start in this way.) After a month or so it stopped, and started up again when the daughter of the house, Diane, reached adolescence. Then objects began to fly around, crockery was smashed, and Diane was often thrown out of bed by an invisible entity.

But it was when she described to me how the poltergeist had dragged her upstairs, with a grandmother clock on top of her, that I realised beyond all doubt that it wasn't her unconscious mind that was responsible, but some kind of 'spirit.' What kind of spirit? The researcher Guy Lyon Playfair, (with Maurice Grosse) of the classic Enfield Poltergeist, quotes a Dutch medium, Dono Gmelig-Meyling, as saying that the Enfield house was crowded with spirits from the local graveyard; in other words, the spirits of the dead.

Now, in a later chapter of this book, there are some other interesting suggestions made. A widow living in Ashington was also a medium, and had noticed that she wasn't alone in the house. The entity ran its fingers through her hair and would even caress her thigh in bed. A friend named Steven Taylor remarked that he was wondering whether the visitor wasn't a poltergeist but an *incubus*. Then there is the following interesting passage:

> The word incubus is Latin, and drawn from *in*, which literally means 'above' or 'on top of', and *cubo*, which means 'I lie upon', 'a burden' or 'a weight.' This in itself highlights the predatory disposition of the entity, which, according to legend, is said to be a sexually driven monster, which preys upon women. The female equivalent of the incubus is

FIRST EDITION FOREWORD

the succubus, who allegedly preys upon men in a similar manner. Supposedly, the incubi are demons of tremendous power and great age. They were even feared by the ancient Sumerians and Babylonians, who believed that they could also control storms, lightning and thunder. According to tradition, incubi constantly attempt to engage in sexual activity with women. Their reasons for this are two-fold. Firstly, they do so because they enjoy it, and secondly because engaging in sexual intercourse with human females is the means by which they procreate. During the act of intercourse, the incubus will draw or 'suck out' energy from its victim – energy upon which it feeds to perpetuate its own existence.

There are two prevalent theories about the nature of both the incubus and the succubus. In some traditions they are said to be two separate genders, male and female, in exactly the same way that humans are similarly divided. In other traditions, however, the concept is a little more complex. One Mediaeval view was that both incubi and succubi are genderless, and are merely two different presentations of the same entity. In other words, the entity will appear as either male or female depending on the type of sexual activity it wishes to engage in. Some scholars suggested that the demon would first appear as a succubus – normally in the guise of a voluptuous female – and have intercourse with its male victim when he was asleep. As soon as the victim ejaculated, the demon would then metamorphose into its male form, as an incubus, and select a female victim. During intercourse with the woman, the demon would ejaculate the sperm it had 'collected' from the male victim and the woman would become pregnant.

The child, although human in appearance, would actually be a demon in disguise that would then go on to promulgate the species in exactly the same manner as its parents. Even though the sperm used in this bizarre form of conception was taken from a human male and the mother was a human female, the resultant offspring was almost always a demon. However, sometimes the resultant offspring wouldn't be fully demonic but actually half-demon and half-human. Such hybrids were known as combions or cambions, and were believed to possess enormous supernatural powers. There are a number of different ways in which an incubus can, allegedly, be identified. When the demon engages in sexual intercourse with a human female victim, its penis is said to feel either incredibly cold or uncomfortably hot. In appearance, the incubus is said to take the form of a hideous dwarf with misaligned and deformed features. Some say that before it materialises in fleshly form it appears as a small but intense light that will dart through the air at great speed like a firefly, or as a metallic sphere.

In yet other traditions it is said to appear as a swan, a dog, a goose, a dragon or even a large fish. Dealing with an incubus is not easy, and over the millennia numerous defence strategies have been employed with varying degrees of success. In the Christian tradition, predictably, exorcism has been the preferred option. The Roman Catholic Church has said that attending confession may also be helpful, along with making the sign of the cross, which demons are said to dislike intensely.

Unfortunately, even thinking Christians have admitted that such tactics are basically useless. Testimony exists that incubi actually have no fear of exorcisms, couldn't give two hoots about the sign of the cross and, on occasion, have actually drunk holy water and spat upon the Bible in front of their victims. One of the most frightening beliefs regarding incubi is that, as previously stated, they "suck out" the life force from their victims. If an incubus is allowed to do this repeatedly, so it is said, the victim will endure a rapid decline in health and, eventually, die if the demon is not prevented from engaging in its rapacious behaviour.

Later, Investigator Michael Hallowell asks her: 'Have you ever seen elemental spirits in your garden?' to which the lady replies: 'Oh yes, there are elves out there – and gnomes.' This interested me because I am apparently one of the few writers on the paranormal who are willing to concede that such things may exist. In fact, chapter 5 of my book *Poltergeist* is devoted to fairies and elementals. One case that always impressed me is vouched for by my friend Lois Bourne in her book, *Witch Among Us*.

Lois is a 'witch' in the sense of possessing odd psychic powers, of whose reality I have not the slightest doubt. She is an extremely sensible and down-to-earth lady and, in her book, among many stories that psychical researchers will find credible enough, she tells a story that will obviously cause most readers to doubt her truthfulness. Staying on holiday at a cottage at Crantock, in Cornwall, she met another member of a Wiccan coven, and spent an evening at her home. The woman's husband, Rob, asked her if she would like to see a goblin. One appeared, he said, among the rushes of the millstream at Treago Mill

FIRST EDITION FOREWORD

every morning at sunrise, and if she wanted to see him, she had to be up early. The next morning Lois and her husband Wilfred joined Rob at the mill gate, and they crept up to the stream.

'I have never been able to decide, and still cannot decide, whether I really saw that goblin, or if Rob made me see it. Whatever it was, there, sitting on a stone calmly washing his socks, was an elfin creature with a red hat, green coat and trews, one yellow sock on, and one in his tiny hands in the process of being washed. I remember thinking at the time in my sleepy befuddled but practical way "what an atrocious colour combination". Suddenly he saw us and he disappeared... "Now do you believe me?" asked Rob.' I have known Lois for years. I may be gullible and she may be a liar, but I believe her. She is not the type to invent such a silly story. And neither is her husband Wilfred – who also saw it – the type to support a downright lie.

In short, I firmly believe that the world is full of living beings that are invisible to us, and the poltergeist is only one among many. Somewhere is this book Darren speaks of Michael's impatience with doubters, and I am reminded of a comment of William James's friend Professor James Hyslop, who said: 'I regard the existence of discarnate spirits as scientifically proved and I no longer refer to the sceptic as having any right to speak on the subject. Any man who does not accept the existence of discarnate spirits and the proof of it is either ignorant or a moral coward. I give him short shrift, and don't propose to argue with him on the supposition that he knows nothing about the subject.' These are words that every psychical researcher should learn by heart. Why is this book about Contagion? Because one of its basic arguments is that poltergeists are not 'one-offs', as researchers (including myself) used to assume, but seem to be capable of spreading like an infection – a startling idea new to poltergeist lore.

Colin Wilson
Cornwall,
May 2009

FOREWORD

In 2006, Darren W. Ritson and Michael J. Hallowell investigated a major poltergeist case in their home area, the north-east of England. They subsequently wrote a well-received book about it, *The South Shields Poltergeist: One Family's Fight against an Invisible Intruder*. In 2014, they published a sequel, *Contagion: In the Shadow of the South Shields Poltergeist*. In a review I posted to Amazon, I said that I regarded it as an 'important contribution to our understanding of poltergeist phenomena'. The present book is a revised and updated version by Darren. For personal reasons, Michael has stepped back from the field of paranormal investigation, although the two men remain friends. Furthermore, I understand that Michael is happy for this new version to appear under Darren's name alone. As the title implies, it's largely about poltergeist phenomena. It refers back to the South Shields case, which was Darren and Michael's 'big one', and discusses other intriguing cases that they investigated. The book also describes major poltergeist episodes, from both the UK and overseas, that were investigated by other researchers.

The word 'poltergeist' comes from German words meaning 'noisy spirit'. However, the notion that the phenomena are caused by discarnate human spirits is debatable. Poltergeist disturbances (or 'infestations', as Darren calls them) entail recurrent physical phenomena, such as banging and knocking sounds, the movement of objects, and the breakage of glass and crockery. This may sound like the paranormal equivalent of a mindless lout throwing things about. But poltergeist manifestations often display a high degree of technical mastery. For instance, in respect of one of the principal witnesses in the South Shields case, there was an occasion when a series of terrifying text messages was sent to her while she and Michael were conversing on the phone. Darren explains:

> The messages related to things that [she] had said just a split-second earlier in the conversation. It would have been physically impossible for a human being to compose even the briefest of text messages within such an incredibly short space of time, but the poltergeist managed it.

Poltergeist phenomena are typically associated with the presence of a particular living person (the so-called 'poltergeist focus'), often someone who is relatively young (e.g. a pubescent girl or teenager). Indeed, some researchers describe poltergeist manifestations as 'recurrent spontaneous psychokinesis', the assumption being that the phenomena are generated (most likely, unconsciously) by that person. To my mind, however, it's unwise to label phenomena in terms of an unproven theory.

Psychical researchers use the expression 'haunting' or 'haunt' to refer to recurrent paranormal phenomena associated with particular places rather than specific people (McCue, 2002). Haunt manifestations might be wholly *sensory* (e.g. sensing a presence, hearing footsteps, or seeing a ghostly figure), or they might include physical activity (e.g. the displacement of objects, opening or closing of doors, and disturbance of bedclothes). The phenomena might occur over years or decades – albeit, perhaps, intermittently. Poltergeist manifestations generally have a persecutory flavour, giving the impression that some entity or intelligence is *deliberately* giving the witnesses a bad time. In haunt cases, on the other hand, the phenomena, although creepy, might seem less 'personal'.

However, despite these differences, it's not always easy to draw a hard and fast line between hauntings and poltergeist cases. As in hauntings, apparitions are sometimes seen in poltergeist cases; and, as noted, physical phenomena (usually relatively minor) are often reported in cases considered to be hauntings. And although poltergeist cases are usually short-lived, some episodes have gone on for years. For instance, in Chapter 21, Darren outlines a case from Battersea in London that ran from 1956 to 1968. It was also the subject of a recent article by Ciaran O'Keeffe in the magazine *Fortean Times* (O'Keeffe, 2021).

At least a couple of the cases that Darren cites may have been hauntings rather than poltergeist episodes. For example, in Chapter 13, he discusses a case involving phenomena at a flat occupied by five female students in the Bigg Market area of Newcastle-upon-Tyne. There were overlaps with what happened during the South Shields disturbances, and this may well have been another person-centred poltergeist case, albeit of relatively low intensity. But it's not known whether manifestations occurred at the Bigg Market flat before and after the students were living there. In other words, we can't rule out the possibility that the flat was haunted.

In poltergeist cases, disturbances often follow the focal person or afflicted family from one place to another. This isn't said to be typical of hauntings, but it may occur from time to time and perhaps more often than is generally recognised. Rosie, one of the students at the Bigg Market flat, subsequently experienced ghostly phenomena at her mother's home in Cumbria. Before living in the Bigg Market flat, she'd resided in the South Gosforth suburb of Newcastle, but she didn't experience anything odd there.

Some years ago, a woman told me about low-intensity phenomena of the haunting type that had occurred in an old house that she'd occupied (McCue, 2003). She and her family then moved to a relatively new house, where there were further manifestations (although somewhat different from those at the previous house). Of course, it may be that, purely by chance, the family moved from one haunted house to another. Or perhaps my informant acted as a catalyst or 'focus' for phenomena at both locations. Alternatively, did 'something' at the first house 'follow' her and her family to the second one?

Various theories have been proposed to explain poltergeist phenomena and hauntings. A traditional notion (probably more popular with amateur 'ghost hunters' than with scientific psychical researchers) is that the phenomena are produced by 'earthbound spirits' – spirits of people who once lived in, or were associated with, the locations concerned (see, for example, Denning, 1996). Another conjecture (applicable to hauntings rather than poltergeist-type cases) is that events can sometimes leave an impression on a place, and can be 'replayed' at a later time, like a video recording. It's also been suggested that haunt and poltergeist phenomena may be a result of localised magnetic fields affecting people and equipment (see, for example, Budden, 1998; Roll & Persinger, 2001).

Regarding poltergeist cases, I've already alluded to the notion that a focal person may have a psychokinetic ('mind over matter') effect on his or her surroundings. From that perspective, the disruptive phenomena could be seen as entailing a discharge of pent-up emotion (most likely anger). But this implies that, in certain circumstances, someone's 'subconscious mind' (if there is such a thing) can produce a wide array of truly extraordinary manifestations. Another possibility – one that I'm inclined to give credence to – is that a very resourceful and tricksterish non-human intelligence may be at work in poltergeist cases and hauntings, and that it may be behind other anomalous activity as well (e.g. 'high strangeness' UFO phenomena and cattle mutilations). This idea seems similar to the notion of an 'arch-poltergeist' discussed by Darren.

Like its earlier version, Darren's book presents intriguing evidence of 'contagion', a process whereby poltergeist phenomena can spread out from the home of the principal witnesses and affect others, such as members of their extended family, or investigators. However, although people affected by contagion will probably find their experiences perplexing and frightening, it seems that the activity becomes diluted as it spreads. Darren and Michael speculated that contagion could be either 'active' or 'passive'. With the former, someone who is connected with the afflicted person or family would be *deliberately* targeted by the intelligence behind the phenomena. In passive contagion, however, the process would occur *automatically*, like accidentally catching a cold from a friend.

It appears that disturbances – or, at least, a transient negative effect – might sometimes result from the receipt of a physical item, such as a letter. That reportedly happened in a case that Darren and Michael investigated in Jarrow. It involved a couple – referred to, pseudonymously, as Derek and Mandy – who'd experienced paranormal phenomena at two successive homes. By the time that Darren and Michael became involved, the couple and their young daughter were living at the second of these homes. Derek had an unusual hobby: collecting memorabilia associated with notorious criminals. He'd apparently taken up this macabre interest more by accident than intention. To add to his collection, he wrote to some serial killers in the UK and the USA, thinking that if they responded, he'd have not only their autographs but also entire letters to accompany them. To his surprise, a number of these convicted killers replied.

Some came across 'like really nice people', but others were different. For example, one of them was initially 'really pleasant', but then – in a subsequent letter, I presume – he declared that he was going to arrange to have Derek killed! Not surprisingly, Derek was scared and didn't write back. But there was an incident that particularly intrigued Darren and Michael: One morning, a letter arrived for Derek, and, as he reached inside the envelope to extract it, the room suddenly felt icy-cold, and everything in it took on an icy, blue-white appearance. He had the feeling that he was surrounded by something totally evil. His wife and mother were present, and they, too, reportedly experienced the same thing. It transpired that the letter was from one of Britain's most notorious serial killers. This happened when the family were living in the second of the two homes, and this particular letter presumably wasn't responsible for the phenomena they'd experienced previously. But maybe Derek's possession of crime-related memorabilia was exposing him and his family to malign influences.

At points throughout this book, Darren refers to strange coincidences associated with anomalous phenomena. For instance, in Chapter 14, he refers to an occasion when one of the cuffs of Michael's dressing gown caught fire mysteriously while he was wearing it. That was the day after Michael and some others, including a medium, had visited the home of an elderly woman who was reporting odd phenomena (although not of a typical poltergeist type). Fortunately, Michael managed to extinguish the flames without incurring serious injury. Later that day, when he was speaking on the phone to the aforementioned medium, some food she was preparing started to burn, setting off a smoke alarm. That was before Michael informed her that his dressing gown had caught fire. Of course, in itself, this incident with the burnt food may have entailed nothing paranormal. But did the correspondence of events – the dressing gown catching fire and the food getting burnt – arise purely by chance, or was it somehow orchestrated by a mysterious intelligence? In the introduction to this book, Darren reminisces that he and Michael spoke of how:

> ... every paranormal investigator dreams of their 'big case'; a circumstance so bizarre and so verifiable that it truly seems to prove that the world is not just stranger than we know, but [...] stranger than we possibly can know. [We] well and truly stumbled across [our] 'big case' with the South Shields poltergeist.

In a similar vein, at the beginning of Chapter 14, Darren states:

> After [our] investigation into the South Shields poltergeist had drawn to a close [...I] wondered whether [we] would ever get such an opportunity again. Cases of that degree of intensity are incredibly rare, and [I] felt it unlikely that the gods would smile down upon [us] twice.

This raises an intriguing question: Did Darren and Michael's wish to get their teeth into major poltergeist cases help to engender the very phenomena they wound up investigating? In other words, did a 'cosmic joker' or 'arch-poltergeist' hear their wish for 'big cases' and then oblige them, by orchestrating poltergeist disturbances at a number of homes in their local area? More generally, it seems that when people investigate paranormal phenomena, their presence and interest may have a bearing on whether manifestations occur.

This reminds me of quantum physics, which deals with events at a very small (i.e. atomic or subatomic) scale. Events at this level seem to defy the rules that apply to the larger-scale world. Take, for instance, the famous 'double-slit experiment' (described by, for example, Al-Khalili, 2013). In essence, it works as follows: A stream of photons (particles of light), electrons, or atoms is directed at a screen with two small slits cut in it. Beyond this screen, there's a space and then another screen, which is fitted with detectors that can register where the photons, electrons, or atoms land. It turns out that if one of the slits is shut, the photons, electrons, or atoms arrive at the second screen as if they were bullets being fired from a machine gun. But if both slits are open, they travel through the apparatus like waves, which split into two sets of waves at the slits. An 'interference pattern' is then registered on the detector screen as a result of the peaks and troughs of the waves intersecting and enhancing one another or cancelling one another out. However, although an interference pattern appears on the detector screen, the individual photons, electrons, or atoms still arrive as 'pin pricks' (i.e. as if they were particles) – it's the distribution of these 'pin-pricks' that makes up the interference pattern. All this is quite strange, because it means that the nature of the phenomenon – whether the photons, electrons, or atoms behave like waves or particles before they reach the detector screen – depends on whether one or both of the slits are open. But there are other strange findings from the experiment. For example, if an extremely fast shutter closes one of the slits after a photon, electron, or atom has gone through the first screen, but before it has reached the detector screen, it travels like a bullet, not like a wave. It's as if the photon, electron, or atom 'knows', after having already passed through the first screen, that one of the slits has been closed. These effects are accepted as genuine by physicists but are inexplicable in terms of the old ('classical') physics. In short, it seems that the very process of trying to determine precisely what's going on at the quantum level at any given time may determine what happens.

However, there's a significant difference between what happens in the double-slit experiment and what's observed in poltergeist disturbances. In the former, the results (although strange) are always the same if the experiment is performed the same way. But in poltergeist cases (and with paranormal phenomena more generally), manifestations don't usually occur in a perfectly predictable manner.

In conclusion, I've little doubt that readers of this book will find the case reports fascinating and Darren's speculations very interesting.

References

Al-Khalili, J. (2013). Double slit experiment explained! https://www.youtube.com/watch?v=A9tKncAdlHQ

Budden, A. (1998). *Electric UFOs: Fireballs, Electromagnetics and Abnormal States*. London: Blandford.

Denning, H. M. (1996). *True Hauntings: Spirits with a Purpose*. St Paul, Minnesota: Llewellyn Publications.

Hallowell, M. J. & Ritson, D. W. (2009). *The South Shields Poltergeist: One Family's Fight against an Invisible Intruder*. Brimscombe Port, Stroud: The History Press.

McCue, P. A. (2002). Theories of haunting: A critical overview. http://www.richardwiseman.com/resources/theories-of-hauntings.pdf

McCue, P. A. (2003). Haunting phenomena at two successive homes. The Paranormal Review [a magazine of the Society for Psychical Research], Issue 26. Pp. 5-9.

O'Keeffe, C. (2021). The Battersea poltergeist. *Fortean Times*, 404 (April). Pp. 24-36.

Ritson, D. W. & Hallowell, M. J. (2014). *Contagion: In the Shadow of the South Shields Poltergeist*. Limbury, Luton: The Limbury Press.

Roll, W. G. & Persinger, M. A. (2001). Investigations of poltergeists and haunts: A review and interpretation. In J. Houran and R. Lange (eds), *Hauntings and Poltergeists: Multidisciplinary Perspectives*. Jefferson, North Carolina: McFarland. Pp. 123-63.

Peter A. McCue, Ph.D.
East Dunbartonshire,
May 2021

INTRODUCTION

In 2006, Darren W. Ritson and Michael J. Hallowell made a life-changing decision: to investigate an alleged case of poltergeist infestation in an otherwise normal family home in the town of South Shields, Tyne & Wear. The only caveat that needs to be added to this fact is that, at the time, they had absolutely no idea that what they were about to do would change their lives to such an incalculable degree.

In their book about the affair, *The South Shields Poltergeist: One Family's Fight Against an Invisible Intruder*, they spoke of how every paranormal investigator dreams of their 'big case'; a circumstance so bizarre and so verifiable that it truly seems to prove that the world is not just stranger than we know, but – as Heraclitus the sage (or Isaac Newton, according to some) once said – stranger than we possibly can know. Darren and Michael well and truly stumbled across their 'big case' with the South Shields poltergeist. Over the course of several months, they found themselves confronting a cruel and mysterious force that seemed to break all the known rules that govern our universe. The poltergeist was invisible – most of the time – and also cunning and violent. It could throw objects around, send death threats to mobile phones via text messages and, when it felt so disposed, slash the flesh of those it chose to target.

During the period of time in question, Darren and Michael realised that the case they were investigating was truly extraordinary, possibly even unique. They believed that the world should know about it, and were convinced that both the poltergeist and their investigation of it would go down in the history of psychical research as a groundbreaking case. Renowned author and researcher Colin Wilson recognised the book as 'one of the great classic works on the poltergeist.' To this day the researchers have not changed their minds about how significant the South Shields case really was. Long before the entity dissipated into the ether, hopefully never to return, Darren and Michael began to write their book about the affair. The South Shields poltergeist ended at the point where the bizarre phenomena that had plagued the family so intensely *seemed* to have stopped. Perhaps naively, the researchers believed that a long, incredible chapter in their lives was drawing to a close. True, they would never be the same again, but they remained convinced that eventually new cases would beckon and they would be able to move on with their lives. It wasn't to be. Like a dark, brooding presence the shadow of the South Shields poltergeist, as incredible as it sounds, continued to haunt the investigators as it had once haunted the family it terrorised; just not in the same way.

Darren and Michael have learned many lessons from their experience during the South Shields investigation. They have learned that human nature can, when plunged into the correct set of circumstances, be every bit as dark and untrustworthy as the poltergeist itself. They are now less trusting of those they meet in their professional lives and see the society they are part of in a far less favourable light. The lessons they have learned should be taken on board by every paranormal investigator.

In February 2008, whilst Darren and Michael were lecturing to a class of university students at Northumbria University, (which had then become an annual event for Darren and Michael) who had an interest in the subject, Michael spoke bluntly of how he found it difficult to be tolerant of sceptics who dismiss the poltergeist experience out of hand. This is something that Darren feels very strongly about, too. The researchers both struggle to be polite towards cynics who have never been in close proximity to a poltergeist let alone witnessed its devastating handiwork. How can they speak with such authority on a subject of which they have had no personal experience?

The poltergeist phenomenon is normally seen by new or inexperienced researchers as a purely paranormal one: strange things happening to or around ordinary people that simply cannot be explained. However, there is another aspect of poltergeist infestation that *some* seasoned investigators often give weight to, and it's sometimes referred to as contagion. This is, allegedly, a process whereby the bizarre antics of the poltergeist spread outwards from the home of the principal witnesses

INTRODUCTION

and start to affect others around them; extended family members, friends, colleagues and investigators who choose, or accidentally wander into, the arena of metaphysical conflict. Like a communicable disease, the poltergeist phenomenon can attach itself to others. The only small mercy is that those who are seemingly subjected to such contagion normally don't suffer poltergeist phenomena to the same degree as the principal witnesses at 'ground zero.' As the contagion spreads, it seems to become diluted.

One part of the poltergeist phenomenon – we can argue about the validity of the term poltergeist later – that often goes unrecognised even by experienced researchers is the destructive effect that the poltergeist experience can have on other aspects of people's lives. The poltergeist is not only a little-understood entity/force that frightens its victims. The poltergeist also has an almost unbridled ability to cause devastation in the fields of employment, relationships, physical well being and emotional/mental health. If you think, as the researchers once did, that the presence of a poltergeist merely generates fear in its victims and leaves the other aspects of their lives untouched, then, putting it bluntly, you are deluded. The poltergeist infects its victims and those around them in the same way that the HIV virus infects those who contract it. It soaks itself insidiously into every fibre of their being, leaving no part or aspect of its victims untouched. Poltergeists – whatever they are – don't only affect people; they infect whole families and even communities.

The truth is that, despite the researcher's optimism, the South Shields poltergeist had *seemed* to come back – and with a vengeance. This time, Darren and Michael would be forced to do battle yet again with the poltergeist, but under the auspices of radically different rules of conflict. This book is essentially the story of the researchers' on-going struggle against the invisible intruder that once resided at Lock Street – an invisible intruder that had, since the days of their first encounter with it, grown far stronger, more cunning and infinitely more dangerous.

What you are about to read in the following pages is a true account. The researchers are well aware that some readers will find the notion of the poltergeist's return under such bizarre circumstances extremely hard to believe. In anticipation of this, they have proposed a number of different hypotheses to explain why the entity that they thought had disappeared for good was able to re-enter their lives with such consummate ease – and why the researchers were once again singled out as targets for its dark malevolence. During the researcher's first investigation, the poltergeist sent a chilling text message to the mobile phone of one of the principal witnesses. It said, quite simply, 'I'm back.' They now acknowledge that potentially, in part, those words were meant for them.

The South Shields poltergeist case has sent powerful ripples coursing throughout the world of paranormal research. Both in the UK and abroad, the book *The South Shields Poltergeist: One Family's Fight against an Invisible Intruder* has caused incredible debate, much of it heated. Drawn into the fray have been academics and armchair enthusiasts, TV personalities and film producers, journalists and psychic mediums, legal experts and radio presenters. And, through it all, the grim legacy of the South Shields poltergeist has been sustained. Perhaps, now that the full truth is about to be told, it can finally be laid to rest.

Darren W. Ritson, 2020

PART ONE
POST SOUTH SHIELDS

1

DEFINING MOMENTS

Darren W. Ritson and Michael J. Hallowell, like every reader of this book, can look back over their lives and pinpoint defining moments that were, to use a modern expression, watersheds; that is, points of no return or events that change one's life permanently and irredeemably. Michael remembers the passing of his grandparents, and the day when he fell prey to an undiagnosed heart condition, which took him to the brink of death. Darren recalls the time when he first saw his baby daughter, Abbey, seconds after she was born. A taxi driver, whilst taking Darren to the hospital, commented, 'you don't know what love is until you see your new-born child for the first time.' Darren later reflected on how true those words were.

Both of the researchers, however, will testify that they share a common defining moment in their lives: the day, in July 2006, when they were first *invited* to investigate the South Shields poltergeist. Darren and Michael are [now] experienced paranormal investigators. They have written many books, articles and columns on both ghosts and the hunting of them, as well as about other paranormal phenomena. Diligently, they have travelled the length and breadth of the British Isles – and sometimes beyond – in the search for evidence that there truly is some form of existence beyond this vale of tears. Both would admit candidly that they haven't been disappointed, although they know full well that not every insubstantial wisp of mist or shimmer of light is proof positive that there is more to this life than flesh-and-blood alone would testify.

Paranormal investigation is in some respects akin to the exploration of an uncharted wilderness. Those who delve into the darkest reaches of the Amazonian Basin, for example, never know just what (or whom) they'll encounter. If they're lucky, they may stumble across a hitherto unknown arachnid or two, or even a new variety of orchid. Perhaps a brightly-plumed bird of uncertain provenance may wing its way overhead, reinforcing the fact that, despite civilisation's relentless march across the natural world like a cancer, there are still some wondrous things left to discover. Indeed, to illustrate this point, in February 2021, the BBC reported that scientists could have discovered what is known to be the 'smallest reptile' on Earth, when two of the lizard species (referred to as Nano-Chameleons) were accidentally discovered in Madagascar during an expedition there by German, and Madagascan exploration teams.

Sometimes, of course, explorers stumble upon discoveries of an altogether darker nature: a bacillus or parasite that perhaps devastates their digestive system or covers their flesh in obscene lesions. They may even run into a hitherto unknown carnivore that displays no reluctance whatsoever when it comes to dining on humans. Well, it's a tough job, but someone has to do it. Darren and Michael aren't suggesting for one moment that paranormal investigators are subject to the same dangers as explorers, either by nature or degree. However, they know full well that their chosen field of endeavour may certainly be no bed of roses, either. Turn on your TV, and at any given time you'll possibly find at least half a dozen channels airing programmes dealing with the supernatural. Stage-bound psychics may be passing on messages from the deceased, and studio-based reporters will be revealing details of the latest UFO sighting. Society, in the main, has a thirst for the unknown. Of course, you can't believe everything you see on TV, in much the same way you can't trust everything you read in the papers. But it isn't all bunkum. Beyond the media-hungry snake-oil salesmen who peddle their psychic wares to the highest bidder, there is a truly unknown world that usually lies just beyond our senses. Sometimes, researchers who may have spent decades investigating low-level hauntings may find themselves catapulted into the uncharted regions of this world unceremoniously.

In the main, Darren and Michael have been fortunate. Their forays into the dimly lit world of paranormal phenomena have caused them relatively little grief. True, Michael *believes* he once came uncomfortably close to the legendary Bigfoot when he was sailing down the Dorcheat Bayou in Louisiana, and Darren was rather unnerved on one occasion when he felt what he *thought* was a ghost walk straight through him in a large old haunted house in Sunderland. But they have never been forced to confront anything truly malevolent or face up to an entity that could quite possibly, if it so wished, do them great harm both physically and psychologically. Except once, that is, when they were invited to go to the house in Lock Street, South Tyneside.

In their book, *The South Shields Poltergeist*, Darren and Michael described in graphic detail how a young family was almost hounded out of its home by an invisible, brooding entity that seemed hell-bent on snatching from them every ounce of happiness they possessed. The researchers found themselves in the daunting position of trying to help the family to deal with this nightmare situation. Over a period of months, the poltergeist danced merrily with the investigators, leading them into a number of blind alleys as they desperately searched for a way to overcome its terrible influence. It proved to be an expert in psychological warfare. One minute it would pass itself off as the spirit of an innocent toddler and the next it would manifest itself as an old woman or a tall, black-clad man with sallow features and a grim countenance. At times, the investigators didn't know whether they were dealing with a single entity, or two, three, four or more.

In October 2006, the researchers sought the advice of a colleague who, without pouring cold water on the idea that the entity was indeed a poltergeist, suggested that it might in some way be feeding on electricity. The householders were asked to turn all of their electrical equipment off at night instead of just leaving them on 'standby'; and, combined with a number of other things, outlined below, it worked. More or less overnight, the poltergeist vanished completely, leaving behind an exhausted and very much relieved family. With the researchers' help, they slowly began to pick up the pieces. However, the thought also occurred that the poltergeist, or whatever it was, had naturally – and coincidentally – burned itself out as so often these things do. After all, it had been almost a year since it first manifested itself at Lock Street.

This, too, was a defining moment in the investigation of the South Shields poltergeist. And there were more to come. In their book, *The South Shields Poltergeist* the researchers attempted to clarify the true essence of the poltergeist. They desperately wanted to understand the nature of the beast they were dealing with. In some respects, they were successful. They came to see how the poltergeist would time its intrusions to perfection, calculating perfectly when to strike for maximum effect. They noticed how, after protracted bouts of activity, it would seemingly rest, as if exhausted. They also discovered ways in which they could make it angry and provoke it into action. Day by day, as they came to understand the activities of the poltergeist better, they were able to chip away at its defences until, one day, it left its abode in Lock Street for pastures new.

But if the researchers were successful in unmasking the poltergeist in some respects, they struggled in others. On reflection, they can see that what they discovered were things relating to what a poltergeist does, but not truly what a poltergeist is. They still held to their original belief that the poltergeist was essentially a form of latent energy that builds up inside its host before externalising itself and creating havoc in its environment. They still believed that the trigger factor to a poltergeist infestation in most cases was intense stress within the host, and that if the cause of the stress was neutralised, then the poltergeist would likely disappear.

All of the above may or may not be true; but again, on reflection, the researchers can see that they made a number of unwarranted assumptions that prevented them from understanding the nature of the poltergeist more accurately. Part of this book will be devoted to rectifying this defect. As the reader will see, there were a number of incidents that forced Darren and Michael to re-evaluate their understanding of one of the world's most baffling – and terrifying – enigmas. What they discovered made them more disturbed, not less. If they believed that the entity known as the poltergeist was truly malign before, they now came to see that it could, at the apex of its power, be nothing short of appalling.

2

PRINCIPLES OF CONTAGION

In the physical world, the process of infection and contagion is well understood. Our planet is literally teeming with untold numbers of bacteria, viruses, fungi and protozoa, which can, under the right conditions, invade our bodies and cause sickness. All invading microbes have the ability to compromise our immune systems to some degree. Sometimes, the damage will be so slight that we may be unaware that anything is wrong. Other times, such infections may kill within hours. The methods used by invading organisms to find their way into our bodies vary. Some are airborne and can be inhaled. Others are transferred from one person to another when body fluids are exchanged. Some are ingested with tainted food and water. However, the relevant factor is that, in almost all cases, the recipients of a specific invading microbe will, if the organism is allowed to take hold, display the same set of symptoms. This is why medical personnel can sometimes identify infections purely by observing the visible symptoms, even before blood tests are carried out.

Indeed, as previously mentioned at the beginning of this book, and at the time of this re-edit (March 2020 – June 2021), the world is in the midst of a terrifying strain of the latest Coronavirus known as 2019-nCov, simply referred to as Covid 19. Covid 19 has been sweeping across the planet relentlessly since November 2019, killing thousands of people while the world's authorities desperately try to take control of the situation by implementing travel bans, the prohibition of mass public events such as concerts and sporting fixtures, and issuing daily bulletins and advice on how to go about limiting the spread of the deadly virus and staying safe. Creating a vaccine that will bring Covid 19 under control, however, had been proving to be a rather difficult task and no one knew at that particular time where this would eventually lead, although it had been suggested by the World Health Organisation (WHO) it *might* have taken up to eighteen months to produce an effective vaccine. However, writing in February 2021 it is clear now that a number of vaccines *have* indeed been produced and are being rolled out presently. One can only hope that this vaccination development and enrollment is a success over the Covid 19 virus. It is very likely that as you read these words, you will have no doubt been given 'your' injections, although the world may never be the same again.

No one would now doubt the reality of physical infection. We know of ways in which the rate of infections can be slowed down or even halted altogether. Good hygiene, inoculation, medication such as antibiotics and anti-viral agents – all of these have a part to play. However, we should remember that it isn't that long ago when the entire concept of communicable disease was dismissed as nonsense by the world's most eminent medics. It was the Persian Avicenna who first understood the concept and popularised it back in the 11th century. Avicenna was also the first person to suggest quarantine as a means of reducing the spread of disease. But it wasn't until the time of Louis Pasteur, in the 19th century, that the idea of contagion, as we understand it, became widely accepted.

It seems, then, that as long as we restrict ourselves to observing the physical world we will get little or no opposition when we suggest that disease can be spread from one person to another or from an infected substance to a living organism. But it is different when we enter the realm of the non-physical. Take a stroll across the psychic or spiritual landscape and you will find scientific open-mindedness far less evident.

However, if we just pause for a moment and give the matter some thought, we will see quite easily that the concept of contagion is obviously not something that is restricted to the world of the flesh. Surely we all know of cases where a depressed person has, through their behaviour and actions, caused those they live or work with to become morose, too. Conversely, the presence of an upbeat, positive-minded person can cause those in close proximity to embrace a better outlook. When we say that a person's presence is 'a breath of fresh air', what we mean is that when they are present, those around them feel better. How often have we heard a person's sense of humour described as 'infectious'? Emotions, then, can be contagious also.

On a broader front, we also must recognise that ideas and concepts can be contagious. Communism, capitalism, socialism, racial hatred (or tolerance), sexism, atheism, theocracy and democracy are all ideas that, for good or ill, had their origins in a fixed place and time and spread out far and wide, sometimes *infecting* many millions of people across the globe. Sometimes, cultural traits can infect entire generations of a particular family. A good example of this is the scourge of domestic violence. It is well known that the children of perpetrators of domestic violence are more likely to engage in such behaviour themselves during adulthood. In its broadest sense, contagion can simply be described as 'the spread of things.' We may not always understand the mechanism, but it happens nonetheless.

When we enter the world of poltergeist infestation, then, we shouldn't be too surprised to find evidence of contagion there, too. After all, our own world is filled with contagion – physical and non-physical – and the poltergeist operates within our world to a very large degree. What we need to do is look for evidence of such poltergeist-based contagion and, if we find it, determine what form it takes.

It has long been recognised by *some* researchers that those in close proximity to the victims of a current poltergeist infestation may also become infected by the phenomenon, although rarely as intensely. Such contagion is normally both transient and mild. However, the symptoms are usually enough to allow witnesses to conclude that something strange indeed is going on in their abode. As the researchers were investigating the South Shields poltergeist, they believed they witnessed numerous incidents of such contagion. A detailed account can be found in the book *The South Shields Poltergeist*, but it would seem appropriate to recount, briefly, the incidents here.

On Wednesday, 31 August 2006, when the poltergeist infestation at Lock Street was at its most intense, Michael received a call from a friend. The call was made to his mobile phone just before 2am, but, by the time he retrieved his phone to answer it, it had stopped ringing. He rang his friend back, and was mystified when the man denied making any call to him whatsoever. His phone had been sitting on the dashboard of his car and he hadn't used it in hours. However, when he checked his call log he discovered that his phone had made a call to Michael's mobile just before 2am. The obvious mystery was how that phone had, without any human intervention, rung his mobile in the early hours of the morning. But there was a deeper mystery. Later that morning, when his friend paid him a visit, it transpired that at the very time the call was made, the friend had been driving past Lock Street – the abode of the South Shields poltergeist.

Of course, it might just have been an extraordinary coincidence, but it certainly made the researchers think. As Michael and his friend chatted in the garden, he heard his mobile phone ringing in the house. He dashed inside to retrieve it, but, once again, just didn't get there in time. He looked at the screen and saw it had said 'one missed call', which was from the very friend he'd just left sitting in the garden. Michael walked outside, holding his mobile in front of him, saying, 'You're calling me!' Michael's friend immediately pulled his mobile phone from his pocket. It was switched off, and yet somehow it had rung Michael's mobile phone. Just then, Michael received a text message saying that a voicemail had been left for him. He punched in the retrieval number and, to his astonishment, found that the message was actually a recording of the conversation that he and his friend had just had in the garden!

Another example of such contagion occurred on 24 September 2006. Michael and his wife, Jackie, were at a house-warming party held by their two friends from Orion TV, Bob and Marrisse Whittaker. He and his wife stayed over at their friends' home after the party had finished, and, during the night, they were startled by a tremendous crash upstairs, where Bob and Marrisse were sleeping. Later, they found out that when the couple had awoken with a start, they were amazed to see a phosphorescent ball of green light hovering in their room. Bob and Marrisse had been to the house in Lock Street earlier to interview Marianne, one of the principal witnesses.

One of the most sinister examples of contagion concerning the South Shields poltergeist occurred when the researchers sent examples of handwriting left by the poltergeist at the house in Lock Street to a respected graphologist for analysis. As she looked over the pictures in the garden of her London home, she suddenly became aware of a presence behind her. She said she could sense that the presence was that of a tall man wearing a long, dark coat. Her description was identical to that given by Robert, the young child who lived in the house at Lock Street, who had also seen the entity on numerous occasions. The graphologist was deeply disturbed by this incident. Those at 'ground zero' – the Lock

Street home of Marianne, Marc and Robert – had been subjected to a sustained, incessant barrage of poltergeist activity. However, many of those around them – family members, friends and investigators – had also experienced brief periods of poltergeistry shortly after visiting the house in question. Some, like Michael's friend, hadn't even visited the house up to that point, but merely drove past it. It was as if the poltergeist was able to infect those who, directly or indirectly, had somehow been in contact with the family at the centre of the disturbance.

The concept of poltergeist contagion is not a new one, although sadly it has been seldom discussed with very little research being carried out by psychical researchers, but it seems reasonable to suggest that the mechanism by which such contagion takes place has little or nothing in common with the means by which physical diseases are transmitted from one person to another. Poltergeists are not bacteria or viruses, but it seems that they can still infect those with whom they come into contact. The common denominators in such cases seem to be either close physical proximity to the person who is the focus of the main infestation, or, alternatively, a direct or indirect link with them. In the case of the latter, it seemed to Darren and Michael that the poltergeist was able to reach out through a chain of individuals. A good analogy is the way in which a round robin e-mail can be sent by one person to another, who then may forward it on to his or her own friends, and so on. There may be no direct contact between the first sender of the e-mail and the last recipient – they may even live on different continents – but everyone who receives the e-mail will experience the same message. All that is necessary is that each person in the chain is connected to one other person in it. Poltergeist contagion is uncannily similar. All that seems to be necessary for a person to experience poltergeist contagion is that he or she is part of a chain of people, which, directly or indirectly, leads back to the principal witnesses. Having established a *prima facie* case that poltergeist contagion does seem to take place, the next question would logically be, how? As far as we can see, there are two possibilities. We may call them *passive contagion* and *active contagion.*

Passive contagion is the process of infection at work, but without a driving intelligence behind it. If a person happens to be suffering from, say, Hepatitis A – an incredibly virulent infection – they may drink from a glass and leave traces of the virus on the rim. If someone else inadvertently drinks from the same glass, he or she could easily be infected with Hepatitis A. This is passive contagion, because the person responsible didn't knowingly infect the person who drank from the glass afterwards. They didn't intend for the person to be infected and devised no dastardly plan to make such a thing happen. The virus itself didn't knowingly infect the person either. There is a process at work by which the infection was transmitted, but no guiding intelligence making it happen. Active contagion is different, and requires a guiding intelligence to complete the transference of a disease from one person to another. A perfect example involves the dreaded HIV virus. Often the disease is passed on passively, by persons who are not even aware that they are infected themselves. Neither the recipient nor the donor knows that the risk of infection is present, because neither of them are aware that one of them is already playing host to the deadly virus. However, from time to time reports appear in the press of individuals who, knowing full well that they are HIV-positive, still engage in high-risk sexual activity with others. In some cases, criminal charges have been brought against those who have purposely infected others with HIV. One such case involved a man who deliberately engaged in sexual intercourse with a former partner. Later, he confessed that he had wanted to infect his victim with HIV so that, 'he could suffer like I was suffering.' Such cases, tragic though they are, are examples of active contagion: the infection is not accidental – it is designed to happen. The researchers think that *both* forms of contagion may be at work in the poltergeist phenomenon.

Although our knowledge of the poltergeist is at best nebulous, we can see that it seems to operate by a set of rules or at least behavioural patterns. The poltergeist will throw objects around in a family home, but it will not apply for a nursing job in a local hospital. It will make banging and thumping noises in a bedroom, but will not sing opera at the Royal Albert Hall. Like human beings, the poltergeist is imbued with characteristics that identify it for what it is – a poltergeist. There's an old saying: 'If it walks like a dog, barks like a dog and wags its tail like a dog – well, it's probably a dog.' The same principle holds true of the poltergeist.

The problem with the poltergeist is that it represents a type of existence that we know little about. Probably, its type of existence is unique. It isn't physical, and yet it operates comfortably within the physical world. In fact, it often seems to manipulate the physical world far better than humans can. It isn't a purely psychological phenomenon, either, as the poltergeist undoubtedly enjoys some form of objective reality. Enigmatically, though, it operates very much on a psychological level. Because we are dealing with a phenomenon that is unlike any other we have encountered, it makes it extremely difficult to be predictive. By way of example, let us imagine that, tomorrow, a new species of monkey were to be discovered in North Africa.

In one sense it could be said that we know absolutely nothing about the new species as we have only just encountered it, but, on another level, it can be said that we know quite a bit about it. For starters, we know that it is a monkey, and we can predict with confidence that, although it is an entirely new species, it will exhibit many traits found in other types of monkey. We can also predict that it will share many common characteristics of mammalian life. It will eat, breathe, procreate and sleep, for instance. We are able to predict these things because it has a context in which it can be set, and that context tells us much before we have even studied the new species in any way. The poltergeist is different, because we simply have no firm context in which we can set it at all. All we know about it are the few characteristics of its behaviour that we have been allowed to see in cases that have been studied. These characteristics tell us something, but they don't allow us to make any predictions about aspects of its existence that we currently know nothing about. We are, to use a Biblical maxim, 'seeing through a glass but darkly.'

Although we cannot make safe predictions about the unknown aspects of the poltergeist phenomenon, we can hypothesise a number of potentials. For instance, the poltergeist phenomenon may include forms of passive contagion, whereby certain types of connection with an 'infected' person may cause others to be subject to polt-like experiences. This form of contagion is 'passive' because the poltergeist, whatever it may be, has not deliberately caused the contagion to occur. Perhaps there is an unknown but entirely natural process at work that triggers such contagion without the poltergeist deliberately causing it?

But, as already mentioned, there may also be a form of active contagion at work, too. Because our knowledge of poltergeists' abilities is so incomplete, we must concede that it may well be able deliberately to precipitate such contagion under certain circumstances. For all we know, an 'infected' person may open up a doorway of opportunity for a poltergeist to infect others when they establish certain types of connection with them. In ways we don't understand, a poltergeist may be able to initiate the process of contagion when a poltergeist host establishes contact with a previously uninfected person. If one sends an e-mail to a friend, it can influence that friend and that friend only within the context of the initial communication. However, if that friend then sends a reply that contains the visible address of another person previously unknown to us, it opens up a doorway of opportunity for us then to contact that person also. Why? Because a set of circumstances has been created that allows us to operate, to do things that we were hitherto unable to do. The same *may* be true of a poltergeist. By making contact with others, the infected person may be creating a set of circumstances that allows polt-contagion to take place. We may not understand the mechanism of such contagion, but that doesn't mean that it cannot happen. It simply means that there are natural processes at work in this world that we have not yet grasped.

In the final analysis, all we can say with certainty is that people who are connected in some way to victims of poltergeist infestation *may* then become victims of the enigma themselves. We don't know how it happens, but we have seen enough during our research to convince us that it does happen, whether we understand it or not.

3

SHADOWS

As the case at South Shields seemed to be drawing to a close, Darren and Michael began to focus more on their manuscript of *The South Shields Poltergeist*. They had witnessed the poltergeist at work in the Lock Street house directly, and also a degree of contagion when the entity had cast its psychic net further afield and invaded the lives of others less directly connected with the case. Now, the traumatic events were petering out and the family were seeing the poltergeist cast its last throw of the dice. It seemed to be over – almost. The publishers scheduled the release of the book for March 30, 2008, and the researchers set about creating a collection of pictures to accompany the manuscript. As the weeks went by, Darren and Michael began to research new cases.

In January 2008, Michael received a call from Steven Taylor, the owner of Alone in the Dark Entertainment (AITDE). Based in Newcastle-upon-Tyne, AITDE specialises in hosting events that mostly have a paranormal theme: ghost walks through Newcastle city centre, corporate events, murder mystery nights, and hen/stag parties. Steven and his colleagues had been organising an evening of paranormal and psychic *entertainment* which was to be held simultaneously in three well-known public houses – all of them, of course, reputedly haunted

– and he wanted Darren and Michael to play an integral part in the proceedings.

The three pubs faced the River Tyne on Newcastle's historic quayside, and stood adjacent to each other: Bob Trollop's, Offshore 44 and The Red House. The idea was to pack the three inns full of people with an interest in the paranormal, and give them a night to remember. Psychic mediums would be on hand to provide readings for those who wanted them, and, later, Darren, Michael and a guest medium would investigate a disused part of one pub that was reputedly haunted by a rather bad-tempered spirit. They'd go up in the dark, with night-vision cameras strapped to their heads, and the live-action footage would be relayed down to a series of large screens below. Darren and Michael fully accept, of course, that this sort of activity cannot be classed as serious paranormal research; and Steven never claimed that it was meant to be anything other than entertainment. Darren and Michael have no problem taking part in events like this; provided they aren't presented as something they're not. The 'walk in the dark' upstairs was meant to be good fun, scary fun and enthralling. If anything truly paranormal did take place, then it would be an added bonus. Essentially, the whole point of the exercise was to open people's minds to the idea that the world is probably a stranger place than they imagined, and send them away with both a smile on their faces and a question or two in their minds.

Entirely coincidentally, AITDE had organised the event to take place on 30 March, which was the day that Darren and Michael's book on the South Shields poltergeist was being released. The event *wasn't the book's official launch party*, but Steven rightly thought it made sense to use the AITDE event to promote the book, and of course the researchers agreed. Therefore, Steven asked Darren and Michael if they would be prepared to give a talk on the South Shields poltergeist case at the event.

Before the event took place, Steven contacted Michael again and told them that a man from Jarrow, which is not too far from South Shields, had e-mailed him and asked him for some help. Apparently, the correspondent and his family had been disturbed by a series of bizarre incidents that had taken place at their home. At first, they'd dismissed them as coincidences, but eventually they reached the point where they could no longer accept that a rational explanation would make sense of things. Something decidedly irrational was going on in their home, and it was worrying them intensely. Steven asked Michael if he would be prepared to visit the family, along with a so-called respected psychic medium. Michael agreed, and asked if it would also be permissible for Darren to attend.

Something struck Darren and Michael as strange. The family at Lock Street had consisted of a young couple and one young child. Similarly, the family at Jarrow also comprised a young couple and one young child. Also, the events that had been taking place at the Jarrow house had been very similar to those that had occurred at South Shields: knocks, bangs and other strange noises, coupled with incidents of objects being moved from one place to another without anyone in the household being responsible. Of course, most poltergeist infestations begin this way, so the parallels in the symptoms were not surprising in themselves. It just seemed odd that the two families should be so similar. It was probably nothing more than coincidence, they assumed, and henceforth didn't give the matter any further thought.

The event on March 30 went well. The major hiccup in the proceedings was that specialist equipment purchased by AITDE from Japan didn't function as planned, and it was no longer possible to do the 'walk in the dark' upstairs in the disused part of the pub. Nevertheless, Darren and Michael's talk on the South Shields poltergeist went down very well indeed. Afterwards, the crowd milled around and relaxed – buying beer and wine from the bar in copious amounts and generally enjoying themselves. Numerous guests approached Darren and Michael during the night and asked them questions about the South Shields case, which of course they were happy to answer.

One chap, called Norman, said that he'd once had 'an unpleasant experience' with a poltergeist:

'It even pinched food from the refrigerator!' he added, as an afterthought.

'It wasn't a pie, by any chance was it?' enquired Michael.

'I think it was; now you come to mention it. Why do you ask?'

'Because the poltergeist at South Shields pinched a pie from the fridge there, too.'

'Wow!' said Norman, 'What a coincidence!'

'It is, isn't it?' responded Michael, not entirely convinced.

Michael looked at Darren; Darren looked at Michael, and the researchers knew they were thinking the same thing.

4

INVESTIGATION AT JARROW

The house at Pallister Street*, Jarrow, seemed completely unremarkable from the outside. It was a terraced dwelling in a street of privately owned and rented residences. Michael was familiar with Jarrow, as he used to go to school there. The school had long since gone, being replaced by a modern housing estate. Other than that, relatively little had changed since he had last visited the place in 1973. Indeed, his local tuck shop was still there, providing local kids with confectionary and other goodies as it had done for decades. Returning to the location was something of a nostalgia trip.

Earlier in the evening, Michael had packed his bag with various bits and pieces that he always took with him on investigations: a camera, a digital sound recorder, a notebook and a pen. He then had a bath, dressed and prepared some food. At 6pm Darren arrived, and his bag was positively heaving with investigative equipment. Then, at 7pm, Steven turned up, and without any further delay they set off for Pallister Street, which was approximately a fifteen-minute drive away. The date of the researchers' first visit to Pallister Street was March 10, 2008. By the time they arrived it was dusk, but they had no trouble finding the house.

Derek* and Mandy* were a pleasant couple. Both were in their early twenties, and they had a daughter called Ella,* who was less than a year old. Unfortunately, Ella had a really heavy cold and found it difficult to stop coughing. Regardless, she managed a gentle smile as the investigators entered the dining room. Mandy immediately offered her visitors coffee, while Derek opened up and told the investigators a little more about what had been going on. The story had begun when the couple lived in their previous home, a rented flat not too far from their current dwelling in Pallister Street. On several occasions, Derek and Mandy had felt a 'presence' in the flat. It was hard to describe, but they said that it 'felt, very real' and made them feel nervous and uneasy. They never actually saw anything, but they just knew that something was there.

Several weeks after the couple had become aware of the presence in the flat, other, more disturbing incidents took place. One evening in April 2007, while Mandy was heavily pregnant, Derek went into the bathroom and was startled to see that the window was wide open. As the weather was quite inclement, there was no way that either Derek or Mandy would have opened it themselves. They were baffled. Then Derek noticed that something else was wrong. The plastic panel that lined the side of the bath had become detached, and was now simply leaning against the bath instead of being fixed in place. With some difficulty, he replaced the bath panel after closing the window. Darren, at this point, thought back to an almost identical incident involving a bath panel that had occurred at the house in Lock Street. It, too, had been detached from the bath, and hearing this account made Darren focus more intently upon the strange coincidences that he'd noticed could occur within the realms of poltergeistry.

Several days later, Derek again entered the bathroom, but, just as he did so, he thought he could hear his mobile phone ringing. He left the bathroom and went to retrieve his phone, but to his consternation found that it was no longer ringing. He checked the call log, and was puzzled to find no missed calls listed. Just then, he heard the sound of running water from the kitchen area. He walked into the kitchen and was greeted by the sight of the cold water tap over the kitchen sink blasting water into the basin at full pelt. He quickly turned it off. Neither Derek nor Mandy had been in the kitchen, and, even if they had, why would they have left the tap fully turned on like that?

One day in July, after Ella was born, both Derek and Mandy had a disturbing experience in the early hours of the morning. At approximately 3am, Derek awoke for no apparent reason; or at least, he thinks he did. He can't be absolutely sure. To this day he has difficulty recalling whether he was actually awake or asleep, but he distinctly remembers – either in reality or in a dream state – sitting up in bed and looking towards the bedroom door. It was open. To his horror, he could see someone standing in the doorway, silhouetted by the moonlight coming in through the window. Derek said that the person was definitely a male, and that he seemed to be wearing a shroud of some kind with a hood over his head. The really weird thing was that the man's face – or what little he could see of it – was yellow in colour. Slowly, the person staring down at him with hollow eyes disappeared. Derek was terrified, but, working on the presumption that he was indeed awake, attempted to go back to sleep. The following morning, Mandy told Derek that she also had experienced something rather disturbing during the night. Although she's not sure of the time it occurred, she endured a short period of sleep paralysis. She had woken up, but found herself unable to move. She lay there, completely paralysed and frightened, until slumber once again overtook her.

Although the steady rise in anomalous incidents disturbed the couple, the worst was yet to come. After the birth of Ella, Derek and Mandy had got into the habit of visiting two close friends on a regular basis. After one such visit, on Sunday 30 September 2007, they returned to their flat and immediately noticed 'the presence' that had disturbed them on numerous occasions previously. However, it was when the couple entered their bedroom that they were truly shocked.

The room was incredibly small, and only just wide enough to hold a double bed. In fact, to get into bed Derek and Mandy had to crawl across the mattress before climbing under the covers. Strewn across the bed were a pillow, an item or two of clothing, a pair of baby shoes and a rag doll. The couple couldn't remember whether some of the items had been on the bed when they left the flat, but were adamant that the rag doll and the shoes hadn't been. However, the most bizarre thing was that baby Ella's cot had been lifted from the floor and placed in the centre of the couple's bed, its legs at perfect right-angles to the mattress it was standing on. Now Derek and Mandy were really frightened. After composing themselves, Derek took a photograph of the cot in situ, an action for which the researchers later complimented him.

The following day, Derek happened to be talking to a neighbour. Troubled by the events of the previous evening, he mentioned some of the strange occurrences that had taken place in their flat. To Derek's surprise, the neighbour then told him some things about the previous tenant that he hadn't known, but which later made him wonder whether they were connected with the experiences which were now beginning to frighten both him and his wife. According to Derek's neighbour, their flat had previously been rented by a single person: a man who had a severe alcohol problem.

The condition had consumed him to such an extent that his health was in an extremely poor state and his behaviour had become decidedly erratic. On occasions, neighbours had been forced to report him both to the police and the local authorities. The man had, seemingly, also been in the habit of leaving his bathroom window open even during bad weather, prompting the question as to whether the mysterious incident when Derek had found the same window open was in some way connected.

One of the symptoms that can often accompany alcoholism is a raging thirst. The alcoholic tenant of the flat, that the couple now lived in, had experienced this, and was forever drinking water from the kitchen tap. The neighbour testified that as the man slowly descended into an almost permanent alcoholic stupor, he took to leaving the cold water tap in the kitchen running permanently as he simply couldn't be bothered to keep turning it on and off. To most people this would seem bizarre, but, to the mind of a person whose thinking processes have been so severely damaged by drink, it may have made some sort of sense. Derek couldn't help but wonder whether this was connected to the incident when he found the cold-water tap in the kitchen fully open, even though neither he nor Mandy had turned it on.

Although neither Mandy nor Derek had mentioned this, the researchers also wondered whether the previous tenant had, in the later stage of his alcoholism, become jaundiced due to liver disease. This could also have been connected to the ghostly personage that Derek saw standing in the doorway of his bedroom – someone whom he described as having a decidedly 'yellow face.' As Derek recited the litany of strange events that had occurred in their previous flat to the researchers, it was obvious to them that he was deeply troubled – and he hadn't yet begun to tell them about what both he and his wife had experienced in their current dwelling. At this point, Darren asked if he could set about his regular itinerary of scouting out the various rooms in the house and setting up numerous pieces of equipment. Derek agreed. Michael's role would be to interview the couple whilst the other two investigators went about their business.

Darren switched on his portable dictation machine on which the interview would be recorded and placed it in the centre of the dining room table. Then both Darren and Steven made their way up the narrow stairwell to the first floor. As they departed, Michael's mind was catapulted back to their first visit to Lock Street. There, too, he had interviewed the couple while Darren went upstairs to set up his camera and other equipment in order to obtain possible evidence of paranormal activity.

As the tape rolled, Michael started to question the couple about their experiences. Within minutes, it became painfully obvious to the researcher that something decidedly odd was going on. With every question posed, the muscles in Michael's stomach tightened further. With every answer provided by the couple, it dawned upon him, with ever-growing clarity that he had walked this metaphorical road before. In fact, he knew what the answers to his questions would be before the couple even articulated them. To be frank, he didn't like what he was hearing one little bit. After the interview had finished, he took Darren to one side and asked to speak to him privately. 'I'm not going to tell you what's on the interview tape, Darren; just go home and listen to it. Make sure, you're sitting down when you do – because what you hear will knock you for six.'

5

POLTERGEIST PARALLELS

Slowly, almost painstakingly, Derek and Mandy recited the litany of strange incidents that had occurred since they had left their old flat and moved into their new home in Pallister Street. There had been many. As had been the case in their previous home, the couple were again plagued by a 'sense of presence': a disturbing sensation that they were not alone. The feeling wasn't a constant one. Sometimes, days would go by and they would sense nothing. Then, without warning, the house would be filled with a dark, brooding atmosphere that was difficult to describe but nonetheless perfectly tangible. While Mandy, usually in the company of Ella, would feel frightened and vulnerable, Derek would become depressed and moody. In the first days of the couple's residence at Pallister Street, the 'presence' was the only phenomenon they noticed. But then additional things happened. One evening, Derek and Mandy were sitting at the dining room table when the door to a recessed cupboard suddenly swung open. Thinking that a draught may have caused the movement, Derek simply walked over to the door and shut it again. No sooner had he sat down than the door swung open a second time, but only more forcefully. This time the couple became afraid. Desperate to find a rational explanation, Derek ran his hand up and down the adjacent door, which led into the kitchen, hoping that he would feel a draught which would explain why the cupboard door had blown open. There was no draught. Whatever had opened the door, it hadn't been simply a gust of wind.

Several days later, Derek began seeing things out of the corner of his eye. When the researchers asked him to describe exactly what it was, he was unable to tell them.

> I'm not really sure, to be honest. Suddenly, I'll just be aware of something on the edge of my line of vision. It's just like a faint shimmer, or movement, but as soon as I turn my head it'll be gone. I can never see it clearly.

Mandy was having similar, although not identical, experiences. For a fraction of a second, she would see what looked like the shadow of a man standing in the corner of the room, but before she had time to focus on it, it would disappear. It reminded us of the 'subliminal messages' that American companies were alleged to splice into movies back in the 50s: a split-second instruction that read something like, BUY POPCORN NOW or BUY HOT DOGS NOW. The message – so the story goes – was only flashed on to the screen for a fraction of a second, and didn't register with the conscious mind of the cinemagoer. However, it remained on the screen just long enough for the subconscious mind to digest it – and prompt the unwary victim to go to the refreshment booth and stock up on goodies during the interval. To our knowledge, the story is nothing more than an urban legend. But the analogy holds good when compared to Mandy's experiences. The only difference is that the visions of the shadow man did remain long enough for her conscious mind to embrace them, but not long enough for her to focus on any detail.

Perhaps the most disturbing events were what the couple referred to as the 'voices.' Sometimes, when they were downstairs, they would hear what sounded like 'deep, male voices' coming from upstairs. They could never make out the words, but they had no doubt that they were human. On other occasions, they would hear footfalls in the bedrooms upstairs. Several times, Derek dashed up the stairwell and searched the bedrooms, but he never found anything untoward. The cupboard door opening, the voices, the shimmers detected with peripheral vision ... these all occurred regularly, if not frequently. However, there were also a number of 'one-off' incidents that didn't fit any particular pattern. In most poltergeist cases, the infestation will likely begin with unexplained bangs or raps. Mandy and Derek's new home was subjected to such phenomena, but on a very random basis. When the unexplained noises did occur, they were not similar to others. Regardless, they greatly disturbed the couple. Other incidents included a number of household objects, including a coffee cup and a book, being moved from one location to another, although Derek admitted it was just possible that he or Mandy had moved them and simply forgotten. There were other incidents that the couple related to Michael during their taped interview earlier. The researchers think that these are of great significance, and will be dealt with in a later chapter.

As the conversation with the couple continued, there was a knock at the door. It was the medium brought in to the investigation by Steven. She was young, attractive and didn't fit the stereotypical public image of a spirit medium. She had a bubbly personality and an infectious sense of humour. As soon as she entered the living room, she smiled and introduced herself to the couple's young daughter, Ella. After some casual chit-chat she asked if she could have a look around the house to 'see what she could pick up.' Just prior to her arrival, Michael had placed his digital sound recorder in Ella's bedroom upstairs in an effort to record any anomalous noises that may have presented themselves to the investigators. This act later sparked a great deal of amusement amongst the researchers, as the reader will soon see.

Darren, Steve and the medium wandered upstairs, while Michael continued to talk to the couple downstairs in the dining room. The medium says that it's important to sense spirit energies when she 'reads' a dwelling, and whilst standing on the landing at the top of the stairs, she confessed to feeling rather uneasy. She also said she felt somewhat disorientated, as if she were 'tipping over.' Darren was intrigued, as Michael had felt exactly the same sensation in that location earlier. A short discussion ensued with Darren and Steven. Then, just as Michael was ascending the stairwell to join them, the medium announced that it was getting a little crowded and that she needed some space. The other investigators were asked to go back downstairs whilst she went about her business.

Later, the medium said that she could sense the presence of a number of spirits, including that of a rather portly woman who had suffered from heart problems and may well have died in the house. She made no comment as to whether she believed that these spirits were in any way connected with the paranormal phenomena taking place within the home. Darren's instinct at the time was that there was probably no connection; in fact he was rather sceptical about it altogether. Later in the evening, after the bulk of the preliminary investigation was over, everyone gathered in the dining room for a final review of the night's events. As the conversation proceeded, it was suddenly interrupted by a loud thud that seemed to come from upstairs. The researchers quickly ascended the stairs and did a quick check in each room. Everything seemed to be in order, but one thing caught Michael's eye. Derek and Mandy have a computer in their bedroom, which stands on a small desk. Michael noted that the desktop was visible on the screen, and that no screensaver was active. There were only two reasons for this that he could think of; either the computer wasn't configured to employ a screensaver when not in use, which is unusual, or someone had just recently used the computer and the screensaver hadn't yet engaged itself. He made a mental note to look into this further on their next visit.

The researchers then made their way downstairs and re-joined the others. However, after a few minutes Steven looked startled and said that he was sure he'd heard a voice coming from upstairs. The medium said that she'd heard something too, but that she couldn't be certain what it was. Darren did another quick check upstairs, but everything was in order. Later, Michael asked Darren if he'd noticed whether the computer's screensaver had been activated when he had entered the main bedroom, but he couldn't recall. During the conversation, the couple's young daughter, Ella, was sitting happily in her high chair eating. Her cough seemed to have subsided somewhat, and she appeared to be quite content. Then, however, Michael noticed a change. The toddler sharply turned her head towards the corner of the living room where the TV stood, and stared. Then she became quite animated and stretched out her hand, as if trying to reach for something – or perhaps someone. Mandy noticed this, too.

'Does she often do that?' asked Michael.

'All the time,' replied Mandy. 'It's as if she can see someone and is reaching out to them. Sometimes her head turns and it's as if she's following someone as they walk across the room. It's weird.'

Darren and Michael really liked Derek, Mandy and Ella. They were a happy, contented family unit. However, both investigators felt that there was something decidedly odd about their home in Pallister Street, and the vibes they were picking up inside the dwelling were decidedly negative ones. Later, they'd find out why. The day after the investigation, Michael listened to the audio recording he'd made in Ella's bedroom. At first, all he could hear was the sound of the medium, Darren and Steven chatting outside on the landing. Michael listened intently as the visiting medium related what she was picking up 'psychically', before giving Darren a number of alleged spirit messages that she had received and felt obliged to pass on to him. Then Michael heard a faint but distinct click. The conversation continued, interspersed by several more clicks. Darren, Steven and the medium then walked into Ella's room where Michael's audio recorder was. Now that they were standing in close proximity to it, the recording seemed to be much sharper. More clicks, only louder this time. At one point, a succession of clicks interrupted the conversation; indeed, they were so loud that he was amazed that none of those present in Ella's room had commented upon them at the time. Unless they hadn't heard them, of course, which was a puzzle in itself. Later, Michael replayed the sounds to Darren, who was just as mystified as his colleague.

'It's strange,' Darren said, 'I can't recall hearing anything like that at all. Hey ... just a minute! I've just remembered, when our medium, Steven and I were talking on the landing my digital camcorder was running. I'll have to check through the footage and see if anything showed up. Who knows ... maybe we'll find out exactly what those clicks were.'

Darren's words were prophetic. He did indeed find out the cause of the mysterious clicking sounds. Our visiting medium happened to be holding a ballpoint pen as she chatted to Darren and Steven. At one point on the footage she can be seen absent-mindedly clicking the top of the pen as she conversed. Nothing more than the sort of idiosyncratic nervous habit that all humans display every day of the week, then, and certainly not the poltergeist at work! Darren and Michael were slightly disappointed that the noises hadn't been something more exotic, but laughed heartily at the irony of the situation. 'It just goes to show how folk can so easily misinterpret naturally occurring noises for paranormal phenomena', said Darren. 'The fact that I was *with* the medium at the time when she was clicking the pen is even more astonishing as I didn't register it, although to be honest, why would I?' Darren went on to say. 'It paid off then; to be recording the proceedings on video camera otherwise the analysis of this said occurrence could have been drastically misread as potential paranormal knocking or tapping.' Michael agreed.

'It's the first time I've ever encountered a ballpoint pentergeist!' quipped Michael. Darren subsequently groaned at Michael's attempt at a joke.

Although there was nothing at all unusual to be heard on the audio recording made by Michael – except for the 'pentergeist', that is – Darren had still to listen to the recorded interview made earlier. On returning home on the night of the first visit, Darren unpacked his ghost-hunting equipment and put it away in his office, making sure to leave out his video camera and dictation machine. It was rather late when he arrived home that evening – much later than he had anticipated – and Jayne, his (now previous) partner, had already gone to bed as she had an early start at work the following morning. Quietly, Darren crept around the house trying not to awaken her or their daughter, Abbey. Finally, he decided to make himself a bite to eat before going to bed. A sandwich, made with some chicken left over from lunchtime, seemed like a good idea. As Darren buttered two slices of bread, he was disappointed to hear footsteps coming down the stairwell. 'Damn,' he thought, 'I must have woken up Jayne after all.' Then, a sudden 'sense of presence' overcame Darren and he just knew that she was standing in the kitchen behind him having come downstairs, probably to inquire how his evening's investigations had gone, or so he thought. He turned to greet his partner – only to find no one there. He was alone in the kitchen. Darren walked into the hall, stood at the bottom of the stairwell, and stared upwards into the shadows.

'Hello?' he called out.

No answer.

'Hello ... are you there?'

Still no answer. Puzzled, he then began to climb the stairs, wondering what was going on. His heart was beating loudly in his ears, and he was suddenly overcome with an overwhelming feeling that his partner was still fast asleep in bed. He opened the bedroom door, peered in and – sure enough – there she was, lying sprawled across the king-size double bed, fast sleep. Darren was glad that he hadn't disturbed her, but he couldn't help but wonder just who had come down the stairs and stood behind him in the kitchen. He knew that someone had been there. And then it dawned on him. 'My God,' he thought, 'I hope I haven't brought anything back home with me.'

Rather nervously, Darren ate his food, brushed his teeth and went off to bed. Before he knew it morning had arrived, and all was normal. He and Jayne rose from their bed to the sound of their daughter Abbey shouting and singing from her room. She had been awake since 5am, and was impatient to go downstairs and watch children's TV before heading off to spend some time with her child-minder, as Darren and his partner both had to go to work.

'Good night last night?' Jayne asked.

'Yeah, interesting', Darren replied, studiously omitting to mention the incident that had taken place in the kitchen the night before.

Several days came and went. Because Darren was busy with work and family commitments, he didn't have an opportunity to listen to the tape-recorded interview made at the house on Pallister Street until the following Sunday afternoon. Jayne had taken their daughter out to see 'mamar', as she called her grandmother, and Darren had the day free. As soon as he had the time, he retrieved the dictation machine from his study and took it downstairs. Darren put the kettle on and made himself a cup of tea. Then he walked into his living room with note pad and pen, sat down and pressed the *play* button on his recording device. The reels on the tape recorder began to chug round and round and soon a gentle hissing noise could clearly be heard. Darren sat and waited, and waited, and waited some more. No interview, but merely the steady hiss of what sounded like a blank tape. Puzzled by this, Darren fast-forwarded the recording only to find nothing at all. Annoyed and upset, he concluded that somehow he must have made a 'pigs ear' of the recording and never actually taped anything. Then a thought struck him: prior to coming home, the tape had been tested and the interview was definitely there. So where was it now?

Darren remembered listening to a small part of the recording before rewinding the tape (side A) back to its beginning, so that listening to it another day would be made easy. He then double-checked the cassette recorder and took out the tape. To his utter surprise he found that not only had the tape been fast-forwarded to the end of side A, the tape itself had been turned around inside the machine so side B was ready to play. Side B was blank, and that is why the constant hiss was heard rather than the recorded interview. But how could that have happened? Darren distinctly recalled re-winding side A of the cassette after the recording at the house, and he was completely certain that he hadn't turned the tape over.

Later he commented, 'I just don't make mistakes like that. I'm very meticulous with what I do and I would have remembered doing something like that. Furthermore, there was no need for the tape to be on side B as it was completely blank. It just didn't make sense.' This odd occurrence set Darren thinking about the night he had returned from the infected house. He had experienced one or two enigmatic incidents. He recalled the footsteps, which he had heard coming down the stairs, and also the 'sense of presence' that he had experienced in the kitchen. Had some kind of paranormal activity actually taken place within his own home? If so, there was only one explanation that came to mind: contagion.

Darren had told Michael that he had been free from contagion during the investigation at South Shields, although this wasn't strictly true. Darren had been subject to the attentions of the Lock Street poltergeist at his home, but for reasons that will be made clear later in this book, he had kept quiet about it. Once again, the thought overwhelmed him like a dark, brooding cloud. It dawned on him that if this were the case, and contagion had been experienced again, albeit only a little, then the entity at Pallister Street might very well be a poltergeist. Although the investigation at Pallister Street was in its early days, this thought disturbed Darren. He decided to rewind the tape back to where it had originally been left, at the beginning of side A, and play it. This time, the interview that Michael had carried out with Derek and Mandy was there. Darren sat anxiously, waiting to hear what had transpired during the conversation. After a short pause it began.

'You've lived in the house since October last year?' Michael asked.

The reply was in the affirmative.

'Have you ever had, previous to that, together or separately, a history of any paranormal experiences of any kind? Nothing of any major importance... but anything paranormal, no matter how big or small... anything you may have thought was a bit weird?'

'We'd never seen anything... but we have heard stuff before,' answered Mandy.

'Things did happen at the old flat,' added Derek.

'Of course this will remain confidential and is strictly for our records only, but have either of you ever suffered from temporal lobe epilepsy or anything like that?'

'No,' both Derek and Mandy replied.

'Right... Okay', said Michael, as he prepared to ask his next question.

At this point in the recording, Darren and Steve can be heard excusing themselves, as they left to conduct some experiments on the first floor of the house. Michael continued with the interview.

'Have either of you ever been diagnosed as bi-polar?'

'No.'

'Have either of you ever been in a serious accident of any kind, like a car wreck, for example?'

'No.'

'You see, all these things have in the past been known to actually trigger hauntings... I won't go into specifics but it... erm, it's complicated...

but they are relevant. How long were you in the house before the first incident happened?'

'I had the first experience in the first week, when I got that feeling at the top of the stairs,' said Mandy.

Derek then added,

'When we moved in, we had to be put up in a hotel for three days and it was basically straight after that we just felt... uncomfortable.'

'Why were you in a hotel?'

'Because we had a gas leak,' said Derek.

'Do either of you belong to religious families or anything like that?'

'No,' they both replied.

'Right, what was the very first thing to happen here?' asked Michael.

Derek answered first:

'Well I would say the first thing to happen to me was after we had been here a month or so, and I was down here in the living room on my own when I saw a black sort of shape slowly pass by. So I went upstairs rather quickly; that was my first odd experience.'

'So, what was yours?' Michael asked Mandy.

'It was, just after a week or so of living here... when I felt a horrible feeling at the top of the stairs. I had never had anything like that before...'

'Like a sense of presence?'

'Yeah...it was horrible, and then...'

'It might be difficult for you, but if you can, try to cast your mind back and tell me how far apart were those two incidents.'

'I would say just a few weeks,' responded Mandy. 'I never said anything at all to Derek about my experience, as I was staying at a friend's at the time and she thought I was just being silly, so I said nothing to anyone else.'

'Did Derek mention his experience to you, then?'

'Yes,' said Mandy.

'OK, then... if you can cast your mind back... it might be difficult, but don't worry if you can't... but if you can, could you recall whether around that time there was any sort of stress in your house at the time of the sighting? Had you just had a row, were you worried about anything in particular, unpaid bills, debts, or trouble at work or anything that may induce a form of stress or anxiety?'

Derek paused, 'I think the only time we suffered from stress was when we were planning the wedding... but that was last December; that sighting happened well before then.'

Later, after hearing this part of the interview, Darren commented, 'Although the wedding was in the December, they said the sighting happened before that. Doesn't stress occur prior to weddings during the preparation for the big day? They moved into their new home in the October – two months before the wedding. To me, that would suggest they were, like most people, probably stressed out during the wedding preparations, and that is the period during which Derek saw the 'black shape' move across the room.'

Michael continued the interview.

'And what about you Mandy... were you undergoing any form of stress at this time?'

'No... we had just moved in, so we were quite happy.'

'So there was nothing at all at the time that was upsetting you, then?'

'No.'

'Have you noticed any particular pattern to the things that have happened – like certain areas of the house, or certain times within the day?'

'Well,' said Mandy, 'the place I normally feel it most is at the kitchen door, the passage, and the top of the stairs, on the landing.'

'Mine is the kitchen door, too,' added Derek, 'and the landing... and sometimes the main bedroom upstairs... but it's mainly the landing for me.'

'Okay, so that was your first two experiences... so if you could just explain... how did it develop from there after you saw the black shape, and had the strange sensation at the top of the stairs?'

'Well, to be honest, we have both been very scared since, really... and we talk about it every day', said Derek. 'There are little bits and bobs [relatively minor occurrences] happening every day now... like Ella... she'll be looking at the door and there is nothing there... and she's smiling and laughing one minute then she gets very serious.'

'Have you noticed any of the household items being moved around, like... have you seen them in one place one minute, and then notice them elsewhere in the house?'

'Yes... ,' replied Mandy, 'we had a little air freshener thing that had a little fan inside... we left it operating one time and when I returned to turn it off I found there was no bottom on it; it had been taken off somehow – it had to be pulled quite hard to get it off – and we found the bottom smashed all over the floor.'

'That's very, very interesting.'

'Not only that,' said Derek, 'but the air freshener was found on a different shelf to the one we left it on; it couldn't have fallen and landed the way it did.'

'We have also heard things moving while we have been upstairs, too, and we have also heard things in the kitchen – noises that we can't explain,' said Mandy.

Derek had also heard noises, but of a different kind.

'I have also heard my name being called out, too, every few weeks or so when I am in the house... in fact, it happened just 30 minutes before you, Darren and Steven came tonight.'

'Where did the voice come from?'

'From upstairs. I was on the PC at the time, and I even replied to it by saying, "What?" It wasn't Mandy, so God knows who it was.'

'When you think about all the incidents that have happened, do you get any warning that something may be about to occur, or is it with no warning whatsoever?'

'It's always a surprise', said Derek. 'I sometimes get little feelings... like, it's hard to explain; sometimes, when I am sitting upstairs, I'd be fine, and then I'd be really scared... as though I am sensing something, like someone standing really close behind me.'

Michael paused for a moment, and then spoke.

'Now, this probably sounds as though I am splitting hairs, but you'll get the gist of what I am getting at and see the point. Obviously, these things that are happening, we have no reason to doubt you and there could very well be some sort of paranormal activity. There's something going on that is making them happen. Now obviously, these things are unnerving... and probably sometimes really scary, because there is something going on in the house and you can't control it. It's like someone messing around, just in the same way as if you had a real flesh-and-blood person in the house that you didn't want there, wandering around, doing stuff without your permission. So we fully understand that. Now the thing is, although you are scared, are you scared because you don't know what is going on, or what is causing it, or is it that whatever it is that is happening seems *designed* to scare you? Do you know what I mean? You see, what I am saying is that... are the things going on in the house frightening you because they appear to be attempting to frighten you – can you see what I am getting at?'

On reflection, Michael feels that he didn't articulate his question particularly well. What he was trying to do was to establish exactly what it was that was frightening the couple. Was it simply the thought of something occurring in their home that they couldn't explain, or did they feel that whatever was happening was being engineered deliberately to scare them?

'Yes, I know what you mean,' replied Mandy. 'It seems like... you see we are not easily scared; well, I'm not, so whatever it is must be going out of its way to frighten us... and it's working.'

'Okay, can you give us some examples of things that it has done that would make you think that *it* was deliberately going out of its way to frighten you?' asked Michael.

'Right', said Mandy. 'When we were in the bedroom and we heard something running about in the loft... it was like the sound of a person running about... thump, thump, thump, thump.'

'Has it ever done anything, or shown any sense of aggression to you in any way, or done anything that makes you think that, whatever it is, it's angry or aggressive? Or is it just confusing you... do you know what I mean?'

'I would just say definitely yes!' exclaimed Derek. 'There have been times when I have been in the kitchen... when I open the door and suddenly the door next to the kitchen just flies open.'

'But has it ever done anything that makes you think it is angry, like slammed anything, or crashed about in an aggressive manner?'

'Yes,' Mandy added, 'we've heard bangs and thumps coming from upstairs, deafening ones, too; you would think someone was up there stamping on the floor... that, to me, sounded very aggressive. In fact, that night we were going to call the police, as we were that convinced there was an intruder in our house. We heard banging from above... that moved around, and then it sounded like it came down the stairs. The thump, thump, thump, as it came down the staircase... but there was no one there, and we were terrified. You could say there was an intruder in the house, but an invisible one.'

Darren, at this point, nearly spat out a mouthful of his tea all over his living room floor; he couldn't believe what he was hearing, the words 'invisible' and 'intruder' being used in the same sentence. Talk about spooky coincidences!' he thought. At that time Darren and Michael's book *The South Shields Poltergeist* hadn't been released. It was just plain weird that Mandy should have chosen to use two words lifted directly from the subtitle of the book (One Family's Fight Against an Invisible Intruder). Still, it could have been nothing more than a bizarre coincidence. Darren also knew that Michael must have cottoned on to what Mandy had just said on the tape – if it really was a coincidence, it was an uncanny one.

The interview continued.

'Do you know anything about who lived in the house before you?'

'We know where they live now,' Derek replied.

'But do you know anything about them?'

'Not really, just that they were a normal, nice family.'

'Mandy, you mentioned earlier on, before the tape recorder was taping, that you felt something touch you on the leg; again, that is something that is frightening, but have you ever felt any other of your body parts being touched?'

'Just when I walked in from the kitchen one time, and I thought Derek touched my behind in a saucy-but-fun way... but he said it wasn't him.'

'Have you ever experienced other household objects moving around, either seeing them move with your eyes or finding things out of place?'

'Well', replied Mandy, 'it's hard to notice really... with having Ella around, things are everywhere most of the time.'

'What about your lights, do they ever flicker, or do you have problems with the electricity?'

'Funny you should say that', said Mandy, 'The light in the hallway is always blowing, and we have to keep changing the bulbs and fuses.'

'Okay... have you ever come home to find a light on that had been left off, or a light off that had been left on?'

'Don't know... we don't really keep a record... and I can't remember any such instances anyway,' said Mandy.

'Nah...' added Derek. 'Most things we notice are mainly the noises, and the sensing of stuff.'

Then Mandy mentioned something that struck the investigators as odd.

'It's just the constant dreams, the nightmares I am always having. They get me!'

'That's interesting,' said Michael. 'Can I ask you – only as far as you feel comfortable – can you give me some examples of your dreams, please?'

'The first one seemed so real, but it must have been a dream. In the dream I was asleep, then... then I [dreamt that I] woke from it to find I was sitting in bed, although the bed was in a different place. I looked over to where the computer chair is and it moved about three feet across the floor by itself. I couldn't remember if it was real or if it was a dream, so I just put it down to being a dream. In another dream, I came downstairs and went into the kitchen. When I opened the door something invisible pushed me hard, and I fell into the wall behind me. It was terrifying.'

'And this was a dream?'

'Yeah, I always dream that I am asleep, and I wake up... when it happens.'

'Have you ever suffered from any sleep disorders such as narcolepsy or cataplexy?'

'No, I don't think so,' Mandy said.

'What about sleep paralysis, when you wake up and find you can't move, and it feels someone is holding you down in your bed?'

Yeah... that has happened to me a few times', Mandy said. 'The worst one I've had – it was a night terror – was when I woke up one night. This happens quite a lot, and I found I couldn't move a muscle. It felt like someone was holding me down; it was a horrible feeling... the worst bit was when I heard a man's voice growling and whispering right in my ear,' said Mandy. 'I woke up crying that night.'

'Can you remember what was said... in your ear?'

'No, I couldn't understand it,' Mandy replied.

'It's funny you mention that,' added Derek, 'because I remember a night in the old flat when we both had a night terror at the same time and we were both paralysed in our beds. We looked at each other in total fear, but could do nothing about it.'

'Have you ever felt as though someone was straddling your chest, during these experiences?' Michael asked.

'Yes, I have had that a few times,' Mandy interjected, 'Not all the time, but sometimes... I have even been pulled out [of] the bed... I mean, that can't be a frigging dream, can it?'

'This is going to sound bizarre... but have you ever awoken from your slumbers to find that you are wearing different garments from the ones you put on to go to bed?'

'No.'

'Have you ever awoken from your slumbers to find that you are covered in scratches or bruises?'

'I'm always waking up covered in bruises, aren't I?' said Mandy.

'All the time,' confirmed Derek.

'Once, I even woke up covered in scratches,' added Mandy.

'That's very interesting.'

Michael's interest in scratches, and whether they had ever woken up wearing different clothing, was prompted by his determination to make sure that the investigators weren't dealing with another phenomenon entirely; a peculiar set of circumstances known to UFO researchers as the *Alien Abduction Phenomenon*. People who claim to have been abducted by aliens – and there are literally millions of them – have occasionally claimed that when they woke up after an abduction experience they found themselves wearing apparel different from that, which they went to sleep in. On a number of occasions they have even claimed that the clothing they woke up in didn't even belong to them. However, waking up with scratches is also a common symptom of poltergeist infestation. A really peculiar link to the UFO phenomenon lies in the fact that UFO witnesses often report poltergeist-like symptoms in their homes, either just before their sighting, just afterwards, or both. Michael personally investigated just such a case back in 2005. He eventually wrote the story up in his popular newspaper column in *The Shields Gazette*.

In February of that year, Michael was delighted to get a call from Kelly Barton* of South Shields, Tyne & Wear, telling him that she'd filmed some rather odd objects in the sky. Within two hours he was sitting on her living room sofa listening to a very intriguing tale. She surely had filmed something rather extraordinary – but more of this later. Kelly's strange tale actually began several days before her unusual encounter. With hindsight, she now suspects that something truly odd was happening even then, with the subsequent events being linked.

On Monday 14 February, Kelly and her partner Les McFallen* were relaxing in their lounge, watching TV, when, without warning, they heard the alarm clock go off in the bedroom of their oldest daughter, Julie*. It was 9.30pm, and the alarm shouldn't have activated till the following morning. Les went upstairs and switched it off, noting that Julie was still sleeping. Strange, perhaps, that the noise hadn't woken her.

On the following Tuesday, Wednesday and Thursday nothing untoward happened, but Friday proved to be a different kettle of fish, as they say. In the early hours of the morning, Kelly woke up with a start. The first thing she noticed was that the room was unusually cold. She was just about to go back to sleep when she heard a noise – the sound of Julie running along the passage towards her room. Kelly waited a few seconds, obviously expecting Julie to enter. Nothing happened. Curious, Kelly got out of bed and opened the door. No one was there. She checked on both her daughters, and found them to be sound asleep. Whatever or whoever had made the noise, it hadn't been Julie – and yet Kelly is convinced that it was exactly the sound of Julie running along the corridor that she'd heard. The following morning, Les had been messing around with a novelty gadget that he'd had for years; actually a small machine that makes daft noises – don't ask what kind – but it's the sort of thing guaranteed to liven up a party that's been marinating in alcohol for several hours. Their two children loved to play with the gadget, as it would inevitably make them laugh hysterically every time they switched it on.

At some point, Les left the machine on the bed and went downstairs. Suddenly, just like Julie's alarm clock, it burst into life, even though no one had touched it. Les went upstairs, switched off the gadget and brought it downstairs. Neither he nor Kelly could explain why it should have mysteriously burst into life. Les placed it on the window ledge in the lounge and thought no more about it, until later that day when, to their surprise, it suddenly switched itself on again. At the time, the entire family had been in the kitchen. Sunday got off to an interesting start. The heavy grating which underpins the fire in the lounge suddenly decided to disgorge itself and land with a clump upon the hearth. Other, similar incidents followed, for which no obvious explanation was forthcoming.

To sceptics, these incidents probably seem like trivial coincidences, for which rational explanations can be found if we only look hard enough. Believers may assume that what the family were experiencing could be labelled as a haunting or a poltergeist infestation. However, to those who believe in the inherent connectedness of all paranormal activity, strings of odd occurrences like this may be seen as the precursors to something far more profound. This was certainly true in the case of the McFallen family.

It is known that those who see UFOs are often subject to strange occurrences just before and/or after the incident. These may include missing time – where the witness inexplicably cannot account for several hours of their life – and poltergeist-like phenomena wherein objects may move without being touched and strange noises can disturb the tranquillity of an otherwise peaceful home. Many witnesses are subjected to what some researchers call 'the Oz Factor': a strange sense of being disassociated. The term was coined by the UFO researcher Jenny Randles. Many describe this state as 'dreamlike' or 'unreal.'

According to Kelly Barton, Monday 21 February, was 'a normal day.' The preceding days hadn't been entirely normal, for the McFallen family had, as detailed, been subjected to a string of unusual occurrences in their home: electrical appliances suddenly bursting into life, strange noises, and so on. Kelly had just returned home from picking up her oldest daughter, Julie, at school. Whilst Julie and her younger sister, Ivy*, were playing in the lounge, Kelly went into the kitchen to make the tea. It was, she remembers, 4.30pm precisely. At this point the investigators will let Kelly narrate the story in her own words:

> The weather had been very volatile that day: cold with snow, sleet and hail showers, and bursts of sunshine in between. As I went into the kitchen, I noticed that the sky was very dark and completely overcast. I knew another shower was coming and mentioned it to the girls as I went through. I suppose I always look at the [north-facing] window when I go into the kitchen. It's actually facing you as you enter. Anyway, something caught my eye as I looked out, and I could see eight bright lights in the northern sky above the rooftops behind the house. They were in a rather straggly line – apart from one, which was above one of the others. They were moving smoothly and at different speeds to each other, but all quite slowly. They were not in formation or moving together, but rather independently of each other. They were all travelling in the same direction, though, which was westwards. I noticed the white-coloured lights were bright and shaped like hockey pucks. They didn't seem close – in fact I got the feeling they were a few miles away, maybe over the River Tyne. I ran to open the back door and watched them for a couple of seconds before realising that we'd had the camcorder out and charged up to film the kids in the snow the previous day. I turned to find it. Luckily, it had been left on the breakfast bar behind me, so I picked it up and started filming out of the back door. I could see the lights with my naked eye very clearly, but I couldn't tell if the camcorder was picking them up, as it seemed to have trouble focusing. I carried on filming for maybe twenty seconds as they travelled westwards. They seemed to go further away and I lost sight of them over the rooftops. At the same time, a hail shower had started, so I stopped the camera and stepped back in the doorway. The shower lasted for about ten to fifteen seconds. After a few seconds, I saw one light coming back heading east, so I started filming again. Then, I saw a second light, slightly higher than the first, which travelled eastwards for a shorter time [and] then seemed to go downwards behind the housetops. The birds had started flying again after the hail, and I filmed them for a while, trying to compare them with the objects but [I] couldn't see any similarities in movement or appearance. One of the main things that struck me was that the brightness of the lights wasn't altered by the two extremes in weather conditions during the time period I watched them.

What Kelly caught on film is anyone's guess, but computer enhancement tentatively verifies her statement that the objects were 'shaped like hockey pucks.' They were certainly not helium balloons, seagulls or conventional aircraft.

When Michael interviewed Kelly she clearly recalled the date and time of the incident. To reiterate, it was Monday 21 February, 4.30pm. Basic information like this is useful, as it helps investigators to correlate a sighting with others that may have taken place at the same time. The question was, had anyone else seen the flotilla of shining, puck-shaped objects that Kelly had immortalised on film?

At exactly the same time that Kelly was filming her real-life flying saucers in South Shields, two members of an East Boldon family were sitting in their living room, chatting to a friend. Without warning, an intense white light seemed to burst through the window and illuminated the entire room for about two seconds. The family and their friends dashed to the window and looked out, but everything seemed perfectly normal. Intriguingly, Michael discovered later that his own mother, wife and son had witnessed this same intense flash when he was out of the house. They, too, lived in the Boldon area.

More intriguingly, a woman, shopping in South Shields town centre, spotted several bright lights in the sky. She watched them drift slowly behind a cloud, fully expecting them to reappear on the other side seconds later. They never did. This sighting also took place at 4.30pm, although there was some ambiguity about the day. The witness said she was seventy-five percent certain she'd seen the objects on the Monday – the same day as Kelly saw her UFOs – but admitted that it could have been the following day. The woman was happy to share her story, but didn't want to be identified.

The flash of light seen by the East Boldon witness is intriguing, for it came from the opposite direction to where Kelly's 'flying saucers' were seen. This phenomenon is puzzling, and doesn't fit into any commonly recognised category of UFO. The puck-shaped objects seen by Kelly and the lights seen by the witness in South Shields are not so problematical. As UFO researchers will know, they are often referred to as *daylight discs* and are quite common.

Kelly Barton's footage is some of the most intriguing the researchers have ever seen, and Michael appreciated the fact that both she and Les were happy for him to take a copy of it away for analysis. He urged them not to destroy or wipe the original recording. Before Michael left, he asked Kelly if he could jot down some background details: full names, ages, careers, current illnesses, and so forth. As Kelly talked and Michael scribbled down notes, little Ivy hurtled around the living room at breakneck speed on a small, plastic tricycle. Michael remarked to Kelly how he wished he had her energy. Before long she tired, collapsed on the settee and fell into a deep sleep. Kelly continued to furnish Michael with details about her background and family life. As she did so, a small, electronic toy belonging to Ivy suddenly burst into life. It had been lying on the floor next to Ivy's trike, and neither Kelly nor Michael was within arm's reach of it.

'See what I mean?' exclaimed Kelly. 'This sort of thing has happened a lot recently.'

What connection is there, if any, between the UFO sighting and the bizarre occurrences that troubled the family in the preceding days? If there is a connection, does this imply that it had already been ordained in advance – by whom we can only speculate – that Kelly would see and film those mystery objects? Or, could it be that the preceding paranormal phenomena in some way 'set up' Kelly psychologically, and perhaps psychically, for the forthcoming sighting? Such philosophical meanderings only serve to lead us into the uncharted regions of the 'enigma zone', of course. Perhaps the only thing we can say with any certainty is that there may very well be a connection, as other UFO witnesses have been subject to similar phenomena on numerous occasions in the past. However, the exact nature of such a correlation between UFO sightings and the poltergeist phenomenon is still unknown – if indeed, there is one at all. Michael later wrote up the family's experience in his column in *The Shields Gazette*. Another poltergeist case Michael investigated – and a far more disturbing one – took place near Ryhope back in 1995. Here, there were no UFO-related incidents, but the scratches phenomenon was once again apparent.

Michael and his wife Jackie were friendly with the couple involved. They lived in a converted farmhouse in a pleasant neighbourhood, and life seemed to be reasonably happy for the family until a terrifying series of incidents forced them from their home for several weeks. The woman in the house, Freda Longthorne*, received a call from a friend one afternoon. The friend told Freda that she was going to attend a show hosted by a celebrity TV medium that evening, but didn't want to go alone. Would Freda be prepared to accompany her, she wondered? At first Freda was reluctant and refused. She had no interest in spiritualism, and would have much preferred to stay at home and watch TV. However, her friend was persistent, and eventually Freda capitulated. She got dressed and made her way to the theatre in Sunderland.

To be quite honest, I was bored. I just sat at the back and really heard nothing that interested me. Afterwards, I just drove home and thought nothing more about it. Arnold (a serving police officer) and I just had something to eat, watched some TV and then went to bed. He never even asked what the show had been like – I don't think he was interested, either, to be frank.

The following morning, Freda and Arnold awoke. Over breakfast, something seemed to have piqued Arnold's attention and he asked Freda 'whether the show had been successful.'

'Well, I don't think so', answered Freda. 'Nothing funny happened that I recall.'

'Well, I hope you're right', responded Arnold, 'Because I'm beginning to wonder whether you might have brought something home with you.'

Puzzled, Freda asked Arnold exactly what he meant. The story he related to her was startling indeed. After they'd gone to bed the previous night, they both fell asleep. But then, about 2am, Arnold suddenly found himself wide-awake for no apparent reason. Almost immediately, his attention was drawn to a small, glowing light, green in colour, which seemed to be hovering in the corner of the room. As he stared at the object, dumbfounded, it steadily increased in girth until it was approximately the size of a football. Arnold also noticed that there were parts of the light that were slightly darker than others. He later commented that, 'it was as if there was a shape inside the light, but I just couldn't make out what it was.'

Just as suddenly, the light disappeared and Arnold was left in the darkness, trying to make sense of what had just occurred. Before going back to sleep – something which he found difficult, naturally, given what had just occurred – he noticed something else. Beside his bed, there was a chest of drawers, and on top of it stood an alarm clock. Suddenly the alarm clock burst into life, and Arnold was sure he heard the voice of his disabled daughter shout, 'Daddy!' It sounded as if her voice were coming from within the clock itself, over the top of the electronic alarm. It was then that the thought entered his mind – could this bizarre occurrence have something to do with his wife's attendance at the mediumship demonstration earlier?

There really wasn't much that Freda could say. Maybe Arnold had simply had a bad dream. After breakfast, the couple went about their business and dismissed what had happened from their minds.

But then it happened again, the very next evening. Arnold and Freda had gone to bed as usual, and after a short while they'd fallen asleep. Then – again, at exactly 2am – Arnold found himself awake. The sphere of green light was back in the corner of the room. And it was growing.

Essentially, the sequence of events was an exact repeat of what had occurred the previous evening – but with one difference. Arnold noticed that the dark patches within the sphere were more clearly defined now. He couldn't make sense of them, but he felt that he should be able to recognise whatever it was within the light. Before he could make such an attempt, however, the light faded out again as it had done the night before.

The following morning, Arnold – who has sadly died since – told Freda what had happened. This time, she was worried and was beginning to regret going to the display of mediumship at the theatre. Now, for the first time, she was beginning to wonder whether something at the event had attached itself to her. At lunchtime, the gnawing fear was still with her, and she found herself unable to eat. On the third night, the strange light returned to the farmhouse at its now established time of 2am. This time, the object within the light was far, far clearer. Arnold could see that it was a human face. Reluctant though he was to do so, he felt honesty was the best policy; he shared his experience with Freda, who was now becoming very, very frightened. The fear she was enduring had killed her appetite, and she didn't eat a thing all day.

On the fourth night, the light returned and the face was clearer still. It was that of an old woman, and she was staring at Arnold intently. He was also becoming rather scared now, and things weren't helped when the shape within the sphere metamorphosed into a bell shape. Now, instead of just being able to see the old woman's face, he could also see her shoulders. It dawned on Arnold that, with every passing manifestation, the light was slowly but surely becoming more human in shape and size. His stomach turned when he wondered whether, if things persisted, it would eventually materialise into a fully anthropomorphic shape. Arnold realised that the couple needed help. The problem was that he had no idea where they could get it. Arnold and Freda breathed a huge sigh of relief the next evening when, for the first time, they both enjoyed a night of undisturbed sleep. However, if they thought that the nightmare was over, they were wrong. It was only just beginning.

Two days later, Freda had just started to pick at her food again, although it was obvious that she'd lost some weight. The day passed uneventfully, and around 11.30pm the couple went to bed. The following morning they both woke up refreshed, but, as they both lay in bed, Arnold related to Freda that he'd had a really weird dream during the night.

'You're not going to believe this', he said, 'but I actually dreamed that I was wandering around on all fours in the back garden, eating the grass on the lawn! How weird is that?'

Freda laughed. Then, Arnold decided to get up and dress. As he sat up and swung his legs over the side of the bed, Freda glanced at him and said, 'Arnold, what's wrong with your hands?' Arnold stared down at his fingers, and gasped in astonishment. His nails were black – ingrained with soil, mud and tiny flecks of green vegetation. His fingers were also covered in scratches. It looked like – and here's the chilling irony – he'd been crawling around on a wet lawn. Alarmed, Arnold raced downstairs and checked the doors. They were all locked, the security alarm was still activated, and there was no mud or soil to be seen in the hallway or anywhere else. Surely, if he'd been sleepwalking, he would have left traces of his midnight perambulation out in the garden? But there were none. There was, in fact, no evidence to suggest that Arnold had left his bed at all after getting into it – and yet his hands were caked in dirt.

The following morning, Arnold again found his hands covered in soil. But this time, unaccountably, his arms – from his wrist up to his elbows – were also covered in deep scratches. What compounded the mystery was the fact that Freda, who was still not eating and was now a bag of nerves, had hardly slept a wink and knew that Arnold had never left his bed. Her weight had dropped dramatically, and neighbours were starting to comment on her milk-white complexion and how poorly she looked. On the night in question, the couple had slept quite well. The following morning, Arnold rose early and checked his hands. They were clean. He washed, shaved, dressed and then left the house to go to the police station for his shift.

Later that day, Freda arrived at Michael's house. Michael's wife, Jackie, made some tea and the couple listened patiently as Freda poured out her story. She looked ill, and her features were drawn. Whatever was going on in her home, Michael knew that she certainly wasn't faking it. She was absolutely terrified and said resolutely that she wasn't going to go back into her home ever again. That evening, her entire family moved in with Arnold's brother in Darlington. It would be weeks before she'd pluck up the courage to re-enter the house.

Over the coming days, Freda kept in touch with Michael by phone. She fed him snippets of information – anything that she thought might help Michael to unravel the mystery of why her family had been targeted in such a horrific manner. For instance, she discovered that two brothers who had lived in an adjacent cottage many years previously were known to have dabbled in the occult, and had seemingly been adept at using an Ouija board. Their former bedroom looked directly upon the bedroom that she slept in with Arnold. Could there be a connection? Michael felt that it was unlikely. They had lived there for years without any bother. It had only been after Freda's visit to the show at the theatre that they had been subjected to poltergeist-like phenomena. Over the ensuing weeks, Jackie and Freda became good friends.

'Freda, maybe if you go back into the house with a different attitude – a positive attitude, you know that this thing isn't going to beat you – it might just go away. Have you ever thought about redecorating... maybe giving your home a makeover? Perhaps you should just draw a line in the sand and forget the past,' Jackie said.

Freda thought that this was a remarkably good suggestion, but had reservations about its practicality. 'Jackie, I'd love to go back and redecorate... but I'm terrified. There's no way I'd go back there on my own.' 'Well, what if I was to go back with you?' Jackie said, 'We could both do the decorating together.' Freda agreed. And so it was, several days later, that both Freda and Jackie set about decorating the master bedroom in the farmhouse. Not a single incident of polt-like activity took place, and before long both Freda and Arnold had plucked up the courage to return home. They were determined to give it a try. For the first few days and nights, nothing happened. Freda later said that the atmosphere in the house was lighter and she was becoming more and more convinced that Jackie's positive attitude suggestion was working. One day, Arnold left for work and Freda found herself in the house alone. 'It was then... at that exact moment... that I knew that whatever had invaded my house had gone. Don't ask me how, but I knew that it had finally gone and that it would never come back.'

And it didn't...

Moving on with his interview with Derek and Mandy, Michael attempted to glean yet more background information from them.

'You know when friends visit, or family... or anyone really... have they ever noticed anything strange? Has anyone commented by saying something like 'Hey, I just saw... ?'

'Yeah', said Mandy. Most people that come in, they either think they see things out the corner of their eyes, or feel uneasy for no apparent reason while being here.'

'Are these people aware that you think the house is haunted?'

'Just close family', came the reply, 'but no one else.'

At this point in the proceedings Darren came downstairs and into the room where Michael was interviewing the couple. He asked if a small plate bearing the face of the murdered Beatle, John Lennon – that Darren had found smashed – had been broken due to the alleged activities taking place in the house. The couple said no.

'Do you ever have anyone visit the house, probably female, around the age of puberty, like a younger sister, a cousin or someone like that?' asked Michael.

The couple shook their heads.

'Is there anybody who visits this house on a frequent basis who is currently undergoing any amount of stress at this particular time?'

'No, not that we can think of', they answered.

'Do you know what, I think that these troubles here could be me!' said Mandy.

'Wherever I have lived I have experienced strange goings-on. My mother was a sceptic until she saw a ghost in my old house when I was a child, growing up; she said it was me, and that I was 'spooky'! So maybe she was right and they just follow me around.'

Michael pressed on.

'Is there a common denominator? And by that I mean do the phenomena occur only when Mandy is here, or only when Derek is here, or does it occur more when one of you is absent from the house?' Derek was the first to answer.

'I've had experiences when Mandy is here in the house, but when she is out they are not as bad, if you know what I mean?'

'Was she at home when you saw that black shape move across the room?'

'Yes, she was upstairs, asleep in bed, and I was watching the TV.'

Mandy went on to say:

> Now we never spend time alone in here... I used to live on my own in a flat, and was never frightened of being on my own – until we moved into this house; having said that, things only started when I became pregnant with Ella. There was one night, after she had been born, when we went out for the evening to relax and have a few drinks and a meal. When we came back we found Ella's crib, or Moses basket, standing on our bed on its legs! We were terrified, we know it wasn't left like that, and we even took a photograph of it as we couldn't believe what it was we were seeing; you can see it [the photograph] if you want.

'That would be great; Darren and I would love to see that if you don't mind.'

'Another thing is that on the photo, you can see all the bairn's [the youngster's] clothes on the bed and a doll just lying on the bed. It wasn't like that when we went out; it was so eerie.'

'Do you ever have problems with any electrical equipment in your house? I know you mentioned the fuses before, but this aside.' Mandy answered. 'Yeah, when we moved in a lot of stuff broke and wouldn't work in the new house.'

'Could the gear have been broken in transit, during the move?' Mike asked.

'No, they all worked fine before we moved, and we are very careful people that look after our belongings. Anyway, loads of stuff refused to work; what are the chances of them all being broken on the one journey?' Derek had a point. 'There were even times', added Derek, 'when appliances would work when we didn't want them to... I mean, the kettle would boil up on its own about ten times a day, not so long ago. We would walk past it in the kitchen, and find it bubbling and steaming away.'

'The TV has turned itself on, on occasions, too, for no reason', Derek went on to say.

'Do you have any mobile phones?'

'Yes, but they don't work anymore', came the reply.

'Does it ever mess around with your phones... I mean, have you gone for them and they aren't there?'

'Oh, all the time', came the reply.

'And have you ever heard noises in the house, and felt as though something has been thrown over and found nothing out of place?'

'Yes', said Mandy, 'I sometimes notice things moving like Ella's coat, out the corner of my eyes while sitting here watching the TV.'

'Going back to the mobile phones then... have you ever, to your recollection, found your mobiles upstairs in the house after they'd been left downstairs? In other words, does 'it' ever move your mobile upstairs?'

'Yeah, all the time,' they said.

'Fascinating... you see these questions are not trick questions. We are not trying to catch you out. These questions are giving me and Darren, a good indication of what may be going on in your house, the type of activity that is going on, so we are narrowing down and whittling away. Believe it or not, what you have provided us with so far has been brilliant. At this point in the evening we may now have an idea of what might be going on, so the quicker we can work out exactly what is happening, the quicker we can help you deal with it, or at least come to terms with it until it decides to depart from the house... which, if we are correct, we think it will. I am happy to say, but not in all cases, that what you have, although it is intimidating and frightening, can be dealt with quite easily. I say vast majority of cases; there are exceptions to the rule, and Darren and I just recently dealt with one of the most vicious types of poltergeist you can get, and it lasted for almost 12 months.'

'So could this one be like the last one?' Mandy asked nervously.

'I don't think so, simply because cases like the one Darren and I have dealt with are very, very few and far between. The most vicious poltergeist documented at this level before our case was in Enfield in North London, thirty years ago. Thirty years! The chances of [our] getting another case of this magnitude are very slim indeed, so we think you have nothing to worry about there. In fact, we were discussing this very same thing on our way down here in the car, and Darren mentioned this very fact, that 'we are never going to be this lucky twice in a row.'

'I feel it might get worse,' said Derek.

'It has been getting worse', added Mandy.

'I feel that whatever it is, it is getting stronger by the day, and I feel it is going to show itself to me and I don't want it to', said Derek.

'If that happens, rest assured, we are here to help you... like we said at the last house we investigated, we will not cut and run and leave you. We will stay with you until this thing has passed, and your normal family life can resume. That we promise', said Darren.

'Thank you', said Mandy, 'That means a lot; we don't know where else to go!'

Mike then said:

> There will be certain things we can do to help you... methods, techniques, experiments and try to help you rid this thing from your lives... if it *does* get worse. If it is a poltergeist, it can be dealt with. The word poltergeist probably scares you even when you think about it, but if you knew poltergeists and understood a little of their behaviour – like their patterns and the way they work – or even the modern theories that may explain them, you wouldn't fear them as much. If you do have a poltergeist here at the house, it will be typical of the vast majority of poltergeist cases. It will be a poltergeist – a very low level,

sporadic one – that will probably go away in its own time without me or Darren having to do anything but sit it out with you.

Darren admits that the contents of the interview disturbed him. There were certain things said in response to Michael's questions that struck a chord with him. Now he knew why Michael had said, 'Listen to the recording, it will knock you for six.' What he heard had troubled him. Michael had been right. He told Darren that the recording would surprise him, and it had. Echoes of the Lock Street poltergeist came thundering back to the forefront of Darren's mind. The mobile phones being hidden and then found again later on, the mobile phones being moved upstairs purposely by the entity... all echoed the phenomena at Lock Street, including the thundering bangs or poltergeist raps that the couple had described as like having an intruder in their house. Granted, at this stage, the couple didn't even know what poltergeist raps were; and yet the phenomenon was described so ironically by Mandy as like having an 'invisible intruder' in their home. Invisible Intruder – two words that had been incorporated into the subtitle of their as-yet unpublished book on the South Shields poltergeist. This case had 'poltergeist' written all over it, but the thought struck Darren and Michael like a runaway freight train – was this actually the Lock Street poltergeist making some sort of obscene return to their lives? The researchers didn't want to see the South Shields poltergeist resurrected.

When Darren and Michael reviewed the evidence, they were startled to see the number of remarkable parallels between the South Shields and Jarrow cases. Some were relatively general, but others were incredibly specific, as the following chart illustrates:

	Phenomena Present in Both Cases
1	Windows opening and shutting repeatedly
2	Appearance of anomalous black shapes, shadows or silhouettes
3	Feeling of uneasiness and disorientation at the top of the stairwell
4	Feeling of uneasiness and disorientation by the entrance to the kitchen
5	Sounds of footsteps 'running' in the loft

6	Banging and thumping noises emanating from bedrooms
7	Light switch in hallway 'blowing'
8	People being pushed violently from behind
9	Sensation of being held down by an invisible force whilst in bed
10	Hearing one's name spoken by an invisible entity
11	Appearance of anomalous scratches on people
12	Finding a baby's cot on the top of bed in the master bedroom
13	Spontaneous switching on of electrical appliances
14	Translocation of mobile phones from downstairs to upstairs
15	Spontaneous ringing of mobile phones when no call is being received
16	Sounds of 'something falling or crashing' in an adjacent room, but on investigation nothing is found to be out of place
17	Articles of clothing moving, as if being pulled or touched by invisible hands
18	Spontaneous opening and closing of recess cupboard doors
19	Household artefacts thrown around, as if by invisible hands
20	A child seems to follow movement of an 'invisible person' around the room
21	Turning on and off of taps
22	Disappearance and reappearance of household artefacts
23	Anomalous sounds of 'breathing'
24	Sensations of being touched as if by invisible hands
25	The removal of the bath panel

Although to all intents and purposes the South Shields and Jarrow cases were entirely unconnected, the similarities between them were simply too great to ignore.

6

THE HOUSE ON PALLISTER STREET

More than once in previous chapters, the researchers have stated that, from the outside, there was nothing even faintly remarkable about the house in Pallister Street where Derek, Mandy and young Ella lived. Inside, however, it is a different matter. There are things about the dwelling that, to some, would seem truly disturbing, and we will scrutinise these aspects presently. However, there is another element of the investigation that needs to be discussed at this point.

Everyone should have a hobby or interest: something that allows him or her to leave the workaday world for a short while and indulge in something more enriching. Hobbies and interests are really nothing more than a positive form of escapism, and they can be incredibly therapeutic. Darren, when he is not out investigating poltergeists, or writing about them, loves to relax by spending time with his daughter, Abbey, followed by some quality quiet time with a drop of Japanese whisky and a good book. He also enjoys other pastimes: Judo, mountain climbing, wildlife photography and travelling. Michael, for his part, now likes to restore old and worn antiques.

Derek and Mandy also have an interest. They simply love horror movies, and this becomes immediately apparent when you enter their home. A bookcase in the living room is stacked up with CDs and videos of old movies such as *Dracula* and *The Abominable Dr. Phibes* with Gothic-style mirrors hanging upon the walls. To a number of people this would raise a number of potential red flags and suggest an obvious reason for the paranormal activity taking place there. In the minds of some, particularly evangelical Christians, horror movies are all part and parcel of 'the Devil's work' and are likely to attract demonic activity. The researchers disagree. Although the décor in Derek and Mandy's home is certainly unusual, they found it in no way threatening; just the opposite, in fact.

Putting aside the moral and theological arguments, the motivation behind Derek and Mandy's fascination with the horror genre is, the researchers believe, entirely innocent. They simply love the ambience created by the old Hammer films that were so popular back in the 60s and 70s. As you walk from room to room, wonderful actors such as Vincent Price, Peter Cushing and Lon Chaney reach out to you. To Derek and Mandy, there is a complete innocence about it all, and, if anything, a certain charm that actually offsets the brooding presence of the poltergeist. Whatever one thinks of the horror genre, we are not convinced that their interest in old horror movies has anything to do with the paranormal phenomena they are experiencing. It's simply a coincidence.

But there are things about the house that the researchers believe *may* not be so innocent. Regarding our first visit, Michael recalls feeling rather disorientated when he stood at certain locations. This feeling was at its strongest when he stepped on to the landing at the top of the stairs. His chest and stomach muscles tightened, and he felt as if he were going to fall over. The sensation subsided, to a degree after a few minutes, but not completely. This was identical to the feeling that the medium experienced, and Michael doubted whether this was just coincidence. Darren, too, while downstairs earlier on in the evening, commented upon the floor being lopsided, or uneven, as a feeling of disorientation came over him when he ventured into the dining room from the hallway at the bottom of the stairs.

The researchers cannot rule out the possibility that there is a psychic or paranormal element to the strange sensations of disorientation that Darren, Michael and the visiting medium experienced at Pallister Street. However, another explanation suggests itself more forcefully, and it is one that the researchers hit upon during their very first visit. The first thing that struck Darren and Michael was that although the disorientation seemed to pervade the entire house, in most places it was so mild that it was barely noticeable. However, in certain locations the feeling was overwhelming. The obvious question was, why? Was the paranormal phenomenon in the house – whatever it may be – only active in certain hot spots within the dwelling? Or was there another, more prosaic explanation? As soon as Derek and Mandy moved into Pallister Street, they noticed something decidedly odd about the interior; all of the walls, ceilings, door frames, window frames, skirting boards and floorboards seem to juxtapose with each other at odd angles. Few corners are a true 90°, and if one stands in a number of locations throughout the house the effect of all these 'odd angles' upon the eye can be incredibly destabilising. Anyone who has visited the 'Crazy House' at their local fairground will know exactly what this sensation is. The difference is that in the Crazy House down at the fair, one expects to be disorientated and will therefore not be surprised. But one doesn't expect to be subjected to this sort of disorientation in an overtly normal terraced dwelling. To Darren and Michael, the effect of this visually disturbing phenomenon, although not paranormal in origin, shouldn't be underestimated and certainly not discounted.

Derek pointed out another strange thing about the house on Pallister Street. Earlier, the researchers mentioned an incident where a cupboard door had, twice in rapid succession, seemingly opened of its own accord. The cupboard is actually a sunken space built into the wall of the dining room, barely three feet in depth and not much more in width. The unusual feature about the cupboard is not the space itself, nor the door, but the *door handle*. Most householders are familiar with interior door handles that are lockable from one side only. Commonly, such handles are fitted to bathrooms and toilets, enabling the user to lock the door from the inside and prevent unwelcome intrusions. It is just such a handle that is fitted to the small, recessed cupboard in the dining room at Pallister Street. The puzzle is *why*.

Obviously, fitting such a handle with the locking mechanism on the outside of the cupboard would be superfluous unless one wanted to lock someone inside the cupboard and prevent them from getting out. This is a disturbing thought, but the handle in question is fitted the other way round, with the locking mechanism on the inside of the cupboard. Bizarrely, this would only be of use to someone who wanted to lock themselves *inside* the cupboard to prevent others from getting in. There is, of course, a patently obvious solution to this enigma. Possibly, the previous householder had such a handle spare, and, even though the cupboard door didn't need a locking mechanism, he or she utilised the handle simply because it would be a waste if they didn't. We may never know why a handle with a locking mechanism was fitted to the inside of the cupboard. Perhaps there is an innocent explanation; or, just – perhaps – there is a more sinister one.

Darren suggests that the cupboard may have been used as a 'darkroom' – although it is quite small – for developing photographs. The handle on the door would pull the door shut from the inside, and the lock would prevent any accidental opening from the 'outside' keeping the light out, in order to develop the prints without any light contamination. Michael decided to keep an open mind, recalling that two incidents of possibly paranormal provenance had been connected with the cupboard. He also felt – it was nothing more than a hunch – that something malign had connected itself to that small space in the wall. He didn't know what it was, and, to date, he has not been able to verify that there was anything other than sloppy DIY involved in fitting a locking handle instead of a non-locking one. The jury, as they say, is still out.

It was at this stage that another thought struck the researchers. During the investigation at Lock Street, there had been a recessed cupboard almost identical in appearance to the one in the dining room of the house on Pallister Street. The only difference was the location, the cupboard in Lock Street from the South Shields case being situated in the bedroom of young Robert. However, he also recalled another recessed cupboard in the kitchen at Lock Street. It wasn't so similar in appearance, but it was more similar in regards to its location. Both of the cupboards in the house at Lock Street had been subject to the work of the poltergeist: the doors would open (and sometimes close) without human assistance. It struck the researchers as strange that both entities seemed to operate in such similar ways.

7

CATALYST

Even before the researchers had begun their investigation into the Lock Street case, they were aware of the almost universally acknowledged belief that every poltergeist infestation has a focus: that is, a person from which the poltergeist seems to emanate, or is in some way attached to. Many other researchers believe that the majority of poltergeist foci are young teenage girls who are either going through – or have just emerged from – puberty. No one seems to know just why this is so, but accept that in the *majority* of cases the notion holds good. Lock Street had been different. There was no pubescent teenager living in that house, and, according to the residents, none who even visited it on anything like a regular basis. This also forged a peculiar parallel with the case at Pallister Street. There, too, the typical pubescent, female focus was notable by her absence. Indeed, D. Scott Rogo makes an interesting comment about the 'absence' of young teenage catalysts in his book, *The Poltergeist Experience* (p. 110) when he states, that William Roll (1926-2012), a well-known psychical researcher,

> ... has in one way promulgated what I call the 'poltergeist myth'. This is the commonly held but mistaken notion that all poltergeists will

centre on a disturbed adolescent. Many investigators overlook the fact that many cases don't centre on children.

Nothing in the world of paranormal research is ever absolute. There are no exact sciences. If paranormal researchers were to be brutally honest with themselves, they'd have to admit that they are, almost all of the time, groping around in the dark. Be this as it may, we can say with some certainty that most paranormal phenomena have a catalyst: something that precipitates events or experiences that are currently beyond our knowledge. Naturally, then, the researchers were keen to establish just *what* the catalyst was at the house on Pallister Street. The first piece of evidential information that came to Darren and Michael's attention was that whatever was going on at Pallister Street, it hadn't begun there. The couple had experienced a number of bizarre incidents at their previous home – enough to suggest that it was there, and not at Pallister Street, that the poltergeist – or whatever it was – had possibly originated.

It had simply followed them to their new abode. This fits in well with the belief held by many researchers that the poltergeist phenomenon, whatever its nature, is person-centred as opposed to place-centred. This in itself needs a few words of explanation. Most seasoned researchers will tell you that ghosts or apparitions are place-centred; that is, they seem to be attached to a particular location. When you move house, you'll leave any ghosts you may have encountered behind. Poltergeists are different. They seem to be attached to people rather than places. Move house, and your poltergeist will likely move with you. The researchers, having established that the entity – call it what you will – that was currently troubling the family at Pallister Street had seemingly moved with them from their previous dwelling, were thus leaning towards the idea that it was indeed a poltergeist infestation that they were dealing with.

Darren and Michael never seriously entertained the notion that the family's interest in old horror movies was the catalyst in this case, so something else had to be at the bottom of the phenomenon: but what? The second visit to Pallister Street took place on Tuesday, March 25 2008. This time, Darren and Michael would be joined by Mark Winter, a member of Darren's long-standing research group the *North East Ghost Research Team*. The weather was rather miserable: dull, clouded skies accompanied by a steady stream of rain. At 6.30pm, Michael caught a bus from his home and alighted at Jarrow. Then he walked the short distance to Pallister Street. Again, memories flooded back of his time spent at the now-demolished school, which he'd attended. Apart from the fact that the school was no longer there, the area had changed little in over thirty years.

Essentially, the second visit was almost a re-run of the first. Recording equipment was set up in various rooms and Michael, not as technically minded as Darren, sat on the sofa and talked to both Mandy and Derek. Rather than focus upon the strange phenomena that the couple had been witnessing, Michael tried to elicit more background information from them. Where had they worked? How had they met? What other interests did they share apart from a love of horror films? It was at this point that Derek mentioned something, almost casually, that struck Darren and Michael as truly significant.

Apart from horror movies, Derek had another hobby: he collected memorabilia associated with famous people. Memorabilia collecting is like most other hobbies, inevitably more complex on the inside than it appears to be to the outside observer. When Michael was a child, his cousin Robert gave him an autograph book filled with the signatures of sporting heroes, including the legendary speedway champion Ivan Mauger and the runner Brendan Foster. The autographs were not in any particular order, but to Michael they were precious. Serious collectors wouldn't be satisfied with this, however. Those who are into collecting memorabilia in a big way usually specialise. They may collect the signatures of footballers, cricketers or rugby players. Alternatively, they may specialise in photographs of movie stars, bone china containing images of members of the Royal Family, or books written by famous authors. Darren, for example, collects both old and new books on the subject of ghost-hunting that have been signed by the authors; indeed, he has a rather good collection, with *some* of his books containing personal messages to him from the late Peter Underwood, Guy Lyon Playfair and Colin Wilson. Darren even owns a very rare, signed, 1936 first edition of *Confessions of a Ghost Hunter* by the late great Harry Price (1881 – 1948). For Derek's part, he specialised in collecting memorabilia associated with some of the world's most notorious criminals.

To some, this would seem an incredibly macabre pastime. Indeed, it is, and it is something that neither Darren nor Michael would care to indulge in themselves. However, it is important to note that Derek does not seem to have engaged in this specialised form of collecting for any dark motive. He takes no delight in the notion that there are people out there who have robbed banks or single-handedly slaughtered dozens of innocents. He has no liking for the personalities of homicidal maniacs – particularly those who have killed not one person but many. Neither Darren nor Michael had gained the slightest impression that there was any distasteful motive behind Derek's hobby.

Strangely, though, it seemed that Derek had chosen his specialist field more by accident than design, and would probably have been just as happy collecting photographs of opera singers, Formula One racing drivers or pugilists. Unfortunately, though, innocence of motive is not enough in itself to protect oneself from malign influences. Some years ago, Michael accompanied members of the Dubberly Volunteer Fire Department in Louisiana on a training exercise. One grizzled fire-fighter, who had obviously been around the block, as they say, told Michael; 'You know, when someone shouts 'Fire' you may not be inclined to believe them – but that don't mean there ain't no fire.' And he was right, of course. Derek had innocently engaged in a hobby that may seem strange to some, but he had no dark agenda. However, there was no guarantee that his innocence of intent would protect him from any malign influences that his hobby would generate. The more Derek told the researchers, the more concerned they became.

Derek's collection had started almost by accident. He'd contacted a fellow dealer who happened to mention that he had a particularly rare specimen for sale connected to a notorious American serial killer. Even better, he was able to offer it to Derek at a knockdown price. Sensing a bargain, he snapped it up, and decided to go hunting for more of the same. Later, he expanded his collection, by purchasing an artefact that had allegedly been associated with another well-known American criminal. True, it wasn't much, but he felt it would enhance his collection, and so he bought it. To build his collection even further, he decided to write to a number of serial killers in both the UK and the USA. If they responded, he figured, he'd not only have their autograph, but an entire letter to go with it. To his surprise, a number of them wrote back. The researchers were intrigued, and asked Derek what their responses had been like.

'It differed', he told Darren and Michael:

> Some actually came across like really nice people – they'd ask what the weather was like in England, and so on. There was nothing in their letters that would give the faintest clue that they were mass murderers, or whatever. Others were different. From the outset, you could tell there was something creepy about them. They'd be arrogant

and boastful about what they'd done, even if they didn't mention their crimes directly. Others were different again. They'd be nice at first, and then, suddenly, their tune would change. One guy was really pleasant at first, and then, out of the blue, he said that he was going to arrange to have me killed. It was scary. I never wrote back to him after that.

There was one particular incident, however, that intrigued Darren and Michael more than any other. One morning, a letter arrived. Derek inserted the tip of his forefinger under the flap and slit the envelope open, but as he reached inside to remove the letter something extremely unpleasant happened.

It was weird. Suddenly the entire room turned icy-cold. I looked around, and it was like being at the North Pole. Everything in the room took on an icy, blue-white complexion, and I had the feeling that I was surrounded by something completely evil.

The letter was, in fact, from one of Britain's most notorious serial killers. The researchers asked Derek if anyone else had been present at the time.

'Yes', he responded. 'My wife and my mother were there, and they experienced exactly the same thing. I'd never experienced anything like it, and I never want to again.'

Later, after the strange disturbances began in their home, Derek's mother actually suggested that his collection of criminal memorabilia might have been in some way responsible. The researchers were beginning to wonder if she was right. But there was a large problem looming on the horizon for Darren and Michael. Their gut instinct was that there might well have been such a connection. Unwittingly or otherwise, Derek had established contact with a number of people who, by any rational definition, were consumed by evil and the need to destroy the lives of others. Even if one reduces the concept of contagion down to a purely psychological level, it is hard to deny that corresponding with people whose souls are saturated with such malevolence could quite easily have a detrimental effect.

The difficulty that faced the researchers was the way in which that negative effect had manifested itself. Had Derek simply read the letter and been disturbed by its contents, there would have been no mystery. Had he suddenly been consumed by regret for having established contact with a maniac, then there would have been no enigma. But this wasn't the way it happened. When Derek first opened the envelope, it was as if a torrent of pure evil had gushed forth from within – and this was before he even knew whom the letter was from. This *suggests* that something preternatural *may* have occurred, for such an experience cannot be explained within the confines of modern scientific understanding. It seemed to the researchers that, in some way they couldn't understand, the evil within the heart of one of Britain's most notorious murderers had somehow attached itself to that letter and touched the souls of Derek and his family as soon as it was opened in their presence. Darren and Michael couldn't deny the process, but they couldn't figure out the mechanism. They believed they knew what had happened, but they were at a loss to explain how.

Michael suggested an experiment. He urged Derek to remove his collection of memorabilia from the family home in an effort to see whether their absence would make any difference to the level of paranormal activity they were experiencing. If, by removing the collection to another location, the bizarre phenomena reduced or stopped altogether, then it might hint to a connection between the two. The problem was where such a collection could be stored.

'I suppose I could ask a friend to keep it', offered Derek.

'I'm not so sure that's a good idea', responded Michael. 'If your collection of memorabilia is generating the phenomena [that] you're experiencing in some strange way, your friend might end up with the problem too.'

Derek said that he'd give some thought to the matter.

'Maybe I can think of a friend who won't mind keeping the collection – even if he knows why I'm asking him.'

During the rest of the evening, Darren, and Mark Winter made several trips upstairs to check on their cameras and other equipment. On one such occasion, they were standing just inside the door of the master bedroom when something decidedly odd happened. Without warning, a pre-recorded video tape shot out from under the couple's bed and landed at their feet. The investigators looked underneath the bed but could see nothing that would have caused something like that to happen.

'It was as if someone had been under the bed and simply thrown the tape towards our feet', Darren later recalled. 'I also couldn't help but notice the title on the tape; it was '*Friends*.' I don't know why, but I thought there was something creepy about that.'

At one point, when everyone was gathered in the dining room, a loud thud seemed to come from upstairs, followed by the gruff sound of a man's voice. Michael went up to investigate, but found nothing. However, as on the previous occasion, he noticed that the desktop image was clearly visible on the screen of Derek and Mandy's computer. He decided to resolve the issue once and for all. He shouted down the stairwell for Mandy, and asked her to join him. She walked up the stairs, followed by Darren and Mark. Michael explained to her that he would like permission to look at the settings on the computer to see whether the screensaver feature was active. Mandy said she had no problem with that, and Michael asked her to watch over his shoulder as he did so. He felt uncomfortable about trawling through someone else's computer unless they were present. Sure enough, the couple's computer was configured so that the screensaver would 'kick in' after exactly four minutes of inactivity.

On each occasion when Michael had glanced at the computer screen, far more than four minutes had passed. So, why hadn't the screensaver engaged after the required period of inactivity? Michael then noticed that there were no programmes currently open on the computer. This jogged his memory, and he remembered that some operating systems had a *glitch* that sometimes prevented the screensaver from activating unless there were programmes open on the desktop. Michael opened up a programme at random so that the desktop wallpaper was no longer visible. Four minutes later, the screensaver was automatically activated. Essentially the mystery seemed to be solved – except for one curious occurrence. When Michael moved the mouse and automatically disengaged the screensaver, the wallpaper that had previously covered the desktop – a photograph of the Beatles – had disappeared and been replaced by a blank, orange screen. A short discussion ensued, during which Michael apologised for losing Derek's photograph of the Beatles. Eventually, Michael simply shrugged his shoulders and walked downstairs, followed by the others. As Michael got to the door he turned and glanced in the direction of the computer, just in time to see the screensaver engage itself.

Hardly had the householders and the investigators got back downstairs when the voice returned: gruff, domineering and decidedly male. Again, it was frustrating not to be able to make out the exact words. The investigators all dashed upstairs to investigate. Everything looked normal, except for the chair next to the computer desk in the master bedroom. Michael could visualise the position it had been in when he had last left the room, and was reasonably certain it had moved. Mandy, Michael recalled, had 'seen' the computer chair move in one of her dreams. Hopes were raised when Darren reminded Michael that his camcorder had been running in the master bedroom all the time. Sadly, however, it turned out that the chair next to the computer desk was just out of camera shot. There was no way of establishing whether it had moved or not.

Before the investigators left, they enjoyed another cup of coffee provided by Mandy. During the ensuing conversation, Derek mentioned that both he and Mandy had been members of a local paranormal research group at one time. This also intrigued the researchers, for witnesses who have a predisposition to investigating 'the unknown' have to be treated rather differently from those who have no interest in the subject whatsoever. Both Darren and Michael have known occasions where just such a disposition had coloured their own view of what they were witnessing, to such a degree that the accuracy of their recollections could no longer be accepted without question. In this case, however, Derek and Mandy's interest in the subject seemed to be quite superficial, and a telling factor was their reluctance to offer any suggestions as to what was going on within the confines of their own home. In Darren and Michaels' experience, amateur researchers and armchair experts are usually chomping at the bit to offer a plethora of different theories about a whole host of subjects, especially if they are at the centre of the alleged paranormal activity. This wasn't the case with Derek and Mandy, however, and the researchers concluded that their previous interest in the unknown shouldn't be allowed to unduly colour any judgement they would eventually make about the case.

Darren, Michael and Mark packed up their gear and put on their jackets before venturing out into the rain. Before they could make for the door, however, the entity decided to entertain them one more time. Mark jumped; 'Did you hear that bang?' He said. 'I heard that voice again', answered Michael, 'but I didn't hear any bang or thump.' 'Well, I never heard the voice, but I definitely heard the bang!' said Darren. This reminded Michael of something that had occurred years earlier, when he'd been investigating another poltergeist case. Again, the parallels were eerie. When Stuart and Lauren Smith moved into their terraced house in 1995, they were under the perfectly reasonable impression that they would be the only ones residing there. They were wrong. One day, Stuart was watching TV in the living room when he noticed a peculiar odour. It was the smell of aromatic pipe tobacco. What struck him as odd was that no one in the house smoked a pipe.

It only lasted for about five seconds, but it was quite strong. It was as if someone was smoking a pipe right there in the room. Then it disappeared just as quickly as it had come.

From that point, barely a day passed by without Stuart or Lauren noticing other odours in the room, such as strawberries, perfume and even the smell of roasting meat. However, not all the smells were pleasant: Sometimes the room would be filled with the cloying stench of either dog excrement or vomit.

The smell of vomit is the worst; sometimes, it's so strong you actually feel like being sick yourself. Sometimes, it can last for a few seconds, other times for three or four hours. The smells even follow you from room to room. It's as if they become attached to you as a person.

Eventually, the couple were forced to consider the possibility that their house was haunted, and a number of other bizarre phenomena seemed to reinforce that idea; a pair of shoes belonging to Lauren disappeared and was never returned. One minute they were there, and the next they were gone. The same thing happened to a pair of silver earrings, which vanished from the top of the TV.

Several months passed by, and then the bizarre occurrences intensified. Stuart was standing in the bathroom one afternoon when he heard the distinctive sound of the gas fire being turned on in the living room. As the weather was particularly balmy, Stuart shouted, 'Lauren, why have you put the fire on?' But Lauren hadn't put the fire on. She was sitting in the living room at the time, but hadn't touched the fire. Strangely, although she was sitting adjacent to it, she hadn't heard the sound of it igniting. In fact, the fire wasn't on at all.

From that day on, virtually anyone who used the bathroom would hear the same, distinctive noises: click and woomph, the 'click', being the sound of the ignition button being pressed, and 'woomph', being the sound made as the gas actually ignited. Those who heard it were unanimous that what they could hear was the sound of the gas fire being ignited, and yet the fire never went on. What truly baffled them was that the noise could only be heard whilst standing in the bathroom. When Michael visited the dwelling to investigate, Stuart and Lauren made both him and his colleague Craig* some tea. Then they gave the investigators a demonstration: they ignited the fire; so that Michael and Craig would be able to recognise the sound if they heard it again.

Michael and Craig then entered the bathroom and shut the door. After just a few seconds, they heard the sounds, and again another time shortly thereafter.

They knew from the outset that Stuart and Lauren were not hoaxing the event: One could only hear the sounds when standing in the bathroom. Michael and Craig later determined that it wasn't coming from the heating system, any other appliance or equipment in the house, or from the adjacent property. The investigators experienced this weird phenomenon several times. Once, Michael clearly heard the sound of the ignition button being pressed, but not the sound of the gas igniting. Craig, to Michael's amazement, said that he had clearly heard the sound of the gas igniting but hadn't heard the sound of the ignition button being pressed! Eventually, the investigators became convinced that the phenomenon had a paranormal origin of some kind, but they couldn't figure out what it was. Lauren told Michael and Craig that the smell of vomit wasn't consistent. 'Sometimes it smells like someone has just thrown up their lunch', she stated, 'but other times it has a milky odour, like baby sick.' Stuart said he had also begun to notice another odd smell:

> It's just like the smell of a shaggy dog that has been out in the rain, Musty and damp. Sometimes I can smell perfume, but Lauren will be in the same room and detect nothing but the overpowering smell of dog excrement.

Readers should be able to see the parallel between the two cases immediately: at both locations there were aural or olfactory impressions. However, in the two cases, some witnesses would experience one sensation, while (at the same time) others would experience something different. The researchers recalled an occasion, at Lock Street, when some investigators heard what they described as a 'piercing scream', whilst others heard what they said was a 'throaty growl', or even nothing at all: one more parallel – and many more questions. Darren and Michael felt that their experience at Lock Street had definitely given them a better understanding of the poltergeist phenomenon, but it was far from perfect. Some bits of the jigsaw puzzle were stubbornly refusing to fit. The relatively low level phenomena at Pallister Street compared with that in the South Shields case led Darren and Michael to believe that the poltergeist at Pallister Street was a mere 'babe in arms.' What they didn't know was that the entity there was watching and waiting, patiently biding its time.

8

THE HAUNTED LOOM

Steven Taylor telephoned Michael in March 2008 and told him that he had yet another 'interesting case' and wondered whether he would like to get involved. Michael asked Steven for some more details, and what Steven told him certainly piqued his interest. Apparently, Steven had been contacted by the owner of a small store in Blyth, Northumberland, who told him that there were some strange things happening on the premises. The store was actually a craft shop that provided materials and equipment for a wide range of traditional crafts such as card making, cross-stitch and scrapbooking. The proprietor had seemingly purchased two large weaving looms from a university that she had formerly attended and had installed them in a room above the shop. Since then, a series of peculiar events had taken place, which led the owner to conclude that the looms themselves, as opposed to the shop premises, may have been haunted.

Strange noises had been heard emanating from upstairs, including voices; and, on more than one occasion, passers-by had seen an old woman staring down from the upstairs window in the room where the looms were situated. Perhaps the most disturbing incident took place when Victoria Nesbitt, the proprietor, was sitting in the room where the looms had been reconstructed, going about her work. Vicky was in the habit of playing the radio, and as she went about her work the presenter of the programme that she had tuned in to listen to, played a series of popular songs. Suddenly, the song that was currently playing was interrupted by static, or – as Vicky described it – as 'an electronic hissing noise.' The noise disappeared as quickly as it had come, but the music didn't return. Instead, there was a short period of silence, which was punctuated by a female voice. It uttered one word: 'Vicky.' Then, there was another burst of static before the music returned and everything went back to normal.

The strange interruption of the radio broadcast was peculiar, but what frightened Vicky was the voice, which had clearly spoken her name. She ran out of the room in fear, and didn't return for over two hours. On another occasion, she was using the older of the two looms to weave a scarf. One morning, she sat down at the loom, as usual, to continue her project, and was amazed to find a second scarf lying underneath the one she'd woven herself. To this day, she has no idea how the second scarf came into existence, and, furthermore, she hasn't been able to work out how it could have been woven on the loom without her own scarf being removed first – which it wasn't.

The scant details provided by Steven had Michael fascinated, and he said he would appreciate being able to visit the premises. On Friday March 28 2008, the day of the investigation, Steven phoned Michael and said that his car had broken down. His father was making an attempt to fix it, but he would be a little late in arriving. Complications ensued, and Steven ended up having to drive through to Sunderland to borrow another car from a colleague. Originally, Michael and Steven had planned to arrive at Blyth mid-morning, but, due to the transport problems, it was early afternoon before they got there. Because of work and family commitments, Darren couldn't attend this investigation. Michael's wife, Jackie, accompanied her husband and Steven on their journey. Her interest in paranormal phenomena is not as intense as Michael's, but she enjoys card-making as a hobby, and the idea of a visit to a new craft shop – coupled with the knowledge that Michael would, of course, have his wallet with him – made the trip well-nigh irresistible!

The craft shop sat on a gable end of a street in Blyth, and was a delight for crafters like Michael's wife. On entering, Michael was taken with the warm atmosphere and overall pleasant ambience of the store. The shop was airy, decorated in a modern style and bore little resemblance to what lay upstairs on the first floor. To the left of the counter was a narrow stairwell that led up to the room in which the 'haunted loom' was situated. Vicky ascended first, followed by Michael, Steven and

Jackie. As Michael approached the landing in the middle of the stairs, he felt the muscles in his chest tighten ever so slightly – something he usually interprets as a sign of paranormal activity.

At the top of the stairwell there were two rooms. On the left was an office and storeroom, and on the right a workroom that contained the two looms and several other bits of equipment, along with a kitchen bench and kettle for making refreshments. The doorway that led into the workroom had no door, and the aperture was covered by a blanket that had to be pushed to one side to gain entrance. Vicky held the blanket back and allowed Michael to enter first. It was at this point that he noticed something distinctly odd: even though the room and the landing outside were only separated from each other by a thin blanket, the difference in temperature was absolutely incredible. The temperature on the landing was warm, cosy even – but inside the workroom it was as cold as a refrigerator. Michael was immediately reminded of his first journey to Lock Street in South Shields, when a sudden temperature drop had occurred in the living room. On that occasion, Michael felt as if he'd been dropped into a bath of ice water, and it actually caught his breath. This was no different. As the others trooped into the workroom one by one, they all commented on the temperature of the room.

'Wow!' said Steven, 'I can't believe how different the temperature in here is compared to on the landing. It's amazing.' 'It's always like this', replied Vicky. 'Sometimes it's colder than others, but it never gets warm. We just can't understand it.' Steven – who, like Darren, is more familiar with the technical side of ghost hunting – immediately began to take readings with a digital thermometer. Then he used his EMF meter in an attempt to detect fluctuations in electromagnetic frequencies. None of the readings proved to be of great interest, and were well within normal limits. During the course of the next hour, the investigators accumulated much information about the history of the haunted loom and the strange phenomena that seemed to have begun when it was re-housed to the craft shop. Michael then decided to take some audio recordings. Over the years he had been incredibly lucky when attempting to record 'EVP' – that is, electronic voice phenomena. During some investigations, he would even record entire [anomalous] conversations – conversations held by people who weren't visibly present in the room at the time. Over the next hour, he made three separate recordings on his digital recorder. The results proved interesting indeed.

Recording one was the least interesting, but did contain one enigmatic sound. At 3 minutes and 40 seconds into the recording,

POLTERGEIST PARALLELS AND CONTAGION

an anomalous noise could be heard: a distinct woomph. Michael is convinced that the noise hadn't been audible when the recording was in progress.

On recording two, at precisely 2 minutes and 10 seconds into the recording, a distinct crack could be heard. At 2 minutes 32 seconds, a faint but distinct voice uttered the word 'Wow.' The word was repeated at 4 minutes 47 seconds. Finally, at 7 minutes 19 seconds, there was another clear crack.

On recording three, after 1 minute 5 seconds, a voice could be heard. However, it sounded muffled and it was impossible to make out specific words. At 1 minute 54 seconds, a voice could be heard saying, 'Hah', finally, at 3 minutes 8 seconds, there was what sounded like a chair being dragged across a wooden floor.

After Michael had finished making his digital recordings, he switched off his recorder and watched intently as Steven started to make some of his own. Steven was obviously hearing noises through his headphones. Every minute or so he would suddenly stiffen and say, 'Hey ... can you hear that?' At first they couldn't, but intermittently Steven would hear things that were also audible to the others who were listening without headphones. On one occasion, everyone present in the room could distinctly hear the sound of music. Michael commented later:

> It was faint, but clearly audible. To me, it sounded like a harp being played, as well as a piano. The music was melodic, but also sad. It had a haunting quality to it – if you'll excuse the pun – and seemed to echo. To be honest, I'd never heard anything like it before.

At one point, Steven spoke openly and asked, 'If there's anyone present... could you make a noise of some kind just to let us know you're here... maybe a bang or something?' Almost immediately there was a loud crack, which seemed to emanate from the vicinity of the workbench at the back of the room. Vicky jumped and looked quite scared. Whatever the cause – natural or preternatural – its timing was perfect. Steven and Michael immediately walked over to the bench and attempted to see what could have caused the noise. After an exhaustive examination of the bench and its contents, they determined that nothing they could see could have produced the noise – with one possible exception.

Upon the bench was an electric kettle with an on/off switch located adjacent to the handle. Occasionally such switches can jump and turn themselves off without human assistance, particularly if the mechanism is faulty or the temperature gauge isn't working properly. However, this usually only happens when the kettle is hot, having just been freshly boiled. Michael checked the kettle; it was stone cold. He then flicked the on/off switch back and forth several times. As it switched position it made a series of dull clicks, but nothing like the sharp crack they had heard minutes earlier. Michael asked Vicky if she'd ever had any trouble with the kettle before, or noticed whether the on/off switch was faulty. She was certain that the kettle had never acted up, and she'd never known the switch to jump spontaneously.

The final proof that a faulty switch on the kettle couldn't have been responsible lay in the fact that, when the investigators examined it, the switch was set to OFF. Had it jumped, then, the switch must have previously been set to ON. However, the electrical flex for the kettle was plugged into the wall socket, and the switch on the wall socket was also set to ON. This meant that had the kettle switch been set to ON also, the kettle would have begun to boil. It hadn't, which meant that the kettle switch must have been set to the OFF position for some time – probably since it was last used to make tea. Whichever way you looked at it, it just didn't seem possible that the strange noise, made in swift response to Steven's request, could have come from the kettle. Frustratingly, there seemed to be nowhere else it could have come from, either.

Steven openly admits to being sensitive; sometimes, on investigations, he *allegedly* picks up things about the history of the building and its former occupants. The thoughts just seem to pop into his head. As he stood in the room, he suddenly began to stare into space and declared, 'I'm getting the name Edward.' He then went on to say that he believed someone called Edward had formerly lived in the building, although he couldn't ascertain any further details. Later, after Michael returned home, he received an e-mail from Vicky:

> Hi Michael,
> Thank you for your visit; it was very interesting. I wanted to let you know I found a man called Edward Spencer in the 1901 census. He was born in Blyth, and was a railway driver. I have left my CCTV cameras on in the shop to see if we can see anything, but they only record for 3 hours. Let me know if you find anything interesting on the recording.
>
> Thanks again,
> VICKY

As he read the e-mail, Jackie came into the study.

'There was a call for you earlier on when you were over at your mother's house. It was a man, but he wouldn't leave a number. He said he'd ring you later.'

'Did he leave his name?'

'Yes... he was called Edward.'

Michael, curious and somewhat disturbed by the coincidence, went to the phone and looked at the call log. The last call received was registered as NUMBER WITHHELD. There were several things that bothered Michael about this seemingly trivial incident. Firstly, it seemed odd that the man had been called Edward, the very name that Steven had allegedly picked up during the visit to the craft shop. Secondly, it was even stranger that Jackie should have told Michael about the call at the very moment he was reading Vicky's e-mail. But there was more. During their investigation at Lock Street, the South Shields poltergeist had displayed a fascination – perhaps even an obsession – with telephones. It had sent messages – sometimes vile and threatening – to Marianne, the occupier of the house. It repeatedly removed mobile phones from where they had been left and took them upstairs into the bedrooms. Also, as noted previously, it had caused a phone belonging to a friend of Michael to ring Michael's mobile when the man was driving past the house in Lock Street, even though he knew nothing about the investigation into the South Shields case at the time.

But the most disturbing thing of all, to Michael, was the fact that *Edward* had withheld his number. Michael's phone will not accept calls from withheld numbers – but somehow *Edward* had circumvented the system. Michael had seen this sort of trickery with phones before: it had been the work of the South Shields poltergeist. He noticed a number of parallels between the Blyth case and the others, which he and Darren had investigated. The most obvious was the utterance of a name. In the Blyth case, it was that of the proprietor, Vicky. Another was the inexplicable temperature variation in adjacent rooms, and a third was the presence of clicks, bangs and other anomalous noises. With every passing day, these bizarre coincidences were becoming more obvious – and increasingly harder to rationalise.

9

CONTAGION – LOCK STREET FRIENDS & FAMILY

During their investigation into the South Shields case, Darren and Michael had been made privy to numerous instances of what seemed to be contagion. Mostly, these involved members of Marc and Marianne's extended families, along with several friends and work colleagues. Some of these incidents weren't mentioned in our original book about the case.

Marc had told Darren and Michael of an incident that occurred at a relative's house when the investigation at Lock Street was at its height. The woman of the house had been dusting and vacuuming the living room in her home. When she'd finished, she took the vacuum cleaner into the kitchen and stood it against the wall, intending to put it away later. Then she returned to the living room and continued with her housework. Sometime later, when she walked back into the kitchen, she was astonished to find that the contents of the vacuum cleaner's bag had been disgorged onto the floor. Baffled, she took a brush and swept the dust and detritus into a pile with the intention of depositing it in the bin when she'd finished dusting the living room. When she returned to the kitchen yet again, she was shocked to see that the neat pile of dust had been disturbed. It had been scattered across the floor, but not in a random manner. As she stared at the mess she could see that the dust and muck had been carefully arranged into a pattern. In fact, it had been arranged in such a way that it actually spelt a word: Marc.

On another occasion – again, at the house of one of Marc's relatives – one of the residents had on display an attractive arrangement of ornamental candles. Several small candles, each ensconced in its own decorative holder, floated in a larger dish containing water. When lit, they created an atmosphere of serenity and cosiness. Until the poltergeist got to work, that is.

When the young woman's attention was distracted, the poltergeist picked up several of the candles floating in the water and poured the molten wax onto the surface of the water itself, where it immediately solidified. When she noticed what had happened she was naturally bemused, but her confusion turned to alarm when she saw that the wax on the surface of the water spelt out a word: Marc.

Another incident of contagion involved a male relative of Marianne. He'd taken Marianne's young son, Robert, for a ride in his car and during the journey suddenly became aware of what he later described as 'a presence' beside him. The researchers have been unable to ascertain whether or not the man actually saw anything, but when the story was related to them they distinctly recall being told that he was terrified. Young Robert, apparently, was unperturbed by the incident and merely said, 'Its Sammy.' Sammy was an imaginary childhood friend of Robert's, and, as Michael found out later, the poltergeist at Lock Street had no reservations about masquerading as 'Sammy' when it suited. Seemingly, that is exactly what happened in the car on that very day. Darren had always been dubious about the 'imaginary childhood friend.'

Perhaps the most disturbing incident involved a work mate of Marianne called Kara*. During the investigation at Lock Street, when several investigators were present, Marianne, perhaps unwisely, sent a text message to her colleague claiming to be from the poltergeist. Marianne did this as a joke, but it naturally frightened Kara. The poltergeist, seizing a golden opportunity, then sent Kara a text message of its own, which was far more chilling. The ability of the poltergeist to be so spontaneously creative in its wickedness was something that the researchers saw demonstrated time and time again.

The researchers noticed something else. The spelling of Marc's name – on one occasion with dust from a vacuum cleaner and on another with molten wax – was eerily reminiscent of the way the poltergeist had audibly recited the names of other victims in different cases.

10

OUR CONTAGION

On Monday, July 24 2006, whilst Darren and Michael were fully immersed in their investigation of the South Shields case, an incident occurred that demonstrated the reality of the contagion phenomenon. Marc, one of the main witnesses in the case, had lost his credit card. He searched the entire house, but couldn't find it. Sometime later, he found the card on the stairwell of the house in Lock Street. It was standing vertically on edge, upon a stair, as if held in an upright position by invisible fingers. The following day, Marianne's travel pass disappeared. Later she found it on the stairwell – in exactly the same place that Marc had found his credit card the day before. Alongside the travel pass was a lottery scratch card that had gone missing several weeks earlier. These incidents were the first in a cluster of occurrences, which acted as a warning that the poltergeist was becoming increasingly active.

That evening, as the entire country basked in a heat wave, Marianne's son Robert was playing contentedly in his bedroom. Marianne and Marc were also there. Suddenly, Marianne became aware of something extremely strange. Bizarre flashes of white light seemed to be dancing hither and thither around the room. Sensing that the poltergeist might be about to engage in some of its malign tomfoolery, she removed her mobile phone from her pocket and switched on the video camera facility. Marc grabbed his mobile and did the same. As both Marc and Marianne fumbled with their phones in an effort to activate the camera facility, Robert clambered upon the bed and lay down. He looked hot, which wasn't surprising, considering the soaring temperature.

Not wanting to alarm Robert, Marc tried to maintain an air of normality. At the beginning of the footage, extracted later from Marianne's phone, Marc can be heard chatting. He sounded nervous and breathless. He suggested that Marianne take Robert downstairs for something to eat. This, the researchers think, was probably an attempt by Marc to remove Robert from the room, so that he wouldn't have to endure whatever it was that the poltergeist was about to do. Robert pointed towards a cupboard door in the room and muttered something, as if in conversation with someone. At that point, the clip ended. When Michael visited later, Marianne forwarded the footage to Michael's mobile phone. After Michael returned home he decided to download it to his computer. He made a fresh pot of tea, washed, and then got to work.

In his study, Michael inserted into one of his computer's USB ports the wireless 'dongle' that could pick up multimedia files remotely. Then he activated the connection between his phone and his PC and prepared to download the footage. It was at this point, as the files were transferring, that he noticed something distinctly odd. Three files, not two, were now sitting on the desktop of his PC. Files 1 and 2 contained the footage that Marianne had sent to Michael's phone. The third file was different, and had an unrecognisable grey and black icon. What baffled Michael even more was that the file had no name – there was just the strange grey and black icon.

Michael was reluctant to open the file, wondering whether it was malicious – perhaps containing a virus. Regardless, he took the risk and double-clicked on the icon with his mouse. The file opened in QuickTime, a multimedia player. The screen was perfectly white, but in the centre, in large black letters, were the words, HA HA. Michael immediately wondered if he could save the file onto his desktop with a name, but before he had time to even think about carrying out the operation, the media player shut down and the file disappeared from his computer's desktop completely. He could find no copy of the file on his phone, and nor on his computer. It was as if it had never existed.

Had the file actually been on his phone to start with, or had it simply appeared alongside the transferred movie clips on his computer? The researchers don't know. Michael also experienced other instances of contagion, some when Darren was present, and others when on his own. Despite his years of research into paranormal phenomena, Michael was still apprehensive about the possibility of his own home being subjected to contagion – not for himself, but because of his wife and others who visited it. On one occasion, this heightened sensitivity to the possibility of contagion led Michael to misinterpret something completely innocent.

After the North East Ghost Research Team had engaged in one of its Lock Street investigations, Michael was dropped off at his home just before sunrise. His wife, Jackie, was still out, as she'd been required to do an overnight shift at her place of work. Michael made some tea and unpacked the equipment he had taken with him on the investigation, before deciding to take a bath. As he walked up the stairwell of his home he noticed an object lying on the upper landing. It was an air freshener – the type that plugs into an electrical socket and expels regular doses of one of several heady aromas during the day. The device had been plugged into a socket in the upper hallway at the top of the stairs. What Michael couldn't understand was what it was doing lying on the floor. He picked it up and plugged it back in, but he was disturbed by what ostensibly was something of little or no importance.

During the investigation at Lock Street, Darren had taken photographs of a night-light: the type that parents plug into sockets, which discharge just enough of a glow so that children can make their way to the bathroom safely from their bedroom, should they need to pay a visit during the hours of darkness. The night-light, which was approximately the same size, shape and colour as the air freshener, had discharged itself from a socket in the upper hallway of the Lock Street house on two separate occasions. To Michael, the sight of the air freshener lying on the floor in his house was a chilling and eerie reminder of the Lock Street events. He was seriously wondering whether contagion was at work.

When Jackie returned home later that day, Michael made her something to eat and then gently broached the matter. He asked her whether the air freshener had been in the socket before she'd left the house the previous day. 'No it hadn't', she replied. She'd been in a hurry to get to work and had suddenly realised that her mobile phone needed charging. She'd removed the air freshener from its socket and plugged in the mobile phone charger. She had fully intended to replace the air freshener in the socket before leaving the house, but had simply got distracted. The mystery was over, but Michael had learnt a valuable lesson: no matter how weird or supernatural things *might* seem, a rational explanation may be waiting just around the corner.

As mentioned earlier on, Darren had experienced his own incidents of contagion, although during the Lock Street investigation he kept them very much to himself, not even telling Michael about them. There was, in Darren's mind, a sound reason for this. The proximity of Michael's home to the house in Lock Street was influencing how the authors carried out their investigation. Darren then lived in North Tyneside, several miles away from Lock Street and on the other side of the River Tyne. Logic dictated, therefore, that the researchers spent far more time at Michael's house than vice-versa, as it was much closer to Lock Street if they needed to go there. Whether it was because of the geographical distance between Darren's (former) home and the house on Lock Street, or for some other reason, the instances of contagion that occurred seemed to take place largely at Michael's home – at least, in the early part of the investigation. Even the instances at Michael's house were few, but at Darren's home they were virtually non-existent. Darren, quite naturally, was happy at this state of affairs. His partner had just given birth to the couple's daughter, and Darren was deeply worried that contagion events might occur at his home when his partner was alone there with her. Eventually, though, things did start to happen at Darren's home too.

Being a paranormal investigator, Darren had to spend many nights away from his partner during his on-site research, and it was on one such occasion, after he had left his home to go to South Shields one evening, that an incident of so-called contagion occurred. His partner had needed to pay a visit, to use a polite metaphor, and popped upstairs to the bathroom. While she was up there, she noticed something move out of the corner of her eye. She turned, looked and saw to her utter surprise that a round bath sponge – known colloquially as a 'white puff' – was moving. It suddenly jumped from the holder it was sitting in and landed in the bath.

Darren returned from his overnight investigation, and his partner informed him of what she had seen the previous night. Darren tried to play it down, and suggested a rational explanation. He didn't want to alarm her with the possibility that the South Shields poltergeist had made its presence known at their own abode. However, she knew there was no rational explanation for what she had seen. But then, on March 10 2008, Darren had felt the unnerving presence in the kitchen when he had been making a sandwich. That changed things. Whereas previously he had harboured a hope that the bath sponge incident his partner had witnessed may just have had a mundane explanation, now he knew that something strange was going on. Eventually, he confessed to Michael that contagion might now have become an issue at his own house, although he still decided not to tell his partner about the incident of March 10. Quite simply, he didn't want to frighten her.

After March 10, until the last week of April, there were no further incidents at Darren's house, but then, on April 28, Michael received an e-mail from Darren out of the blue. There was something that he wanted to get off his chest:

Dear Michael,
During the past few days at home I have been very jumpy and on edge. To be honest I didn't want to say anything, because as we are writing this new book about 'contagion' I thought it would sound rather cheesy – or as if I was making something up to go in the book. I AM NOT. During the last few days I have been seeing fleeting shadows at home out [of] the corner of my eyes. One instance was upstairs on the landing and another at the bottom of the stairs near the wall mirror. The latter one I saw from the kitchen while preparing some food. Sometimes I think I see things. I turn my head quickly and nothing is there – well not until last night. I was in bed, but I was snoring and keeping Jayne awake. I decided to go downstairs and sleep on the sofa so that I didn't disturb her. At some point I woke up, and I saw an elderly woman standing in the middle of the floor. She was bent over and looking at me with a puzzled expression on her face. Her head was moving in a way that resembled a robot – turning her head, moving it up, down, left, right in a subtle, slightly jerky manner. To be honest, it looked as if she was giving me the once-over. It was fucking creepy. I looked at the clock – I suppose that's the ghost-hunter in me – and it was 12.20am. What happened next I can't be sure, but somehow I thought that I'd gone back to sleep, only to be woken up by Jayne's mobile phone. Someone was sending her a text through the night. It seemed as if ages had passed since seeing the old woman, so when the text came through and woke me up again I presumed I'd been asleep for a few more hours. Jayne phoned me this morning on my way to work and told me about the text that she'd received. I'd forgotten about the text coming through the night, so never mentioned it to her this morning. In any case, I certainly never mentioned seeing the old woman. The text was from her sister telling her that a new baby had arrived in the

family. The girlfriend of Jayne's nephew had given birth during the night. The text had arrived at precisely 12.21am; just one minute after I'd seen that old woman! I thought I'd been asleep for [a] few hours after seeing the woman, but it was really only a few seconds later. [I] Don't know if there is a link – not even sure if I was dreaming or not – but it has spooked me. Must talk more to you about it sometime soon.
DARREN

Superficially, it seemed that Darren had gone through a number of strange experiences but there was nothing about them that would directly link them to the entity that had so terrified the family at Lock Street. Seeing strange shadow-shapes out of the corner of your eye and witnessing the apparition of an old woman in your lounge would alarm most people; but Darren is a sensible and experienced investigator for whom such experiences were nothing more than an occupational hazard. On reflection, it's likely that he was unnerved for one, simple reason: he suspected deep down that the South Shields poltergeist *might* have been back. Such suspicions were not to be taken lightly. The researchers found out to their cost that the poltergeist at Lock Street was a master of disguise and deception, so Darren could have no confidence that the old woman he had seen during the night wasn't really the poltergeist. Also, it could easily have been responsible for the 'shadow-figures' Darren had seen on a number of occasions.

Whatever the truth, there was no denying the possibility that Darren, as well as Michael, might now have been subjected to instances of contagion. It wasn't a pleasant thought. There was one instance in particular that had occurred when both Darren and Michael had been present. To the researchers, it was highly indicative of contagion at work.

On Friday, 25 August 2006, when the South Shields case seemed to be reaching its zenith, Darren and Michael had been at the house at Lock Street. On this occasion, it was extremely active and carried out a series of intimidating stunts in full view of three investigators and the principal witnesses. After Darren and Michael left the house, it completely trashed one of the bedrooms, leaving it in such a state that one could be forgiven for thinking that a tornado had hit the place. The researchers went back to Michael's home to assess the situation.

Darren and Michael sat in front of the computer, typing up case notes and looking for anything significant. After a while, they took a break and walked into the kitchen. Now it just so happened that in Michael's office, upon a bookshelf, was a hardback copy of George B.

Hodgson's *The Borough of South Shields*. This volume – the definitive work on the Borough of South Tyneside's capital town – weighs almost four pounds. As the investigators walked away from Michael's office there was an almighty bang emanating from behind them. They both flinched and ducked simultaneously. When they turned round, *The Borough of South Shields* was lying in the middle of the office floor.

'Do you think we've brought something back with us?' asked Darren.

'I hope not', said Michael. 'Jackie will hit the roof.'

The almost humorous notion that the investigators might have brought something back with them to Michael's home wasn't made with any seriousness. They would later come to see how gravely they had misjudged the situation.

11

TIME AND TIME AGAIN

Let's imagine a hypothetical scenario. A body is found in an apartment in a run-down area of Staten Island, New York City, and the deceased person has obviously been murdered. The victim has been brutally strangled, and the killer has left a 'calling card' upon the torso – a playing card, *specifically* the Five of Hearts. Over the succeeding weeks, further bodies are found in the same area. Again, all the victims have been strangled and a Five of Hearts playing card has been left upon each body. Even before the murderer is found and arrested, homicide detectives will be able to determine two things with a high degree of certainty. Firstly, after autopsies have been carried out and forensic evidence analysed, they will be able to announce that the victims were indeed murdered and didn't die accidentally or of natural causes. Secondly, the presence of a Five of Hearts playing card at each murder scene is highly indicative of the fact that the same individual has carried out each homicide.

Murder, sadly, is a common occurrence in our society. No one would suggest that all of the hundreds of murder victims found each day have been slain by the same individual. People commit murder for a wide variety of reasons. Of course, we know that the murderers all belong to the same species: they are all human. Beyond that, it may or may not be possible to narrow down the number of suspects to *one particular* human in any given case. Even the *modus operandi* of the murderer may not be enough. Strangulation is a common method of killing, so just because two murder victims are found strangled in the same city on the same day or even in the same week does not mean that the same person killed them. However, when the killer leaves a unique 'calling card' or 'signature' at the scene of each crime, the situation changes. Leaving a Five of Hearts playing card on the body of each victim is so specific – so unique – that it strongly suggests that a serial killer is at work.

What can we learn from this? Well, we can see clearly that some actions merely allow us to narrow down suspects to a species, whilst others are so unique that they allow us to state that one individual is responsible, even if we haven't yet determined exactly who that individual is. When the homicide detective finds a body with a Five of Hearts playing card on it, he knows that he is looking for one particular killer as opposed to just 'a killer.' Basically, it's all to do with characteristics. Some traits are widely prevalent throughout an entire community or race, whilst others are specific to one person only. This feature of human behaviour would become crucially important to the researchers as their investigation into the contagion phenomenon progressed.

There was one other incident of contagion that occurred at Darren's home that the researchers have not yet detailed. Shortly after Darren and his partner's daughter was born, the child was given a cuddly toy as a present – a stuffed bear. When Abbey would drift off to sleep, the bear would be at the bottom of her cot. One evening, Darren went in to Abbey's room and found to his surprise that the bear was now 'tucked up' under the blankets with his daughter. The question was, how had it got there? Abbey wasn't yet able to walk or crawl; how could she have retrieved the bear from the bottom of her cot and placed it under the blankets beside her? More, how could she then have tucked the blankets around herself, cocoon-like, without help? She simply wasn't old enough to accomplish this. Darren asked his partner if she had placed the bear next to Abbey under the blankets, but she answered firmly in the negative.

There were two occasions when the poltergeist at Lock Street did something similar with the toddler Robert. On one occasion, it removed him from his bed and placed him on the floor with a quilt wrapped very tightly around him. On another occasion, it placed him in a wardrobe in the next room. It would also take Robert's toys and place them in his bed. On one occasion, it took a stuffed toy duck and placed it next to him under the blankets – exactly the same as had happened at Darren's home.

Darren happened to be talking to his colleague Darren Olley, and mentioned the incident with the bear that had occurred all those months ago. Darren Olley had also played an integral part in the investigation of the South Shields poltergeist, and had visited the house at Lock Street on a number of occasions. Perhaps this makes his reaction to Darren's recollection all the more intriguing.

> It's funny you should say that. My girlfriend and I had a similar experience when we lived in Gosforth (Gosforth is a suburb of Newcastle-upon-Tyne, in the UK, and lies a mile or so north of the city centre). The flat we lived in had a spare room with a wardrobe in it. The wardrobe was on the right just as you walked in the door, and on top of it there were some stuffed toys – you know, teddies. There was also a stuffed toy donkey that used to sing 'Happy Birthday', which had been sitting on top of the wardrobe for several months. One day, when my girlfriend walked into the room, it started to sing and dance. She nearly had kittens. This had never happened before, and has never happened again.

When Darren related his friend's account to Michael, he knew it set bells ringing in his head. At Lock Street, the poltergeist would often place cuddly toys on top of a wardrobe that stood against the wall on the right-hand side of the relevant bedroom as you entered it. It seemed an extraordinary coincidence to Darren and Michael that both incidents involved cuddly toys on top of wardrobes – and that in each of the two houses, each wardrobe happened to be in a corresponding position within the bedroom concerned. Another fascinating coincidence then struck Darren. At South Shields, a stuffed *Tigger* toy was found on top of the wardrobe. At Darren Olley's flat, the donkey that had burst into life was actually *Eeyore*, and the teddy bear that was moved in Abbey's cot at Darren's house had been none other than *Pooh Bear*! Three stuffed toys, all characters from the same series of children's books written by A. A. Milne.

Later in the day, Darren sent an e-mail to Darren Olley and asked him when the incident had occurred. He couldn't quite remember, so Darren Olley in turn e-mailed his girlfriend and asked her. She e-mailed Darren Olley back and stated that they had lived in the flat in Gosforth between May 2006 and March 2007 – coinciding with when the South Shields poltergeist investigation was at its height. Darren and Michael strongly suspected that Darren Olley and his girlfriend had been subjected to poltergeist contagion.

As if this wasn't enough, both Darren Olley and his girlfriend had experienced another strange occurrence in the flat. One day, the girlfriend needed her passport, and looked for it in the place where she thought she'd left it – a drawer. It wasn't there, and consequently she was forced to carry out a thorough search of her entire home. The search was fruitless, and so she once again checked the drawer where she thought she'd left her passport: still no luck. Frustrated, she checked the drawer a third time. As Darren Olley watched her searching, he too became frustrated and said, 'Where did you actually put it?'

In response, his girlfriend opened the drawer once again and replied, 'Darren, I put it in here!' Both Darren and his girlfriend stared down into the drawer, and saw, to their astonishment, that the passport was there in plain view on top of the rest of the drawer's contents. 'I saw her search that drawer on several occasions', Darren Olley commented later, 'and I can tell you that it definitely wasn't in there.'

This also made Darren recall a specific incident at Lock Street. On the afternoon of Thursday, 21 September 2006, Marc suddenly realised that his employers' ID card was missing. Concerned, he began to search for it systematically. On two occasions, Marianne checked a drawer in the kitchen. On the first occasion she took a cursory peek inside, but on the second she ransacked the drawer completely, until she was absolutely satisfied that Marc's ID card wasn't inside. Unbeknownst to Marianne, Marc had also searched the drawer thoroughly. After thirty minutes of fruitless searching, the ID card appeared in the drawer, sitting on top of all its other contents. The parallels between what had happened at Lock Street and what was happening in other cases that the researchers were either investigating or being made aware of were uncanny.

From the time when Darren and Michael began to investigate the South Shields poltergeist, they had become aware of a series of strange 'coincidences.' In themselves they were nothing startling, and, in fact, Darren and Michael had often joked about them. The first incident of its kind came just before Darren found out about the infestation at Lock Street.

One evening, Darren had telephoned Michael and they were discussing a number of different paranormal subjects, including the poltergeist phenomenon. Darren said, 'wouldn't it be great, Michael, if we got a really big case to investigate... like Enfield?' Michael agreed, and responded,

'It would be. Who knows? One day we might.'

As the conversation continued, a thought struck Michael: 'You know, I also think it would be a great idea if we were to write a book together.'

Darren paused for a moment and then said, 'Are you serious?'

'Absolutely.'

'What would we write about?'

'I don't know – something will turn up.'

Astonishingly, only a few days later, Darren was told about the infestation at South Shields. It not only turned out to be their big case, but they also wrote an extremely successful book about it – now into its third edition. But there was another strange parallel that the researchers had noticed. During the Enfield case, back in 1977, Maurice Grosse (1919-2006) had been the first investigator to take up the challenge of investigating it. Guy Lyon Playfair (1935-2018) had then joined Maurice in his endeavours. Darren once commented to Michael,

'You know, that's exactly what happened at South Shields. I got the case and then a month or so later, you came in on it.'

To the researchers, this was nothing more than an amusing coincidence. Or at least, it seemed that way at the time. Another similarity was the fact that just before the Enfield case broke, Maurice had become a member of the Society for Psychical Research (SPR). Just before the South Shields case broke, or at least just prior to the book being released, Darren had also joined the Society for Psychical Research. Unlike Enfield, however, the South Shields case itself wasn't an investigation formally looked into by the Society for Psychical Research, although Darren and Michael lectured about it at one of the society's meetings in December 2007, and Guy Lyon Playfair was heavily consulted by the investigators as their research proceeded. Their investigation into the Lock Street case, along with a reasonable amount of the accumulated evidence was later vigorously assessed by Alan Murdie – then the Chairman of the Spontaneous Cases Committee – and given an extremely positive review in the *Journal of the Society for Psychical Research* (Vol 74.2, No 899, April 2010, pp129-132). Interestingly, at the time of this edit, (June 2021), a thorough investigation into the South Shields case and its accumulated data is currently underway, being conducted by American parapsychologists James Houran, Ph.D., and Cindy Little, Ph.D. This effort is being heavily assisted by Darren W. Ritson and the three hope to publish a number of papers in scientific journals, including the *Journal of the Society for Psychical Research* (JSPR).

In 2003, New Dominion Pictures, in conjunction with the Discovery Channel, started producing a series of dramatised documentaries called *A Haunting*. Each hour-long programme featured a dramatic and supposedly true-life case, some of them being of the poltergeist type. When the first edition of this book was being written, the programme was in its fourth season. But now, it seems that episodes are no longer being made. It was well produced and hugely popular. Two episodes in the series, both produced in 2006, proved to be of immense interest to Darren and Michael. As the South Shields poltergeist first reared its head in the latter part of 2005, and the infestation lasted for almost a year, we can safely say that the filming of the programmes in question overlapped in whole or in part with the South Shields investigation. The series was first shown in the UK in 2008, thus reducing almost to zero the possibility that the principal witnesses had seen the two episodes concerned. This is important, as cynics will inevitably suggest that the family at Lock Street copied incidents contained within the documentaries. There is no doubt that such criticisms will be levelled, for the parallels between the relevant episodes of *A Haunting* and what occurred at Lock Street are nothing short of mind-blowing.

Episode nine of the second series was titled *'Demon Child'*, and concerned a family from western Kentucky. The child at the centre of the drama, given the pseudonym Cody to protect his real identity, started to display disturbing character traits at the age of seven, including the use of foul language in front of his nanny or child-minder. Cody then claimed to have an invisible or imaginary childhood friend called 'Man', who purportedly died at the age of seven. Slowly but surely, Man exercised an ever-increasing influence over Cody, whose behaviour spiralled out of control. His mother began to suspect that Man wasn't really the spirit of a young child at all, but something far, far darker. A Native American shaman was brought in to help the family, and he showed them how to perform cleansing rituals with the aid of incense made from sage and sweetgrass. The entity eventually manifested itself before Cody's mother, appearing, first, as a young boy. However, she soon realised that it was no child, as it metamorphosed into a large, anthropomorphic creature with a hideous countenance.

The poltergeist – for that is what Darren and Michael concluded the entity was – had simply been masquerading as the innocent spirit of a young boy who had died in tragic circumstances. Those who have read *The South Shields Poltergeist* will realise immediately how close the parallels between the two accounts are, for the Lock Street poltergeist also masqueraded as an imaginary childhood friend, called Sammy. As with the western Kentucky case, Sammy turned out to be a full-blown poltergeist in disguise, which ended up terrorising an innocent family.

As the researchers watched the programme, they were struck by other bizarre similarities. Both Robert and Cody liked to play with a toy fire truck, for instance. On one occasion, Robert's stepfather, Marc, found the toy in a cupboard, soaking wet. The South Shields poltergeist once urinated on the floor in Robert's room. The mother in the west Kentucky case found her son's closet soaked in urine, although, to be fair, Cody did seem to admit responsibility for it. 'Man', he said, had 'encouraged him to do it.' The poltergeist at Lock Street seemed to have a fascination with stuffed cuddly toys, including a teddy bear. In the west Kentucky case, Cody's father found his son cutting up a teddy bear with a pair of scissors. Man had told him it would be fun. Also, in the west Kentucky case, the poltergeist would arrange the child's stuffed toys theatrically in the middle of the bedroom. The South Shields poltergeist did exactly the same thing. The poltergeist that invaded Darren's home (during an episode of contagion) messed around with his daughter's teddy bear; and the entity that infiltrated Darren Olley's flat also had a fascination with cuddly toys. The west Kentucky poltergeist repeatedly threw a teddy bear across the lounge.

But perhaps the strangest coincidence involved a scene in the dramatised documentary when Cody can be seen playing in his room. On the floor, just under the bedroom window is a play mat, which contained roads upon which toy cars could be driven. Michael had a similar play mat when he was a child, as did Darren. When Michael first noticed the play mat, it rang a bell with him, so to speak, and he was sure that he had seen an identical mat in Robert's room at Lock Street. Michael looked through the dozens of photographs they had taken in the Lock Street house, but he couldn't see any such item. He decided to e-mail Darren and asked him if he, too, had any such recollection:

> Hi Darren, I know this sounds like a stupid question, but can you remember whether Robert had one of those play mats containing

roads and stuff for toy cars? I'm sure he had, but I can't see it on any of the photographs.
MICHAEL

Darren replied within a few minutes:

Hi Michael, yes he did. It's on the full version of the picture of me examining the warped table.
DARREN

This refers to an occasion when the South Shields poltergeist turned its attention to a plastic table in Robert's room. When Michael found it, it looked as if it had been melted: the legs were bent and the surface of the table warped beyond recognition. Later, Michael took a 'record' shot of Darren examining the table. There, underneath Darren's feet, was an identical play mat to the one featured in *'Demon Child.'* When Michael looked through the photographs before contacting Darren, he'd glanced at the one of Darren examining the table but hadn't noticed the play mat on the floor. After Darren's reply arrived, he looked at the picture again.

Not only was it an identical play mat, but it was also positioned in exactly the same location on the floor – directly under the bedroom window. Michael found it very difficult indeed to believe that this ostensibly meaningless parallel was simply a coincidence. Whether the 'real' Cody had had such a mat in his room, the researchers didn't know. Perhaps it had simply been added to the dramatised reconstruction. To Michael it didn't matter – the parallel was there in any case, in all its stunning simplicity.

Another coincidence – if such it was – involved the employment of a Native American shaman who showed the family how to 'smudge' with sage and sweetgrass in an effort to rid their home of the entity. *The South Shields Poltergeist* details how Michael – who has Native American heritage – used almost identical smudging rituals at the behest of Marc and Marianne, in an effort to combat the entity at Lock Street. The herbs he used were also identical: sage and sweetgrass.

The next episode in the series was called *'Sallie's House'*, and detailed the experiences of a family who had just moved into a house in Atchison, Texas. The couple's son suddenly started to communicate with an imaginary playmate called Sallie. At first, she seemed to be the spirit of a young girl. However, mediums who visited the house soon identified the presence of an older, 'very powerful' spirit that was really pulling the strings, so to speak. Again, the entity at Lock Street also presented itself as an imaginary childhood friend to the youngster, Robert, who lived there.

During the Atchison infestation, the poltergeist would make eerie, threatening noises over the baby monitor, which led from the child's room. The poltergeist at Lock Street did exactly the same thing. The Atchison poltergeist would slam doors and trap the occupants inside rooms. The Lock Street poltergeist did exactly the same thing. The Atchison poltergeist would sometimes appear as a woman looking out of the upstairs window. The South Shields poltergeist did this on one occasion, as did the entity at the craft shop in Blyth and the west Kentucky poltergeist. The west Kentucky entity would pull books from shelves and throw them on to the floor. The South Shields poltergeist did exactly the same thing. The researchers could go on listing many more coincidences, but it isn't necessary. The point is that in all the cases detailed by Darren and Michael – both in the UK and abroad – there are uncanny parallels that undeniably demonstrate an intimate link between them; and there will be more case-parallels presented in chapter 21 of this book.

In the west Kentucky case, the entity (according to the TV documentary) eventually showed itself to Cody's mother in its true form. In the dramatised documentary, the entity is shown with blue, deformed skin. During the Lock Street investigation, Michael interviewed young Robert, a toddler at the time, and asked him what 'Sammy' was like:

'What does Sammy look like?'

'He has blue skin.'

'Really?'

'Yes. His skin has bubbles on it.'

The truly disturbing common denominator between all these cases is that the poltergeist – whatever one conceives it to be – repeatedly masquerades as something innocent to hide its dark, terrible nature. Slowly and systematically it will insert its psychic hooks into its victims and then, when it is too late, reveal itself as it truly is.

12

I'M SICK OF THE BASTARD!

On 15 February 2008, Darren was informed of a poltergeist-like experience that had the hallmarks of a bona-fide and very interesting case. Darren feels it warrants inclusion in this volume because the witness is known to the author and is considered by him to be an utterly reliable source. It must also be stressed that this particular narrative is a first-hand account and, as it had occurred fairly recently, the details were still fresh in the mind of the principal witness.

Darren stumbled across the story purely by chance whilst chatting to a former neighbour, Doreen*, at the bus stop one morning. Darren – neither shy nor reticent by any standards – took the opportunity to tell Doreen about the book *The South Shields Poltergeist* which he had co-authored with Michael and which was due for release in little over a month. He warned her that what she would read, if she bought it, would undoubtedly be questioned, since the phenomena it described were so bizarre. Darren gave her several examples of the experiences detailed in the book. She turned to him with a stern look on her face, and said, 'I was forced out of my last house by a ghost, only for the damned thing to follow me. I'm sick of the bastard!' Darren, by now very much intrigued, asked Doreen to tell him more.

At the time, she'd been living in a house in North Tyneside with a friend, and had experienced some things that, to seasoned investigators, would certainly hint at the presence of a poltergeist. After moving into the house, everything was initially fine: nothing of a paranormal nature occurred, and she was happy, content and at ease with her surroundings. Then, out of the blue, the disturbances began. Doors opened and closed on their own, a chair in the living room slid across the floor one day, and three tins of peas were removed from the kitchen cupboard and placed one on top of another in her bath!

This reminded Michael of a case he investigated in 2003 and subsequently wrote up in his newspaper column. It involved a man from the Cleadon Park area of South Shields who, on two separate occasions, found four bottles of fresh milk standing in his bath. Was someone playing a prank? A likely explanation, until you analyse the facts. The man lived alone. No one else had a key to his flat. Plus, on the second occasion, he had used the bath just ten minutes earlier. Again, he was the only person at home. The upshot was that this otherwise rather tough individual became too frightened to stay in his house. It was, he said, 'really scary. If someone gets in my face I would normally just hit them – that's my way, the way I was brought up – but I couldn't fight this; it was invisible.'

It is hard to overestimate the negative effect that such experiences have on those who witness them. When bizarre events – events of which we can make no sense whatsoever – invade our lives and instil fear in us, that fear is exacerbated because we are dealing with an enemy that we can neither see nor touch. If someone wants to burgle your house, you can take action to stop them by purchasing an alarm, but how do you stop an entity which seemingly stalks your house whilst you are in it and fills your bath with milk bottles – or tins of peas – when your back is turned? Sometimes people treat these experiences lightly and make fun of them, and that was true in this case.

> My mates were laughing at me, and saying things like, I hope you can train it to put the tea bags and hot water in as well, or does it put the empties on the doorstep? It was okay for them to laugh; they didn't have to live with it.

Those that make fun, the mockers and cynics out there, may think they're being clever and funny, but they would be laughing on the other side of their faces if a poltergeist decided to pick on 'them'. It would be nice if one did, then they would *know* how it felt. Nevertheless, these days a lot more people talk more openly about the paranormal. It's no longer deemed as *taboo* to believe in ghosts. In fact, it's got to the point where if you haven't seen a ghost or had a 'paranormal experience', then 'you' are the odd one out – however, there are still cynics in abundance! But more incongruous phenomena are things that few will admit to experiencing. The reason, of course, is simple. There are just some things that are just *too* strange to be believed, and, should we admit to them, we will inevitably be labelled as delusional or downright liars.

In the case of Doreen, knocks and bumps were also heard, as was a gruff voice that called out her name. Later, Michael would recall how the owner of the craft shop in Blyth had also had her name called out by the entity, albeit over a transistor radio. In July 2006, Darren took part in an investigation at a location in Durham City, where on this occasion, an anomalous voice calling his name was actually recorded on tape. With Darren, there were a number of other investigators, from a local paranormal research team that he'd co-founded in 2005. During the investigation, a number of anomalous voices were recorded under controlled conditions. They weren't heard at the time, but could be heard with crystal clarity when the tapes were replayed later. The voices didn't belong to any of the investigators present. One voice was that of a female with a distinct brogue. Some of the investigators, including Darren, were convinced that the accent sounded distinctly Irish; others disagreed. At any rate, chillingly, the mysterious voice could be heard to plead, 'Can you help me?'

After this recording was made, Darren later returned to the room with another researcher, Suzanne Hitchinson, to carry on with the investigation. What happened next is taken from Darren's own account in his book, *Ghost Hunter – True Life Encounters from the North East*:

> We settled down in the office and proceeded with the investigation. Just on the off-chance, I decided to leave my audio-dictation machine running whilst in there, and in retrospect I'm glad I did as yet another anomalous voice recording was made. It wasn't until the day after the investigation, when I played the tapes back, that I heard something that I had recorded. Suzanne and I were in the office upstairs, and were 'calling out' to the woman who had previously asked, 'Can you help me?' Unbeknown to us at the time, another voice had been recorded, only this time it was that of a man. The disturbing thing about this recording was that he said nothing but my name, 'Darren.' To hear

such a weird recording of what some researchers would presume to be that of a ghost or spirit is one thing, but to hear one call out your name is something else.

Later, Darren recalled a number of peculiarities about the incident that made it even stranger. Firstly, he has no recollection of actually hearing the voice at the time, and yet he must have heard it, because on the recording he can clearly be heard responding to it, by saying, 'Hold on.' The conversation between Darren and the entity, short though it was, sounded completely natural: someone called out Darren's name, and Darren responded by saying 'Hold on!' – essentially asking him to wait a moment. The second peculiarity is that the other investigator present, Suzanne, didn't hear the anomalous voice, and neither did she hear Darren's reply. Had she heard it, she would have undoubtedly asked whom Darren was responding to.

Perhaps the strangest aspect of the incident concerns the fact that the disembodied voice sounded uncannily like Darren's own. These enigmas may give us a hint regarding the nature of the disembodied voice. Had Darren subconsciously heard the voice, thereby explaining why Suzanne didn't? Perhaps he also responded to it subconsciously, not actually uttering the words, 'Hold on', but merely thinking them. Of course, this only deepens the mystery, for if neither the entity nor Darren physically uttered the words, how on earth were they picked up on tape? The only other explanation is that Darren deliberately uttered his own name and then responded to it, essentially having a conversation with himself. However, this doesn't explain why Suzanne, who can be heard talking in the background, didn't hear either Darren utter his own name or his response to it; this is simply because he didn't deliberately utter his own name and then respond to it!

At the time the recording was made, all the investigators, except for Darren and Suzanne, were in another part of the building, and therefore couldn't have been responsible. Had it been another investigator shouting Darren's name, then both Darren and Suzanne would have responded to their call. However, on the tape the voice, although clear and distinct, is not loud. It is also obvious that the entity that uttered Darren's name was in close proximity to the recording device. The more one studies the tape, and the circumstances in which it was made, the more baffling it becomes.

In the case of Darren's former neighbour, Doreen, household objects began to move around on their own, personal possessions seemed to disappear for weeks-on-end and then suddenly re-appear in exactly the same place where they had been seen last. One particular article, a music CD, was placed on the mantelpiece for just a moment while Doreen tended to another matter. When she turned around to retrieve the CD, it had gone. It mysteriously reappeared on the mantelpiece one week later. Other phenomena occurred, too. Picture frames that were placed upon the walls came thundering down the stairwell after they had been pulled from the wall. No one, of course, was upstairs at the time. On occasions, the frames actually jumped off the wall when more than one person was in the room to witness it.

One of the more alarming incidents of this case was when two apparitional children were seen inside the house. While a friend of Doreen's was sleeping on the settee one night, she was awoken by the sound of what she described as a plastic bag rustling. Stirring from her slumbers, the friend noticed that with every passing second the sound became more pronounced. By now she was wide awake, but still lying down; yet the rustling continued. Darren felt that this was significant, and indicated that this particular symptom couldn't have been caused by what is known as the hypnopompic state.

The hypnopompic sleep state is experienced when an individual is waking up from a deep sleep. It is a transitional state of semi-consciousness and has been described by parapsychologists as a time when subjects are more likely to experience visual or auditory hallucinations. Many allegedly paranormal encounters are experienced during this time. We have all heard stories about people waking up during the night and seeing someone at the end of the bed, or hearing footsteps in the room as they lie there in total darkness. This hypnopompic state is said to be responsible for misinterpreting dream-like events as paranormal phenomena. The same principle applies when the individual is drifting off to sleep in what is called the hypnagogic state. Darren and Michael have no problem accepting this, as they believe that on occasions they, too, *may* have experienced bizarre symptoms of these sleep states themselves. On one occasion, Darren thought he heard a voice calling out to him as he was dropping off to sleep and jumped up with a start. On another occasion, he distinctly felt someone sit on the end of the bed, but upon looking there was no one there. Michael has had similar experiences. Often, just as he is dropping off to sleep or waking up, he'll think he hears the phone ringing or someone knocking at the door. The noises for the most part are illusory, although on several occasions he has experienced anomalous noises that, although superficially similar, were almost certainly of paranormal provenance.

Creepy though such instances are, the researchers don't believe that their houses have resident ghosts, and therefore they believe that these experiences were probably symptoms of these two sleep states. Having said that, strange things *have* indeed occurred, at their homes, as already noted, but only when they were dealing with poltergeist cases elsewhere. As stated earlier, however, Darren believes that this is not the case with Doreen's friend, as she clearly specified to Darren, when they met, that she had woken fully by that point and yet the rustling sound still continued.

After hearing the bizarre noise, she then turned around and was stunned to see two children in the room with her. When she called out to ask what on earth was going on, they simply disappeared. The rustling sound ceased immediately at this point, too. Doreen then informed Darren that her best friend henceforth refused to stay over at her house, because it was too spooky. Eventually the phenomena became so intense and frequent that Doreen decided it was time to leave. It sounded like a good case to follow up. Whether it was a poltergeist at work or just a normal haunting – if you can define hauntings as 'normal' – it didn't matter at the time. Of course, when investigating things of this nature, one has to be careful not to get certain phenomena mixed up with others, leading an investigator to wrongly diagnose what is occurring in the infected house. For example, a doctor doing this with his or her patient could be deemed incompetent, and risk being struck off the medical register.

There is no *official* code of practice or any governing body that supervises ghost and poltergeist investigators; therefore, too many researchers/investigators/ghost hunters, these days, seem to be reading from *different* hymn sheets, which can result in false conclusions being drawn. The closest we *do* have to a 'code of practice' is a set of guidelines recently updated and re-written by a colleague of Darren's, named Steven T. Parsons. The seventy-page booklet, entitled *Guidance Notes for Investigators of Spontaneous Cases – Apparitions, Hauntings, Poltergeists and Similar Phenomena* was published by the Society for Psychical Research in 2018 and now comes with an accompanying booklet called, *Using Equipment: Guidance Notes for Investigators of Ghosts, Hauntings, Poltergeists and Similar Phenomena*, also by Steven T. Parsons. Should the aficionado wish to conduct spontaneous case investigation in a serious, professional and ethical manner utilising up-to-date scientific methodologies, then these publications are strongly recommended.

Darren and Michael, over the years, have heard countless stories of well-meaning amateurs, accompanied by their team mediums, entering a household or a property of some sort and seemingly discovering not one ghost but an overabundance of them: one upstairs in the bedroom, one on the stairwell, one in the kitchen, two children in the living room, a spectral dog, a phantom cat, the ghost of a goldfish called Jaws, a poltergeist in the garden shed, and let us not forget the resident 'merciless demon' that often shows his face once in a while! The householders end up more frightened and confused *after* the investigators have visited than they were before they came. Often, after the gross misdiagnosis has been made, they'll leave the troubled abode never to return!

This actually happened at the house on Lock Street, and the family in question were at one point informed that no less than six entities resided in their abode. In Darren's opinion, this was more than likely to be utter nonsense. Darren and Michael believe, however, that there *are* potentially reputable mediums out there that *can* help, but not many; one just needs to be careful which ones you choose. The renowned psychical researcher Patricia Robertson – former president of the Scottish Society for Psychical Research and an associate of Darren's – would wholeheartedly agree with the researchers on that one, based upon her outstanding work with the late Prof Archie Roy into mediumship and communication after bodily death.

That said, Darren and Michael *eventually* came to believe that they had gotten to the bottom of the Lock Street case after months of hard work, dedication and determination – and found that there certainly weren't countless spirits at work at all. Darren and Michael stayed with the family and saw it through with them no matter what it threw at them (no pun intended), until the poltergeist eventually departed from their home – like they promised they would. Darren thinks that there is a fine line between true *full-on* poltergeist activity and an alleged spirit that is merely mischievous. He has investigated literally hundreds of hauntings in private houses, pubs, castles, social clubs, museums, restaurants, community centres and theatres across the UK, and has experienced some quite frightening phenomena during the course of his research. One simply has to be able to determine 'what causes what' when it comes to paranormal phenomena.

Darren recalls one investigation where a trigger object – a crucifix – was left in a locked-off room for a couple of hours.

(For the uninitiated, a trigger object is an item, such as a 'cross', or coins, that are usually placed on a piece of paper, and carefully drawn around. They are then left alone, or locked off, for a designated period of time, in an attempt to entice so-called spirits or ghosts, to come and interact with them. If, upon return to what is now a *displaced* locked off object, this interaction should be indicated with the said object being 'outside' of the drawn pencil lines. This displacement may indicate that ghostly interaction has taken place. If a film-camera is trained on the object, you might just catch a paranormal incident on tape, as long as you can eliminate natural causes for the movement of course, such as winds, or vibrations from outside traffic).

The crucifix was placed on a sheet of paper and a line carefully drawn around it to mark its original position. On returning to the room the investigators noticed that the cross had been moved a distance of one inch from its original resting place.

'Oh, my God!' cried out one of the investigators, 'This can only be described as major poltergeist activity!'

'*Major* poltergeist activity?' asked Darren.

Later he reflected, 'The cross had only moved an inch, for goodness sake! Yes, we had a result, as the cross had indeed been moved by something – but not necessarily a poltergeist.' Darren went on to explain to the investigators, 'Look, if you experienced true full on '*major* poltergeist activity' you would damn well know about it. Furniture moves across the room, cupboards topple over with a crash, objects are hurled at you, you may hear thunderous bangs coming from nowhere, and you may even get dragged out of your bed at night and thrown around the room. That could be described as '*major* poltergeist activity'!'

Later, Darren added:

> Granted, they [the poltergeists] can displace objects such as when the crucifix was moved on that particular occasion, but I don't particularly think *that* was a poltergeist at work. For starters, poltergeists usually need a focus or catalyst. They need to draw their energy from someone to do the things that they do, and that is why most poltergeists operate in normal, everyday households where the foci live, work or visit. As far as we know, poltergeists don't switch from focus to focus (although this point is something that will be mentioned again later in the book), and there was no one attached to the pub at that time that we could even tentatively identify as a focus or host. The truth is that other types of paranormal phenomena *can* cause poltergeist-like

symptoms, so we need to be careful in our analysis... unless of course, this particular poltergeist is a *place-centred haunting* as opposed to a *person-centred haunting*? And this is where things could get really complicated. Personally, I think the chances are that the crucifix was possibly moved by some natural vibrations, perhaps from a passing lorry or some other sort of heavy road vehicle... an accident perhaps, or maybe even human deception.

On another investigation, Darren and a few members of the team witnessed a chair moving in an old room within the bowels of a castle. On another occasion, a coin was thrown across a room – which sent shivers down the spines of those present. Poltergeist activity? Not necessarily: '*perhaps* just a playful ghost or spirit considered to be that belonging to a "haunt" case, that enjoyed toying around.' Darren commented:

> You see, poltergeist-*like* activity is not necessarily from a poltergeist, hence the term "poltergeist-like." It could merely be something else messing with your belongings, maybe trying to tell you something or get your attention. Poltergeists often appear to have a pattern, an agenda, and seem to operate by a set of rules – but not in all cases, as we found out at Lock Street. The typical poltergeist will normally adhere to these patterns and agendas, and it is these predictable aspects that emerge in cases over time. They provide knowledgeable and clued-up investigators with inklings regarding its nature, or at least lets them know what might be going on.

Darren subsequently arranged a time when he could speak to Doreen regarding her experiences, and on the following Sunday he carried out his interview in her home. He settled down at the dining room table with a tape recorder, notebook and pen. Doreen, for her part, provided tea and packet of ginger nuts... and twenty Lambert & Butler cigarettes.

'So, can you tell me how long your house was... infected?' Darren asked.

'Infected? What do you mean?'

'It's just a term we use; what I'm asking is how long did the occurrences go on for?'

'Oh, about three months', Doreen said.

At this point Darren began to think that it could well have been a poltergeist. The three months during which the occurrences took place do indeed suggest a short visit from one. This fact, combined with the actual phenomena that were detailed to Darren a few days earlier, also indicated that a poltergeist was potentially at work. So far then, all the evidence seemed to point in the poltergeist direction.

'Was anyone in their early teens living at the house?'

'No.'

'Was there anyone in their early teens that visited the house regularly?'

'Yes... my niece', Doreen said.

'Tell me about her.'

'What can I say? She is fourteen years old, a nice girl and gets on well with most people – except one or two at her school, bless her; she's having a hard time of it at the moment.' Darren, at this point, realised that another piece of the metaphorical jigsaw had maybe just fallen into place.

'What was going on with her at school, then... and is it still going on?'

'Why do you ask that?' Doreen asked bluntly. 'What's that got to do with this?'

At that point Darren sensed that an uncomfortable situation was arising and presumed the rest of the dialogue was going to be difficult. He pondered for a second or two and then explained why he had asked the question. After delicately explaining the theories behind the poltergeist phenomenon and explaining how her niece's troubles could in some way be directly or indirectly responsible for the disturbances in her former home, Doreen sat back and laughed.

'She's not coming back to this house then!'

Doreen now understood what Darren was trying to explain to her, and she then told him exactly what was going on with her niece at school. It has been decided not to include and divulge the details of the teenager's troubles in this book due to their personal nature. However, as the penny dropped, her face went white.

'She comes to this house a few times a week; do you think that is why things happen here as well?'

'What happens in this house, then?' Darren asked.

'Well, not much really; the odd thing here and there... it's not as bad as what it was in the other house.'

Darren thought for a minute or two, and then asked another key question:

'Is your niece still having trouble at school, then?'

'Not as much as she used to; things are getting a bit better.'

Darren realised that as the trouble at the school was slowly subsiding, and her niece was coming to terms with her *'stressful'* situation, the paranormal activity at Doreen's new house was slowly tapering off, too.

'Right', said Darren, 'I'm going to lay my cards on the table then, and make a prediction. When all her troubles are over and things return to normal, I will bet your bottom dollar that your 'ghost' will go away – for good. I'm confident this will be the case; in fact, there is no need to continue with what we are doing today. Help your niece through her bad time – and just watch!'

This recorded interview took place on Sunday 17 February 2008, and, at this time of writing, Darren understands that all the troubles at the teenager's school and home have ceased. Doreen's niece is now well over her ordeal and is getting on with her life as a normal youngster. When Darren later spoke to Doreen she commented that 'all was well', and she thanked him for his time and his help. However, she had a question that she wanted him to address: 'You know, it's all over now and nothing odd has occurred for months; but remember my friend – the one I lived with at the other house and who saw the two apparitions and heard the rustling?'

'Yes?'

'Well, if all this was down to my niece and the trouble she was having... then how the hell could it follow my friend to her mother's house? My niece had never been there!'

As Darren considered Doreen's question, one word flashed through his mind: contagion.

13

ECHOES OF LOCK STREET

In early 2008, Darren was approached by a young woman called Gemma Gorner, who *thought* she was living in a haunted flat, located in the Bigg Market area in the centre of Newcastle-Upon-Tyne. She told him that she had got his contact details from the curator of Newcastle Keep Museum – Paul McDonald – after a visit there one day with a friend. She had noticed Darren's previously published books, which happened to be on sale there, and told Paul that she, too, 'had a ghost'. Paul then gave her Darren's work number so she could contact him.

Gemma rang during Darren's lunch break. After introducing herself, she explained about the ghost in the flat. Although she and her flatmates had seemingly experienced a number of strange things, Darren felt that a visit wasn't yet justified. The usual array of phenomena had been witnessed, such as objects being moved around, and footsteps being heard inside the property when no one else was around. In all honesty, Darren thought that because Gemma lived with *four* of her student acquaintances, then maybe a lot of the reported phenomena had a normal explanation. With *five* student girls under one roof, there was, perhaps, scope for wrongly attributing innocuous events to something paranormal... but, as always, Darren kept an open mind.

POLTERGEIST PARALLELS AND CONTAGION

On May 30 2008, Darren was contacted again by Gemma, and informed that the 'ghost' (whom they had named 'Tom') was still making his presence known, only this time it had become a little more intense. Darren was told that noises were quite often heard while Gemma was in the flat on her own. When Darren asked her to tell him more about what exactly she had heard, he admitted that it was reminiscent of the poltergeist case that he and Michael had investigated in 2006. Darren was informed that one day, while Gemma was home, a loud noise was heard. She said:

> It sounded like a large spoon or something metallic being thrown down the corridor, only, when I went to see what it could be, I found no explanation for it.

On another occasion, again when she was in the flat on her own:

> I woke up one night to the sound of a banging noise in my room; one minute it was in my room, the next it was coming from out in the corridor. It was really terrifying and I knew no one would believe me, so I grabbed my mobile phone and recorded the noises. But on the recording, they are not as clear as they were on the actual night.

By far the most impressive report of her unwelcome visitor came when Darren asked her if she or any of her flatmates had seen anything move around.

> You know, there was one thing I meant to tell you about, and you have just reminded me of it. My flatmate Rosie went in to her room one night and saw, on her table top, a bottle of water standing on its edge, leaning over 45 degrees, and spinning around. Round and round it went! She couldn't believe her eyes and was rooted to the spot.

Darren could hardly believe it. He then had to ask Gemma if she was pulling his leg. She said 'No,' and he believed her. This led Darren to believe that Gemma and her flatmates may have been experiencing a low-level poltergeist outbreak. Darren then informed Michael, and explained the whole situation regarding the 'bottle balancing' episode in Rosie's room. Well, you could have knocked Michael down with a feather. Darren knew exactly how Michael would react to this phenomenon being reported, and he also knew exactly what Michael was now thinking. The true significance of what Rosie saw will become apparent later on.

Darren immediately arranged a time to visit Gemma in her home and it was planned for Monday, 2 June 2008. The day in question came, and the two researchers arrived at the flat at about 12.30pm. Gemma met Darren and Michael downstairs at the apartment block entrance and took them up to her top-floor flat, where one of her friends, Liz Mills, was sitting waiting. Another flatmate, Jo Risolino, was at the shop getting in some supplies for the visit. In next to no time at all, she arrived back at the flat, and, after a cup of tea was made, the girls delighted Darren and Michael with *more* stories of their alleged ghostly goings-on.

Jo started first. She told Darren and Michael that one night she woke up and saw a dark shadow in her room and, to her horror, realised it was standing over her bed. This actually happened on the night before the visit. She spoke of 'a creeping, ice-cold rush that began at my toes and crept right over my body; then, as quick as it came, it went.'

Gemma then went on to tell the researchers that she had recently heard footsteps walking along the narrow corridor while she was in her bedroom: they ceased after they reached a certain point. Then they were told that Rosie, although not in attendance on our visit that day, had witnessed her TV being turned on in her room when no one else was around. Liz Mills had experienced little or nothing at all.

During the afternoon, Darren and Michael carried out a number of tests and experiments, but little did they know how successful they were to be. They recorded taps and knocks coming from within Gemma's room, and it sounded as if something was clattering about in there. At one point in the afternoon, the flatmates and the researchers went into the hallway that led from the flat to the stairwell outside. Both Darren and Michael switched on their digital sound recorders and placed them on a shelf, after which they found somewhere to sit. Darren and the girls positioned themselves on the stairwell, whilst Michael sat down on the floor. The lights were switched off, and the hallway was plunged into darkness.

After several minutes, Michael's eyes adjusted to the dark. The only light he could detect was a thin column shining through the gap in between the door that led into the lounge and the frame that surrounded it. At some point, Michael slightly adjusted his position on the floor and noticed something odd: if he moved his head slightly to the left, the shaft of light shining through the gap in between the door and the door frame seemed to break into two, horizontally. Then, if he moved his head back again the two shafts of light joined back together to form one. Puzzled, Michael stood up and tried to figure out what was causing this anomaly. It seemed that something three-dimensional was in front of the door, and that the movement of his head – changing the angle of his vision – caused whatever was in front of the door to obscure the light and seem to cut it in two.

At this point Michael felt rather uncomfortable, and developed an overpowering feeling that something was standing in front of the door, even though he couldn't actually see it due to the almost complete absence of light. Slowly, he walked forwards along the hallway towards the door, and, as he did so, the shape of the object became faintly but tangibly clear. It was anthropomorphic, completely black and three-dimensional. When Michael came within two feet of the entity he paused and stared straight ahead. He then called out to Darren and the girls, and told them what he could see. Slowly but deliberately he stretched his right hand forward, fully expecting it to make contact with whatever it was in front of him.

At that point everyone there heard a long drawn-out sigh, which made the women distinctly afraid, and all five could see the six-foot tall, three-dimensional black shadow while they were sitting in the darkened hallway. This was Liz's first experience of the paranormal activity at her home and it was obvious to the researchers that she didn't like it. As the deep sigh echoed throughout the hallway, Darren shouted, 'Michael... was that you?' Michael, not realising that Darren was talking about the sighing sound, replied, 'was that me, what?'

'The sighing sound we just heard – was that you?'

It was obvious that Darren thought the sound might have had a perfectly logical explanation – that Michael may have sighed, perhaps without even realising it. However, Michael hadn't sighed. And then it happened again, and immediately one of the women sitting on the stairs jumped forward with a start.

'I heard it – and it came from just behind my head!'

As the girls became increasingly frightened and rapidly began to lose their composure, Michael continued to stare at the 'thing' in front of him, his arm still outstretched. Darren tried to calm the girls down, and reassured them that they were perfectly safe. The 'thing', whatever it was, suddenly dissolved into the ether, leaving nothing behind but two startled investigators and three terrified flatmates wrapped in a mantle of darkness. All five then decided it was best for now if they proceeded to the lounge area, and into the welcoming light.

Michael had seen this entity – or something very like it – once before. At Lock Street, both he and Marianne had witnessed a similar being stride across the hallway from the bathroom into one of the bedrooms. It had paused momentarily, stared at Michael and then carried on. The 'shadow man' at Newcastle hadn't walked anywhere; it had just stared. This, however, hadn't made Michael feel any easier in its presence. Both Darren and Michael were both aware of what seemed like a strange coincidence: two entities of identical appearance – or was it the same one? – that had appeared in *two* different and seemingly unrelated cases. Michael had seen it the first time; now both Darren and Michael had witnessed it together. A date for a full investigation was then planned, in which Darren and other investigators would place the flat under surveillance with CCTV, video cameras and all the latest mod-cons for a protracted period of time in the hope of recording any alleged anomalous activity.

On the night of 14 June 2008, Darren, and a group of dedicated ghost hunters, the Ghosts and Hauntings Overnight Surveillance Team, arrived at the Bigg Market flat to carry out the full investigation. The *Original* GHOST had been co-founded way back in 2005 by Drew Bartley and Darren W. Ritson after both aficionados had served a few active years with the North East Ghost Hunters, one of our region's earliest – if not *the* earliest – ghost hunting groups. After the founder of NEGH decided to disband the team in 2004, we simply reformed the team and carried on regardless under the new name *without* him. At the time of writing this update (June 2021), we still investigate hauntings and work together as a unit, albeit in a very different way now, and with new, and slightly more clued-up researchers as part of the outfit.

Mark Winter (from the North East Ghost Research Team, founded in 2003) and Darren, arrived at about 10.30pm and were soon met by the rest of the investigators, Drew Bartley, Fiona Vipond, Jim Collins and his brother Paul Collins (now sadly deceased). Michael was unavailable for the investigation. At 10.50pm, two of the team members – under the watchful eye of Darren – carried out initial baseline tests in the apartment and discovered nothing odd whatsoever. Squeaky floorboards were discovered in certain areas of the flat, and draughts and winds from outside were virtually non-existent. The average room temperature was between 20 and 22° Celsius. Motion sensors were then situated in both the upper corridor and lower hallway of this quite spacious two floored apartment; CCTV and laptop were set up; our hand held video cameras were checked and the time synchronised; then finally, our trigger objects were set up in various locations around the flat. The researchers were then ready to commence with the investigation.

After the baseline tests had been carried out, but prior to the first vigil starting, the ghost – it seemed – was already beginning to make itself known. A huge, white light came into view at one end of the upper-floor corridor and moved in the direction of Drew Bartley with great speed. It then, he says, 'shot over my right shoulder and I had to move to miss it'. Not long after this, *four* of the investigators present noticed that the toilet door handle was being moved up and down, and subsequently reported it to Darren. The team then split up into three groups to cover the flat.

The first group comprised four women: Fiona Vipond, Gemma Gorner, and two friends of Gemma's, Rebecca and Karen. They investigated the upper corridor. The second group consisted of Drew, Mark and Jim, who investigated the entrance hall and lower corridor. Darren and the late Paul Collins made up the third group, and stationed themselves in the living room. Throughout Darren's first vigil in the living room, we 'called out' to see if anything would occur, but without result. Darren then tried some voice-recording experiments – this attempt also yielding no results. The only strange occurrence for the duration of this vigil was when Darren was filming with his video camera, and, for no apparent reason, it turned itself off in his hands. Drew Bartley, Mark Winter and Jim Collins, while investigating the entrance foyer experienced something odd when they found that the door, which had previously been closed, had now been opened. Again, no explanation was forthcoming as to how that could have happened as the door was closed with the latch clicking into place. Two of the girls upstairs (Gemma and Karen) experienced a phenomenon that would end up repeating itself later in the investigation in the form of whistling – and it was *inside* the corridor area where they were located.

During the first break, Gemma's flatmate, Liz Mills, had returned home and joined in with the overnight investigation. The researchers then made their way to their new (next) vigil locations, but they didn't stay in them for long. Things began to turn truly bizarre when Drew and his group were in the upper corridor. Darren and Paul were investigating the entrance hall and corridor area down below at the time, and they could clearly hear Drew and his group upstairs. Their vigils were broken up when they heard Drew call out and ask if the *alleged* spirit could make itself known. A distinct *whistle* was then heard by all upstairs – and *also* by Darren and his colleague downstairs. Darren then actually called out to Drew, and asked if the whistle came from any of the folk up there. He was told it hadn't.

After asking out for more phenomena, the investigators heard knocking, which was rather odd to say the least. Then, suddenly, a remarkable series of crashes and bumps was heard coming from the upper corridor.

'Did you hear that?' Drew called out.

'Yes I did, what the hell was it?' Darren bellowed up the stairs.

'I don't know yet; I'm checking it out', Drew replied, as he made his way along the corridor to the scene.

Suddenly, from out of the darkness came a number of choice expletives, too crude to mention here. It turned out that the crucifix trigger object had been *thrown* from its original position on the floor at the end of the corridor, had travelled about four feet across the floor, and had landed just short of the strategically-placed motion sensors. By this time, Darren and Paul had ran upstairs to find out what was going on. They saw the relocated trigger object lying far from its original position. One guest investigator then hurried past them along the corridor and he was clearly terrified. The video camera that had been filming at the time was rewound, so the investigators could all watch it. The noise could clearly be heard as the three investigators stood at the other end of the corridor from where the object was placed. One can clearly see Jim and Mark on the footage, and it shows them both to be at the other end of the corridor at the time. Drew, was with them too, as *he* was filming there. No one was near the trigger object, then, when it was launched with force down the corridor towards them.

The investigators then went downstairs and met up with the girls. They knew something odd was going on, as they too had heard the object as it was thrown but had decided to stay in their current vigil location. During the next break, cups of tea and coffee were drunk in abundance while the investigators excitedly discussed what had just taken place. Darren then took it upon himself to return to the corridor with his EVP recorder and carry out some more tests. Two of the team, along with Gemma's flatmate Liz Mills, accompanied him. He proceeded to switch on his device and began recording. Darren then asked a number of questions, leaving enough time for any *alleged* spirit that may have been present to reply – and they were not disappointed. After posing around ten questions or so, they were rewarded with two replies to two of the questions:

'How old are you?'

On the recording, a distant but clear voice can be heard saying, 'Forty-eight.'

'Do you know that you are dead?'

'Yes.'

Intriguing results to say the least: the EVP recording was immediately transferred onto a laptop computer and analysed. Then, some time was spent excitedly discussing the paranormal events that had taken place there. A séance experiment, lasting over forty-five minutes, was then held in the area where all the excitement had occurred. During it, Darren was seemingly pushed by something from within the darkness. It moved him back a little, and it didn't feel as if it was particularly welcoming. Minor temperature drops and the occasional breeze were also felt by some of the circle members, and then the alleged activity seemed to cease.

This investigation proved to be a productive encounter for all concerned, with some astonishing activity both witnessed and documented. It is also – for the record – *one* of about fifteen to twenty investigation films we made, that Drew Bartley – a film maker as well as a paranormal investigator – edited together, for a DVD document of our night's investigation for our personal use, and of course for posterity; a DVD which Darren still owns to this day. On it, you can see all the above unfold, along with interviews of Gemma Gorner discussing her ghost, Tom, and relaying the incident when Rosie saw the plastic bottle spinning on its edge. The investigation there seemed to suggest that something distinctly otherworldly was occurring and warranted further investigation. However, since the writing of the investigation report based on Darren's findings, it has come to light that the girls have moved out of the premises. Their time at University had come to an end.

A number of disturbing occurrences that were witnessed at the Newcastle residence intrigued Darren and Michael very much. A lot of the phenomena documented during the researchers' visits (Darren twice, Michael once), were typical of a low-level poltergeist at work: objects being thrown around, a nasty sense of presence in the bedrooms, unexplained thumps and strange whistling noises; but during the whole investigation there was one particular incident which grabbed Darren's attention more than any of the other reported phenomena.

When he was informed about it for the first time he almost went white, hardly able to believe what he had just heard. It was the time when Rosie saw the bottle of mineral water in her bedroom spinning around at a 45-degree angle. What the girls at Newcastle didn't know, was that during the investigation at Lock Street, South Shields, Michael had actually recorded almost nigh on the exact same phenomenon on camera: a half-full bottle of water could clearly be seen balancing on its edge of its own volition, although it wasn't spinning around as in the Newcastle case. Darren and Michael had to ask themselves a very simple question: what were the chances of two separate poltergeists both deciding, seemingly on a whim, to entertain their human hosts by balancing a plastic bottle of mineral water on a table, at pretty much the same angle, and effectively defying the laws of physics?

The researchers knew that this was exactly the sort of meaningless thing that a poltergeist will do, but the similarity between the two incidents simply couldn't be put down to coincidence. Also, the appearance of the 'shadow man' in both cases drew Darren and Michael to the cautious conclusion that the Newcastle and South Shields events were, in some way they couldn't yet figure out, linked; but why and How?

∼

An interesting postscript to this account comes almost *thirteen* years after the investigations, and during the updating process of this work. I had wanted to amend and bring up to date the 'acknowledgements' section and add the *full* names of Gemma's friends, as opposed to using only their Christian names (as in the first edition), so I contacted Gemma, as we are still friends and in touch with one another, and asked the following:

> Hi Gemma, I hope you are doing well. I have just a quick question if you don't mind; I was wondering what the surname was of Rosie, the girl you shared the flat with in Newcastle, it's just for an update of a book I am working on... I know yours has now changed, and I know Jo's and Liz's surnames; can you perhaps remember at all? So I can update accordingly.

After Gemma had replied with the surname for Rosie, I took the opportunity – while we were messaging – to scratch a metaphorical itch that I had burning inside of me for some considerable time in relation to the girls packing up and leaving, not long after our investigations there.

'While I am on, may I just ask you one more question Gemma? About 'after' you girls left the flat in the Bigg Market.'

'Yeah that's fine', Gemma replied.

'Okay, my questions is: did any of you ladies ever experience anything 'odd', something that could be ascribed as being 'paranormal', *after* you all left the flat... and in your new homes? Or was it all left behind you when you left Newcastle?'

'Good question; no I don't think so, and I certainly didn't. I can check with the others though.' Gemma said.

'Please do, that would be helpful', I said.

'No worries. I'll message Rosie and see what she says. It would be interesting to know if the people there now experience anything like we did', Gemma said.

'It would indeed. Do let me know if you find anything out regarding the girls.' I requested.

Soon afterwards, I received a text message from Gemma – and what I read surprised me. The following text was sent to Gemma, from Rosie:

> Yes, I would hear scratching/moving noises in the roof above my bedroom in the middle of the night. I even got my mother up at 3am once to listen and she heard it, too, but she told me it would be a squirrel or an animal from the nearby woods. She subsequently got a builder out to go into the roof area and patch up any holes where perhaps anything could get in at night, but they found nothing up there. The builder had said that if there *had* been an animal in the roof space, there would be droppings, and everything would be chewed. Also, my graduation picture that was hanging on the wall fell off and smashed; my mother said it was the wind, and the downstairs CD player would randomly switch on/off; mother said it was probably faulty. I was terrified one night when my mother and father were on holiday and I was actually home alone. I was awoken by the bathroom tap switching itself on full blast, I thought to myself, "Goodness me, there's a burglar in our house and he's washing his hands!" In the morning, the tap was fully turned off. My mother's explanation was her pipes were old.

Interesting comments, but more delving was now needed, as a few questions had arisen due to this rather unexpected response. Rather than asking Gemma yet again to relay my questions to her friend, I simply found Rosie on social media and decided to ask my follow up questions directly.

Hi Rosie, its Darren here, Gemma's friend. Instead of bothering Gemma to ask you my questions, I thought I'd just ask you personally, if that is okay? I can't remember if *we* actually met in Newcastle, or you were away while we visited the flat, but I have to say thank you nonetheless for telling Gemma about what happened afterwards. May I ask you a question or two just to tie things up in relation to what you told Gemma? I won't take up much of your time. Thanks, Darren.

Rosie replied: 'Yes that's fine, no I wasn't there in Newcastle at the time, as I was back at my parents' house, but it was *my* room that you put that flying cross outside.'

'Did you ever see the film we made? We gave one to Gemma. What an odd place you lived.' Darren said. Rosie then replied:

Yeah, I watched it, but it was quite a bad copy for some reason! I do remember you all running down the stairs at one point; this is exactly what we did one night. My sister actually came to visit me one weekend and she flatly refused to sleep there, and went to a hotel instead!

'You said you experienced odd things when you moved back home to Cumbria, but your mother had ideas as to what they all were: old pipes, wind, animals in the roof etc. I was just wondering though, what *'you'* thought the disturbances were?'

'I didn't agree with the explanations. I thought and *still* do think that it was a ghost or spirit: something basically trying to spook me' Rosie said.

'Okay, thank you for clarifying that. In relation to the tap coming on through the night when you were in on your own, did you not feel the need to get up to turn it off? You said by morning it had stopped. I have to say, I would have thought that old pipes themselves wouldn't be able to actually turn the tap on to release water, so that is quite interesting,' Darren said. Rosie replied:

No I was terrified, so I did the whole thing of staying still in bed and not moving. Eventually, I must have fallen back asleep, and when I woke again the taps weren't running anymore. My mother says this happens... which I also thought sounded ridiculous!

That's great; thanks for your time, and thank you for the information. It's been a real help. 'You *are* the one that saw the bottle standing on its edge in the room, are you not?' I asked.

'Yep that's right.' Rosie said.

'Yes, I thought it was you, quite bewildering eh?' I said.

'Yes, you can say that again, I was completely caught unawares, absolutely dumbfounded; never seen anything like it in my life', replied Rosie.

It's interesting to note that Rosie – the only person that lived in the communal flat where the haunting had taken place – was the only individual to seemingly 'take some away' with her after they all moved out. Inquiries revealed that none of the other girls had witnessed, or reported anything untoward that could've been considered paranormal, so it begged the question, why did Rosie experience the phenomena back in Cumbria? I contacted her once more with a final question; I felt I needed to dot the I's and cross the T's.

> Hi Rosie, I should have asked this question yesterday, and, as odd as this may sound, it's a question that has to be asked. At the time of your living at the flat with the girls, and shortly after when you returned home, did you, or indeed any of the girls, have any situations in your life that you could describe as being stressful? Had any of you been going through a rough time, or perhaps been feeling depressed? You don't have to go into it – if you have – and by this, I mean the ins and outs of the pressures; but can you at least confirm if one, or maybe more of you, were 'troubled' at that time?

Rosie replied and told me that for her – on a personal level – she had never been stressed, traumatised or anxious for any reason at that time, and had suffered no ill effect through any traumatic events, essentially ruling her *out* as a potential poltergeist focus. She did, however, explain that *one* of the girls *had* indeed been, for quite some time, going through a stressful period in her life and she was somewhat concerned about her own future at that point. Due to the delicate nature of the details relating to this stress, and to protect the identity of the 'said' individual, I shall leave this here: needless to say, that it is very possible that *this* individual was the focus of the poltergeist activity. It is very interesting, however, that it should have been Rosie that 'took away' the phenomenon from the Bigg Market, and endured it in Cumbria until eventually, it petered out.

Before we finish this chapter, there is one more fascinating and thought-provoking account that must be discussed which bears considerable relevance to the aforementioned phenomena. It came about when I was invited to take part in an online radio podcast in 2021, to discuss the rerelease of *The South Shields Poltergeist* book. Paul Rook, of the incredibly popular *Paranormal Concept Show*, which is co-hosted with Kerry Greenaway and Richard Clements, had expressed a great deal of interest in the case and the book, after reading about the 'bottle balance' footage that had been filmed during the course of *our* investigation in 2006. This subsequently reminded him of an event he had witnessed for himself during a poltergeist investigation that he attended in Frogmore, near Watford, in 2016. During the recorded interview for the podcast, he made mention of a very similar 'balancing' incident to ours, that had occurred in front of a number of witnesses, which of course I was very interested in following up. After the interview, I contacted Paul and asked him for more details in relation to it; he sent me the following:

> In 2016, I was an independent paranormal investigator, when I was invited to join a London based paranormal research team on what had seemed to be an intriguing poltergeist case they had been investigating. The house they were researching was based in Frogmore, near Watford. The case came to the attention of the researchers from three ladies that lived there – a mother and her two daughters – after they had been contacted for advice. We went into the property and I was subsequently introduced to the three residents. We carried out experiments in various rooms of the house, and spoke about the different levels and variations of poltergeist activity that they had been experiencing. We undertook some electronic voice phenomena work (EVP) and although we *did* pick up some responses, they were rather unclear, and it was uncertain if they were caused by the actual residents or even some of the team members present, which rendered them very subjective.
>
> Then, something interesting happened. While all *seven* of us that were present that evening were standing in the kitchen and all chatting together, one of the householders gasped in amazement and pointed over in my direction. On the work surface, and before all our eyes, was a tall slender drinking glass balanced on its edge at a 45-degree angle! Even the fluid that it contained was angled and very still; however, nobody actually saw the glass tilt, but needless to say we were all astounded. The investigating team documented it by taking photographic evidence. There was no way anyone in that room could

have placed the glass in that position without someone else seeing them – this very unorthodox display of poltergeist activity had hitherto not been witnessed or reported in other poltergeist cases, or so I thought, until I read the rerelease of *The South Shields poltergeist* in 2020 – the uncanny coincidence with the bottle of water and 'our' glass, was astounding. This was an experience that will stay with me always, and I still have yet to experience anything like it again.

So, now we have a *third* account of a poltergeist executing a very specific and very unusual 'act' as part of its mind-boggling repertoire; Granted, on this occasion it precariously balanced upon its edge, not a bottle as such, but rather a tall and slender drinking glass. The similarity to what happened in the Newcastle and South Shields cases is astonishing. Further inquiries by Paul, at my behest, regarding acquiring and seeing a copy of the alleged photograph that was taken of the 'tilting glass' sadly yielded no results. Should anyone know who might have it, please get in touch with the author, my contact email address is at the rear of this book.

14

THE INCUBUS – SUCCUBUS PROSPECT

After Darren and Michael's investigation into the South Shields poltergeist had drawn to a close – at least insofar as its manifestation at Lock Street was concerned – Darren wondered whether they would ever get such an opportunity again. Cases of that degree of intensity are incredibly rare, and Darren felt it unlikely that the gods would smile down upon them twice. Michael was a little more optimistic.

> You know, when our book about the South Shields poltergeist is eventually published, it's going to cause something of a stir. My bet is that a lot of people who are experiencing a poltergeist outbreak are going to get to hear about us by reading the book. If they're desperate for help, we could very well be the first ones they'll call. My guess is that we may not just get one more good case, but a boatload of them!

On Monday 28 April 2008, Steven Taylor again rang Michael again at his office. A new case – possibly involving a poltergeist – had come to his attention and he wanted to know if Michael would like to investigate.

According to Steven, an elderly woman who lived in Ashington, in Northumberland, had allegedly found herself under attack from a rather malign entity, which had entered her home without invitation. The woman, a widow, had seemingly been involved with spiritualism for many years, and had gained something of a reputation as a medium. To her, the concept of spiritual beings making their presence felt from time to time was perfectly normal and natural. Initially, therefore, she was unperturbed by thinking that a spirit was in her home. But then it started behaving in ways that left her deeply disturbed. The only other information that Steven had was that the woman had occasionally allowed her home to be used for 'open circle' meetings by local spiritualists. Steven said that if Michael wanted to follow up on the case, he'd arrange a visit and try to accrue further background information. Michael asked whether Steven had any particular time in mind for the trip.

'The thing is, Michael, this woman seems desperate. My feeling is that we need to go as soon as possible,' said Steven.

'Well, I can't make it tomorrow or Wednesday – how about Thursday sometime?' replied Michael.

Steven said he would ring the woman to confirm the visit and get back to Michael. The following day, Steven rang Michael again.

'Hi Michael, I've checked with the woman at Ashington and she says that Thursday is fine. I'll pick you up around 1pm, if that's okay.' Michael said that was perfect, and asked Steven if the woman had been able to tell him anything else that might be of use; Steven replied:

> Well, she did give me a few more details. Apparently, the entity – whatever it is – is getting very up close and personal with her. It's creepy, to be honest. Sometimes she wakes up, and she will feel it running its fingers through her hair. Other times, it will start to caress her thigh. It seems predatory, and you don't have to be a genius to work out that there are some distinctly sexual undertones present. Personally, I'm wondering whether it's not poltergeist at all. I'm starting to think it could be an incubus.

The single mention of the word incubus sent a cold shiver down Michael's spine. More than any other spiritual adversary, the incubus was often reputed to be the most feared.

The word incubus is Latin, and drawn from *in*, which literally means 'above' or 'on top of', and *cubo*, which means 'I lie upon', 'a burden' or 'a weight.' This in itself highlights the predatory disposition of the entity, which, according to folklore, is said to be a sexually driven monster that preys upon women. The female equivalent of the incubus is the succubus, which allegedly preys upon men in a similar manner. Supposedly, the incubi are demons of tremendous power and great age. They were even feared by the ancient Sumerians and Babylonians, who believed that they could also control storms, lightning and thunder. According to tradition, incubi constantly attempt to engage in sexual activity with women. Their reasons for this are two-fold. Firstly, they do so because they enjoy it, and secondly because engaging in sexual intercourse with human females is the means by which they procreate. During the act of intercourse, the incubus will draw or 'suck out' energy from its victim – energy upon which it feeds to perpetuate its own existence.

There are two prevalent theories about the nature of both the incubus and the succubus. In some traditions they are said to be two separate genders, male and female, in exactly the same way that humans are similarly divided. In other traditions, however, the concept is a little more complex. One Mediaeval view was that both incubi and succubi are genderless, and are merely two different presentations of the same entity. In other words, the entity will appear as either male or female, depending on the type of sexual activity it wishes to engage in. Some scholars suggested that the demon would first appear as a succubus – normally in the guise of a voluptuous female – and have intercourse with its male victim when he was asleep. As soon as the victim ejaculated, the demon would then metamorphose into its male form, as an incubus, and select a female victim. During intercourse with the woman, the demon would ejaculate the sperm it had 'collected' from the male victim, and the woman would become pregnant.

The child, although human in appearance, would actually be a demon in disguise, which would then go on to promulgate the species in exactly the same manner as its parents. Even though the sperm used in this bizarre form of conception was taken from a human male and the mother was a human female, the resultant offspring was almost always a demon. However, sometimes the resultant offspring wouldn't be fully demonic, but actually half-demon and half-human. Such hybrids were known as combions or cambions, and were believed to possess enormous supernatural powers. There are a number of different ways in which an incubus can, allegedly, be identified. When the demon engages in sexual intercourse with a human female victim, its penis is said to feel either incredibly cold or uncomfortably hot. In appearance, the incubus is said to take the form of a hideous dwarf with misaligned and deformed features. Some say that before it materialises in fleshly form, it appears as a small but intense light that will dart through the air at great speed like a firefly, or as a metallic sphere.

In yet other traditions, it is said to appear as a swan, a dog, a goose, a dragon or even a large fish. Dealing with an incubus is not easy, and over the millennia numerous defence strategies have been employed with varying degrees of success. In the Christian tradition, predictably, exorcism has been the preferred option. The Roman Catholic Church has said that attending confession may also be helpful, along with making the sign of the cross, which demons are said to dislike intensely.

But thinking Christians have admitted that such tactics are basically useless. Testimony exists that incubi actually have no fear of exorcisms, couldn't give two hoots about the sign of the cross and, on occasion, have actually drunk holy water and spat upon the Bible in front of their victims. One of the most frightening beliefs regarding incubi is that, as previously stated, they 'suck out' the life force from their victims. If an incubus is allowed to do this repeatedly, it is said the victim will endure a rapid decline in health and, eventually, die... if the demon is not prevented from engaging in its rapacious behaviour.

Darren and Michael found the concept of the incubus disturbing, too, but for different reasons. During their investigation of the South Shields poltergeist, they had seen first-hand how devious the poltergeist could be, presenting itself as an old woman, a sweet young child, a middle-aged man and in other ways. They were in no doubt that this ability to switch guises was done for one reason and one reason only – to try to fool and confuse its victims. The incubus does exactly the same thing. But there was another parallel that was even more striking. The poltergeist feeds on human fear, or to employ a rather overused term popular with some paranormal researchers, 'energy.' The incubus was said to feed in almost exactly the same manner, by 'sucking out' the life force or energy from its victim. In one mediaeval legend, the incubus was said to be able to resist exorcism completely, but needed to rest for several days after an exorcism had been attempted.

In poltergeist cases, it is well known that exorcisms, although usually unsuccessful, do sometimes result in a short hiatus before the entity resumes its business of frightening the householders. Again, a strange parallel can be seen between both the poltergeist and the incubus phenomenon. The parallels between the poltergeist and the incubus led Michael and, to some degree, Darren to a rather disquieting conclusion.

THE INCUBUS – SUCCUBUS PROSPECT

Could both phenomena actually be one and the same? In fact, the only meaningful difference between the two that the researchers could see was that in cases of incubus attack, there was a sexual component present, which was normally absent in cases of poltergeist infestation. But then Darren made an interesting observation:

> Maybe there *is* a sort of sexual element in some cases. In a lot of instances of poltergeist infestation – the 'normal' ones – the focus is often (but not always) a young girl around the age of puberty or the beginning of her menstrual cycle. These are both indicators that the young lady in question is reaching a point in her life where her sexual urges will begin and eventually culminate in her reaching full sexual maturity.

This is true, and often at this point in a young girl's life, she may be mixed-up, confused, and going through physical and emotional transformations – hormonal changes, for example. Perhaps the poltergeist, or an incubus, sees this as a golden opportunity to make its attack, striking while the iron is hot, so to speak, when 'the focus' is at its most vulnerable. All in all, the parallels between the poltergeist and the so-called incubus were just too strong not to be considered.

On Thursday, 1 May 2008, at 1pm, Steven called to pick up Michael and his wife Jackie, for the journey to Ashington. Because of a family commitment, Darren didn't go along. The weather was balmy, and, as the trio headed towards their destination, the conversation inevitably turned towards the disturbances at the house they were going to visit. No one had a clue what they might be facing. As Steven, Jackie and Michael pulled into the picturesque square of houses, they could see the guest medium that Steven had brought along to Pallister Street, standing outside waiting for them. Beside her were the homeowner, an elderly lady, and the medium's partner. Within the space of a minute, a troop of intrigued investigators were ascending the stairwell of Minnie's* home. By all outward appearances, it was delightful; parchment-coloured walls were adorned with country-style paintings and ornaments, and cream carpets added to the carefully orchestrated cottage effect that Minnie had created. It was hard to believe that something sinister could be lurking therein. Minnie's living room was airy and well furnished. Gently flickering candles were dotted hither and thither, adding to the ambience. Introductions were made, and then Minnie trotted off into the kitchen to make tea. Another friend, a neighbour of Minnie's called

Vanessa*, popped in to chat to her friend's guests. Michael looked around and attempted to connect with the surroundings. Something wasn't right, but he decided not to say anything until Minnie had returned. The guest medium, he noticed, was also looking rather unsettled and glanced over her shoulder several times.

Minnie's story was as follows: She had spent many years within the spiritualist movement, although she was no longer able to attend church regularly. Nevertheless, she managed to enjoy something akin to a full spiritual life from within the confines of her own home. Others of a spiritual disposition, including Vanessa, had taken part in open circle services and similar activities there. And then, unfortunately, 'it' had arrived.

At first, there was just the usual sense of presence; the irresistible feeling that someone or something unseen was in Minnie's flat, watching her. Initially, this didn't bother her at all; her practice of spiritualism had made her quite accustomed to such sensations, which she accepted as perfectly natural. But then, on one occasion in the early hours of the morning, Minnie had woken with a start. It felt as if someone were running their fingers through her hair. Alarmed, she got out of bed, and after several seconds it stopped.

However, the same thing happened again several nights later. Minnie was annoyed at this unwelcome intrusion, and actually took to wearing a woollen hat whilst she was sleeping. Somehow, that seemed to prevent the entity from touching her head, and she once again found herself able to sleep peacefully. Then, on the third occasion, she awoke to find that 'it' was rubbing its hand up and down the inside of her thigh. This was, of course, a step too far. Whatever was taking such an interest in Minnie had taken liberties, and now she wanted it out of her home.

At first Minnie tried several techniques common within spiritualism in an effort to remove her uninvited guest, including shutting herself down spiritually and asking the spirit to go. Nothing worked. 'I've tried everything to get rid of it... everything.'

'Does it frighten you, Minnie?' Michael asked.

'Oh, no,' replied Minnie instantly. 'I don't think it's a bad spirit. I'm just sick of it and I just want rid of it.'

This puzzled Michael. The entity, whatever it was, had invaded Minnie's home and had touched her in ways that, had it been a human, would have promptly got it arrested. How could she say that it wasn't a bad spirit? Minnie, Michael thought, had perhaps concluded that the spirit was merely lonely and, despite the rather intimate nature of its advances, had really meant no harm; in effect, that it was sad rather than bad. After a brief discussion on ley-lines, after Minnie had mentioned that they ran through her garden, Michael asked:

'Have you ever seen elemental spirits in your garden – you know, pixies, gnomes, elves... that sort of thing?'

To those of an inherently cynical nature, people who believe in elves, pixies, gnomes and fairies will likely be viewed as nutcases. However, thousands of people worldwide do claim to see such entities, and there is, Michael thinks, evidence that they are genuinely experiencing something of a paranormal nature. Darren, on the other hand – although he is *enchanted* by the notion of fairies, pixies, elves and gnomes living at the bottom of one's garden, deep in the undergrowth, or in a magical labyrinth of tunnels in a subterranean world – is, alas, a lot more sceptical regarding their objective reality.

What disturbed him was Minnie's answer.

'Oh, yes... there are elves out there – and a gnome.'

'Do they ever touch you?'

At this point it was Vanessa, and not Minnie, who answered in the affirmative:

'Yes. They often grab my legs when I'm out there.'

Minnie then added, 'I hope it hasn't come in from the garden... you know, there are some awful things out there.'

Michael didn't doubt it for a minute. What disturbed him was that incubi often disguise themselves as elemental spirits in much the same way that poltergeists disguise themselves as discarnate human spirits. The gnawing feeling that something dark and brooding had indeed infiltrated Minnie's flat was even stronger now. Then Minnie dropped a minor bombshell. She had, she said, taken to using 'a board'.

In some spiritual and New Age circles, it is common to employ a device known as a board in an effort to communicate with other realms or dimensions. Such boards come in different types, the most common being the well-known Ouija board – commonly, but mistakenly, pronounced *wee-jee* board by many enthusiasts. Essentially, spirit communication boards consist of a circle of letters, numbers and icons. Perhaps by employing an upturned glass or other artefacts as a pointer, upon which the users place their fingers, the presumed *spirits* will be asked to move the artefact towards the letters or numerals in sequence, to spell out whatever messages they want to convey to those present. Using spirit communication boards *can* be an extremely risky business. For years, Michael has refused to countenance their use under any circumstances whatsoever, because he knows of too many cases where users have allegedly 'opened up a doorway' and attracted the attention of entities that were, to put it bluntly, quite evil. One chap from Leeds told Michael that he had gone through six months of hell after his brother and some friends used an Ouija board when he was in the room. He hadn't actually taken part in the exercise, but something had latched on to him, he said, and had almost driven him out of his mind. In March 2001, Michael wrote the following in his newspaper column after hearing further reports of how the use of communication boards had backfired. A reader called Maureen told him of an occasion when she and some friends visited a pub and then went back to one of their homes for coffee:

> Whilst the kettle was boiling, Jen went into her bedroom and brought out [a] Ouija board, suggesting that we try to contact some spirits. We did – and I can tell you that I'll never use [a] Ouija board again. I don't want to go into what happened, but I nearly ended up in a psychiatric hospital because of it.

And Maureen isn't the only one to have had such an experience. A local postman from South Shields relayed this account of an incident involving his mother-in-law back in the 1960s:

> My mother-in-law, Lilian, who now lives in Kent, used to work as a cleaner at Chatham dockyards during the 1960s. One day, several of the cleaners decided to mess around with [a] Ouija board during their break. They gathered in a small room where they used to drink their tea. It was known as the 'bait room'. Sure enough, the glass started to move as if by its own accord and then toppled over. She said it was obvious that something strange was happening. After a while they put the board away and went back to work, but Lilian was concerned. The others laughed and told her not to be silly. And then, the very next day, it started. Not long after, they heard four sharp knocks on the window – knock, knock, knock, knock. Startled, they looked around to see where the noise had come from. Then it happened again, and they realised that someone was tapping loudly on the window. The knocking continued, and they could see exactly where the sound was coming from. It was definitely someone knocking on the glass.

Michael asked, 'Could it not have been someone playing tricks, maybe someone knocking on the window from the outside?' His informant replied:

> Well, that's the strange thing, you see. The room was on the third floor. You couldn't reach the windows from outside at all. No drainpipes, outside stairwells or anything.

There is an on-going debate about what exactly happens when people experiment with an Ouija board. The traditional view is that the experimenters are making contact with the spirits of the dead. A more scientific explanation is that the 'messages' received are actually produced subconsciously by the experimenters themselves – this is called the ideomotor effect. The point is that whatever causes the phenomenon; it can have nasty psychological consequences, and therefore maybe shouldn't be dabbled with. A colleague of Michael's, who believed that it involved spirit communication, put it this way:

> When you use [a] Ouija board you are opening up a portal to another dimension, which you can neither control nor fully understand. Opening that doorway is easy, but you may find that it is not so easily shut again. Personally, I wouldn't go near [a] Ouija board if you paid me a fortune.

This was how Michael felt about dabbling with spirit communication boards back in 2001, and he has only slightly modified his view. He now believes that communication with entities that are not evil is possible, but shouldn't be attempted under any circumstances. In 2007, Michael took part in a demonstration involving a spirit communication board and the medium conducting it said she 'had a man present' that wanted to talk to someone sitting around the table. When asked to identify who the person was, the glass in the centre of the table, upon which all the sitters had rested their index finger lightly, moved towards Michael.

The spirit person identified himself as Michael's great-grandfather, and, spelled out numerous facts and dates that could only have been known by Michael himself. Then, Michael's grandfather came through for good measure, and also said things that no one apart from Michael himself – and his deceased grandfather, of course – could have known. Michael does not believe the spirits were those of his great-grandfather and grandfather, but they certainly detailed things that no one else around the table could possibly have been aware of. The question was: could Minnie's use of a spirit communication board have opened up a doorway that allowed the malign entity into her home? Michael advised Minnie to desist from any form of spiritual activity for a while: no spirit board communication, no incense and no rituals.

> Every time you engage in something like that, you are effectively opening up a line of communication with this entity and inviting it to stay. The only way to deal with it is to stop doing anything at all that will encourage it. As far as is humanly possible you should ignore it. Hopefully, it will get bored and go away.

Minnie thanked her visitors for their help and kindly insisted that they accept a donation towards their travelling expenses. Michael, Steven, Jackie, the guest medium and her partner then departed. Michael, for his part, wasn't entirely confident that Minnie would be able to desist from engaging in any form of spiritual activity for a protracted period of time. The notion that the entity may have decided to turn its attention to Minnie's visitors never entered his head, but it wouldn't be long before he would begin to wonder. Within the space of a day, something truly frightening would happen that catapulted the concept of contagion into the forefront of his mind.

Thursday 1 May, the day on which the visit to Minnie's home had taken place, was also the day on which the entire country would be encouraged to vote in the local council elections. Michael, intrigued by the day's political events, got up early on the morning of 2 May to catch up with the shenanigans on Sky News. It was slightly chilly when he got out of bed, so he donned an ancient towel dressing gown that was full of holes, but one of his most comfortable pieces of clothing. He then went downstairs into the kitchen, switched on the kettle and made himself a cup of tea. All thoughts of the previous day's visit had left him, and his only interest at that point was to follow the election results on the TV. He picked up his mug, walked into the lounge and turned on the news. For maybe five minutes, he sat comfortably on the sofa as a stream of ecstatic Conservatives and nigh-suicidal Labour supporters were paraded on the screen to offer their thoughts. It was fantastic entertainment.

At precisely 6.10am, Michael detected the distinct smell of burning. It came suddenly, and without build-up. One moment it was absent, the next the overpowering odour of smoke filled his nostrils. Alarmed, he sat up and glanced around in an effort to see where it was coming from. He soon realised that wisps of smoke were emanating from the cuff of the right-hand sleeve of his dressing gown. These were followed by delicate tendrils of flame, at which point his wrist suddenly became extremely hot. The sleeve of his dressing gown was on fire. Instinctively, Michael began to pat the ignited area furiously with his left hand. As he did so the smoke increased, but the flames, thank goodness, went out. The fire was quickly extinguished.

To this day, Michael has absolutely no idea how his dressing gown caught fire. He replayed in his mind a dozen times every action he had taken since he had walked down the stairs, and at no time had he been near a naked flame. What's more, even if he had accidentally set his dressing gown on fire, how on earth did five minutes go by before he smelt smoke and noticed the flames?

A thought struck Michael; as far as he could see, there was absolutely no rational explanation for his dressing gown catching fire. This led him to consider a far darker possibility. One of the most extreme symptoms of poltergeist infestation, and normally one of the last to manifest, is the phenomenon of fire starting. Those who have gone through the trauma of intense poltergeistry will sometimes testify that fires will break out spontaneously in their homes. Usually, such fires are normally small and, mercifully, will extinguish themselves spontaneously, although there are exceptions to the rule in which poltergeist fires have razed entire buildings to the ground. The poltergeist at Lock Street never did get around to full-blown fire starting, but it came perilously close. Marianne, once found a candle in her bed that was still warm, although not lit. The wax was still soft, indicating that it had been lit shortly before she found it. On another occasion, Michael, Marianne and Marc witnessed a build-up of fine smoke in the kitchen. It had no odour, but it distinctly looked like smoke. If the entity at Minnie's house had been a poltergeist – or worse, as Michael suspected, an incubus – there was a possibility that it had, through a process of contagion, attached itself to Michael and precipitated the fire itself.

After sitting for several minutes and getting his thoughts into order, Michael photographed the burnt cuff of his dressing gown sleeve. He then noticed a white blister on the third finger of his left hand, which he believes was caused when he attempted to beat out the flames. The only other physical damage that he could notice was the absence of some hairs on his arm where the cuff of the sleeve had been resting when the fire started. They seemed to have been burnt off, but the skin itself was untouched. Michael photographed the blister and then made another cup of tea before sending an e-mail to Darren. He needed to speak to him urgently. He decided against ringing his friend, as, the night before, Darren had taken part in an overnight investigation at a public house that was reputedly haunted. Darren wouldn't have arrived home till dawn, and would therefore still be in bed resting.

But there was more to come. Michael also decided to telephone the guest medium and see what she thought about this latest incident. What happened next was intriguing. She answered her mobile phone and told Michael that she couldn't speak, as she was just about to start driving her car. She would ring him later, she said, after she had arrived at her partner's flat. After some time had passed, Michael's phone rang. She was returning his call. Michael first asked her what her thoughts had been about the previous day's visit. They chatted for a while, and then the conversation was shattered by an incredibly loud, rhythmic beeping noise. It was the smoke alarm in her partner's kitchen. She was preparing a meal, and something had begun to burn.

'Oh, no!' she shouted. 'I'm cooking and I've set something on fire! I'll ring you back!'

Minutes later she called Michael for a second time. Order had been restored, the smoke alarm was now silent and the only damage that had been done was to the meal that she had been preparing for her partner. Now, it seemed, he would be receiving burnt offerings instead of a more conventional meal when he got back from his business.

Michael told the medium about the incident with the dressing gown. She sounded shocked – not just because of the incident itself, but because of the coincidental activation of the smoke alarm at precisely the moment when Michael had been about to tell her that his dressing gown had caught fire. The activation of the smoke alarm had a natural explanation, of course: as the medium had become engrossed in the first conversation with Michael, she had forgotten about the meal she was cooking for her partner. Inevitably, then, it had started to burn and the smoke alarm had activated. And yet it still seemed strange that the activation of the smoke alarm had occurred just when Michael was about to tell her that an item of his clothing had spontaneously burst into flames.

After mulling over the incident between them, the conversation then took a more general tone and she expressed her feeling that, in the world of paranormal research and alternative spirituality, some people were too eager to believe *anything*, simply because they had read it in a book or seen it on TV. Michael agreed, and related to her an anecdotal tale, which perfectly illustrated the point.

Several years previously, he had listened to a lecture by a colleague on the subject of some mysterious crystal skulls that had been discovered in South America, and during the talk the speaker had stated that one skull was no less than 3,468,242 years old. Michael was intrigued as to how the speaker had been able to state such a precise age with unbridled confidence. Later, at the bar, where both were ordering a drink, he asked her. The woman stared at Michael as if he were an idiot and promptly said, 'I know it's that old, because I read it in a book about crystal skulls. So, that's how I know it's true!'

'Oh, well... if you read it in a book, then it *must* be true,' he replied with no small degree of sarcasm. After Michael had finished reciting the tale to the medium, there was a pregnant pause in the conversation, before the medium whispered, 'My God... my spine has turned to ice. This is creepy!' Michael, puzzled, asked her why.

'Because right now I'm reading a book called *The Crystal Skull!*'

The title of the publication that the lecturer had referred to all those years ago and the book that the medium was currently reading were almost identical. Michael knew that this just couldn't be 'coincidental'.

Later that afternoon, after Darren had woken from his sleep, he rang Michael and was astonished to hear about the incident with the dressing gown. He, too, felt that the notion of contagion couldn't lightly be dismissed. Whatever it was, Michael sincerely hoped that there wouldn't be an encore.

∼

May 3 2008. It had been a long afternoon. Darren's daughter, Abbey, had been to her 2nd birthday party at a local soft play centre where she and a dozen of her little cousins and friends had played riotously for an hour or so before tucking in to a table-full of party food as well as her birthday cake. For the previous hour, Darren and his partner had been running round like headless chickens looking after all the children and making sure they all had a wonderful time. The event went without a hitch and all concerned had a great time.

Darren later arrived home and subsequently took a quick bath. Running around looking after children is seriously hard work. His partner remained downstairs and waited for Darren to take over looking after Abbey. She was headed out to a friend's house to celebrate a birthday, so Darren was left holding the reins, so to speak. At 7.30pm, she left the house and at 8.00pm Darren put his daughter to bed. She was tired after her exciting day and slept... well, like a baby. At 11.30pm, Darren decided to turn in, but rather than go to bed he decided to get comfortable on the sofa and nod off there, at least until he knew his partner had arrived home safe and well.

At 1.00am, Darren woke up and realised that she hadn't yet returned. He paid a visit to the loo, and checked up on his sleeping daughter before returning back downstairs. He lay back on the settee and dozed back off. The next thing he knew was that his partner was opening the front door; she had arrived home. Darren looked at the clock and it read 1.15am. Just as she entered the living room the telephone began to ring. As she picked up the phone to say hello, it went dead.

'Who the hell is that ringing at this time of the morning?' said Darren.

Almost immediately, she rang 1471 to see who had just made the call. As Darren lay there, waiting to see who it was, she began to recite the number of the last person that rang; one by one, the digits of Michael's telephone number were read out.

'What on earth is Michael phoning at this time for?' Darren said.

'Probably trying to ring someone else', she said.

'Give me the phone please,' Darren then said.

Darren then also rang 1471, to check for himself that it *had* been Michael. Sure enough, Michael's number was repeated by the automated voice at the other end of the line.

'I wonder what he wanted?' Darren thought to himself.

Nothing more was thought about it until the next day, when Darren visited Michael at his home. Darren had forgotten all about the incident, when Michael just happened to mention that he had been on the phone to a guy in the United States of America for a few hours through the night.

'Hey, that reminds me', Darren said. 'Why did you phone me up in the middle of the night?'

'Eh?' said Michael, 'What do you mean?'

'You phoned me through the night.'

'No I didn't.'

'Yes you did,' Darren said.

'What time?' 'It was about 01.15 – 01.20am; I know this because it was just as my partner was coming in.'

'Darren, I never rang you through the night!' Michael said sternly. 'Look, I rang this chap in the USA after he sent me an e-mail asking me to do so. He sent the e-mail at 12.30am, and it was only a few minutes after when I rang him. I was on the phone for around two hours. Jackie went to bed around 12.25 that night, so when I received this e-mail, I thought it was a good time to call him.'

'So, what you are saying is that if my phone rang at 01.15am, it must have been another number?'

'Must have been,' said Michael, 'It wasn't me.'

'Look, I know your number; it was your phone, your number – there is no mistaking it'.

The upshot of this is that Darren was adamant that Michael rang him, and Michael was adamant that he hadn't. If Michael was telling the truth – and deep down Darren really had no doubt that he was – then how could his phone have rung Darren? In fact, Michael showed Darren the call log on his phone and – sure enough – it detailed the lengthy call that Michael had made to the USA that night. He had been on the call from 12.30am, until around 02.30am. Darren had been interrupted from his sleep at around 01.15am on the morning of May 4 2008, but by whom, or what? The thought then struck both Darren and Michael that it could have been the poltergeist up to its old tricks. They both knew what that particular entity was capable of.

15

MAYHEM IN MIDDLESBROUGH

On Saturday 4 April 2009, Michael received a call from a good friend of his who had also been an acquaintance of Darren for many years. Tony* is an electrician, and (at the time of writing in 2014) has been married to his wife Linda*, a nurse, for seven years. The couple have four children, and currently reside in Middlesbrough. Tony is an extremely laid-back person, who never takes life too seriously, and, as his friends all testify, he has an infectious sense of humour. Normally, that is; but, on the day he telephoned Michael, he sounded uncharacteristically tense.

During the previous few days, the couple had noticed some odd things happening in their home. Occasionally, they would see what appeared to be fleeting shadows out of the corner of the eye; and, on a number of occasions, household artefacts had gone missing, only to reappear later in rather odd places. At some point Tony, because of his professional background, decided to use an EMF meter to see if he could detect any anomalous readings. He was aware that strong discharges of electromagnetic energy could perhaps cause hallucinations and other physiological effects. He focussed on the main bedroom, and did indeed find that his EMF meter fluctuated wildly in certain spots. Tony wanted to know if Michael had heard of similar cases in which people had hallucinated under the same conditions. Michael said that, as far as he was concerned, the possibility that electromagnetic fields were causing the problem couldn't be ruled out, but there were other explanations that also needed to be considered. Tony said that he would keep Michael abreast of any further developments.

Two days later, Tony telephoned Michael again and said that Linda had gone through a rather odd experience the previous night. Neither of them was sure what to do about it. Tony gave Linda the phone, and asked her to tell Michael exactly what had happened. Around 2am, she'd woken up and gone to check on her youngest child, a baby girl named Holly*, who was only several months old. When she returned to the bedroom, she was astonished to see someone lying in the bed where, just minutes previously, she herself had been asleep.

'The figure', she said, 'was human-shaped, but it didn't look like an ordinary person. It was sort of solid, but looked as if it was made from smoke. It was really weird. You could make out dark patches on its face where its features were supposed to be, but they weren't really clear or distinct.'

Michael asked Linda how long the apparition had been in view:

'I think it must have been for thirty seconds or so, I can't remember exactly.'

Michael also asked Linda whether the figure had disappeared instantly or slowly faded away:

'I don't know, because I was startled and turned my head away. When I looked back, it was gone. The thing is, I wasn't scared at all. In fact, I felt extremely calm. The figure in the bed even looked calm, as if it was totally at peace, serene even.'

The following evening, Linda had yet another strange experience. Once again, she woke up in the small hours of the morning, and was startled to see a woman standing by her bed, looking down at her. The only light entering the room was a dim glow shining in from the hallway, and the figure appeared similar to a silhouette. Nevertheless, Linda could make out some features. The woman had blonde hair with a fringe, and pale blue eyes. Linda sensed, somehow, that the woman was 35 years of age, or at least *had* been when she died. Then the apparition spoke to her:

'My mother doesn't know what happened to me,' it said.

As the figure addressed Linda, she noticed that there were now two other apparitions standing behind the first. The woman in front of her disappeared, and one of the two remaining figures, an elderly woman, stepped forward. This spirit, Linda noted, had been 87 years of age when she had died.

'I don't know how I knew that,' said Linda, 'but somehow I just did.'

'I can't find my husband,' the woman said.

As the second apparition disappeared, the third, a male teenager, whom Linda estimated to be around 18 years old, said, 'I never had time to say goodbye.' He, then, also disappeared.

All three apparitions were, Linda said, dressed in modern, contemporary clothing and didn't appear to be from a distant era. As before, Linda wasn't frightened by her experience; she wondered if she might possess latent mediumistic abilities that were somehow being activated by something in the house. Michael said he would mull over her experiences and see if he could draw any conclusions about them. If he could, then he'd ring the couple back.

On Saturday 11 April, Tony rang Michael again. Linda had had another strange experience, but this one, unlike the previous two, was extremely disturbing. Once more, Linda had woken during the night and had gone to check on the baby. She returned to bed, climbed in, and prepared to drop back off to sleep. At some point, whilst still awake, she turned over and was lying face down in the bed. It was then that she felt what seemed to be a hand pressing down on the left side of her head, effectively pinning her to the bed. Panicking, she tried desperately to free herself, but found, to her horror, that she was now completely paralysed. Worse, she could now sense what felt like another hand sliding in between her thighs, caressing her. She struggled, and tried to shout, but couldn't. Then, after what seemed like an age, the invisible attacker left her and she could once again move.

Linda came to the phone, and told Michael exactly what had happened, filling in several details that Tony had omitted. Her story was punctuated with heartrending sobs, as she struggled not to burst into tears completely. Things were obviously getting out of hand, now, and Michael arranged to visit the couple on Tuesday 14 April.

Tony met Michael and his wife, Jackie, at Middlesbrough train station early in the morning. The three of them then caught a bus to the estate where Tony and Linda live. Their terraced home is not far from the town centre. The dwellings are all over a century old, but possess what aesthetes often refer to as 'character.' On entering, both Michael and Jackie noticed how welcoming the house felt. It was warm and just seemed to radiate friendliness. Linda made tea and then proceeded to explain in more detail just what had transpired over the previous weeks.

'Really, it began when we first moved in here a few months ago… actually within a day or two', said Linda. At this point, Michael interrupted and said, 'Oh, I thought these things had only been going on for the past couple of weeks.' 'Well, they've been worse for the last two weeks, particularly since we changed the clocks for daylight saving time on 29 March,' Linda said. 'But really, there were things happening before that; we just tried to dismiss them.'

Linda had, without being asked, written down a list of the incidents she could recall. The significance of this action cannot be underestimated, and was to help the researchers immensely, later, as they tried to determine exactly what sort of phenomenon the couple were dealing with. Following is a list of the phenomena presenting themselves in the couple's home as recorded by Linda:

- Touch-activated talking cup began talking when no one was near it.
- Banging often heard from Holly's room when no one was there.
- Objects often fell from kitchen benches without being touched.
- Sudden temperature changes. Darius's* bedroom felt cold.
- Crying heard on three separate occasions. Tony and Linda heard it once; Linda heard it twice, outside the bathroom door.
- A friend of Linda's saw a boy aged about 6 – 7 in the downstairs passage.
- Darius's baby-walker had played music by itself.
- A smell of urine and excrement was noticed in the living room at times. Also a smell of women's perfume.
- Feelings of being watched.
- Holly often felt as if she were being followed.
- Holly had three scratch marks on her stomach after being in the upstairs shower.
- Linda often sensed the presence of a little girl, normally by the living room door, mostly when she was on her own.
- Linda had seen numerous shadows, all around the house.
- Tony saw someone in the corner of our bedroom.
- Lights often flickered, sometimes constantly, despite new fuse boxes being fitted.
- Holly and Linda heard drumming noises coming from Darius's room during the night.
- When Linda was in Holly's room, the top drawer of her chest of drawers suddenly opened.
- A computer has acted erratically.
- Things went missing, and then appeared somewhere else.

- Weird draughts, really strong, seemed to be come into the living room from the passage.
- Tony would wake up with scratches all over his torso. They looked as if they had been made by a child's hand.
- Something poked Linda in the back when she was in bed.
- Linda saw an apparition lying in bed between her and Tony.
- Linda felt paralysed in bed, and as if something was on top of her.
- Temperature variations in Tony and Linda's bedroom throughout the night.
- Clicking sounds in Tony and Linda's bedroom.
- Linda walked into Darius's room and it was all foggy.
- The cat sometimes went 'crazy'. It had recently been jumping up at the fireplace a lot.
- On occasions, Tony (and Linda, to a lesser extent) had noticed a strong earth-like smell.

There were a few things that Linda had written down that needed exploration. What was the talking cup for instance? Linda explained that Tony had a large, ceramic tea mug with the face of a modern rock star moulded on to the front. When lifted up, a tiny sensor on the base of the mug activated a digital recording of the rock star saying something extremely witty. To activate the recording, one had to move the mug by, for example, picking it up. However, the mug had started playing the recording without being moved at all. Darren and Michael had seen this sort of trickery before, where a poltergeist had manipulated talking toys and novelty items to ramp up the tension in the household. It had been at South Shields.

The baby-walker incident also caught Michael's attention. Linda explained that there was a toy on the front that Darius could play with. By manipulating or banging the toy with his hand, the toddler could make the toy play tunes or musical sounds. Like the talking cup, the baby-walker had suddenly started playing music spontaneously, without being touched at all. As noted above, Linda had referred to the family's computer acting erratically. Michael asked the couple exactly how it was malfunctioning. Tony explained:

Well, sometimes bizarre things happen with it that we just can't explain. Take the other day, for instance. I booted up the computer, but the monitor wouldn't come on. The power light was activated, so

I knew the electricity was getting through, but it just refused to work. I repeatedly turned everything off and then back on again, but it took fifteen minutes before the monitor began to work normally.

Michael asked Linda and Tony what it *was* about some of the incidents that made them think something paranormal was going on. After all, we can all put something down and forget where, and, in any home, electrical appliances – particularly children's toys, computers and novelty items – will sometimes malfunction. The couple accepted that, when examined in isolation, some of the incidents didn't look that odd. But taken together, they seemed significant.

'It's like... well, everything started happening together,' said Tony. 'We went from nothing strange happening at all, to loads of stuff within a short space of time.'

'Could it not be that you're looking for strange occurrences, now the idea is in your head?' asked Michael.

How can that be? It's not just the little things, like objects going missing and toys playing up, but the big stuff. Holly and Tony have both been scratched. Two of my friends have seen apparitions in the passageway. Tony has, and so have I. Everything – all of the weird stuff – has started happening all at once.

To be honest, Michael found it hard to fault Linda's logic. Something was precipitating a regular stream of seemingly paranormal occurrences. If there was a single, guiding intelligence behind the activity, then it certainly had a wide repertoire of party tricks under its belt.

Michael asked Linda and Tony if he could leave his digital sound recorder running in the master bedroom for a while to see if he could pick up any anomalous sounds. Then he and Tony talked for a while, whilst Linda and Jackie chatted in the kitchen.

Twenty minutes later, Michael retrieved his recorder and played it back. There were no anomalous sounds at all to be heard, except one: about two thirds of the way through the recording, there was what sounded like a rustling noise followed by a gentle click. It definitely sounded as if the noise had been made in close proximity to the recorder. There was another puzzle about the recording, however, that was more difficult to explain. When Michael had activated the recorder, he said, 'Right, that's recording...' Tony and Michael then stood talking for several minutes about the anomalous EMF readings before going downstairs. Just as they left the room, Michael said, for the benefit of the recording, 'Right... shutting the door.'

When Michael played the recording back, both he and Tony were astonished to hear that there was no gap at all in between Michael saying, 'Right, that's recording...' and, 'Right... shutting the door.' What happened to the five-minute conversation in between those two short utterances? Both Michael and Tony are adamant that they had a lengthy conversation in between those two points – in that very room – and yet, the recording seemed to have been *edited* to remove it.

Later that morning, Tony and Michael took a walk to a nearby street, which had been famous in the 1970s because of a poltergeist infestation that had occurred there. Michael wanted to take some photographs. Just before they left, Linda asked if Michael would leave his digital recorder behind. Would he mind if she and Jackie used it to see if they could capture anything strange? Michael said that was fine. All in all, Michael and Tony were out of the house for approximately thirty minutes. When they returned, Tony's parents and grandfather were there. After introductions were made, Michael asked Linda whether she and Jackie had managed to record anything anomalous.

'Actually,' said Linda, 'the recorder is still running up in the bedroom.'

Jackie went up to the bedroom and, as she expected, the recorder was where she had left it. The red recording light was still glowing. She picked it up, switched it off, and promptly went back downstairs where she handed it to Michael. Michael was intrigued as to whether, unlike the first time, the girls had actually managed to capture any substantive anomalous noises. Michael switched the recorder back on, and was immediately puzzled by the digital display on the screen. The last recording was numbered *six*. When Michael had arrived at the house with Jackie earlier, there had been *three* recordings already stored on the machine, which were entirely unconnected with the case. The first attempt Michael had made to record anomalous sounds in the bedroom was, then, stored as *four*. This meant that the last recording made by Linda and Jackie should have been stored as *five*. But it wasn't. It was stored as *six*. Superficially, this seemed to indicate that the girls had made not one recording, when Tony and Michael were out of the house, but two. However, both Linda and Jackie were insistent that only *one* recording had been made.

Linda told Michael, 'Jackie turned the recorder on, pressed the record button and left it. We were only in the room for seconds, and the machine was definitely recording when we left.' Michael pressed the play button to activate recording five, and everyone in the room listened, expecting to hear the beginning of a recording that should have lasted nearly forty-five minutes. However, after just twelve seconds the recording ended. Both Jackie and Linda looked at each other in astonishment. Jackie was the first to react:

'Eh? Where's the rest?'

Michael looked at the recording time on the screen. It was exactly twelve seconds long, no more and no less. All that could be heard at the beginning of the recording was a faint click as the switch was pressed and the recorder began to work, followed by a faint shuffling noise as Jackie went to leave the room with Linda. Then, after twelve seconds, there was a louder rustling noise. Someone had seemingly picked up the recorder. Just as it ended, all that could be heard was the faint click as the stop switch was pressed. Someone had stopped the recording just twelve seconds after the machine had been activated, and it hadn't been Jackie or Linda.

But there was another mystery; if the only recording made by Jackie and Linda was *'five'*, what on earth was the recording now, stored on the machine identified as *six*? His curiosity piqued, Michael pressed the play button once again. There was a faint click, followed by a short rustling noise, as if someone were touching the recorder. Footsteps could be heard, faint at first, as Jackie entered the room and picked the machine up. Again, one can hear a short rustling sound followed by a click as she turned it off. The entire recording lasts 10 seconds. Piecing together the length and content of the recordings, plus the sequence of events, it is possible to work out exactly what had transpired:

> 11.22 hrs: Tony and Michael leave the house.
> 11.26:13 secs: Jackie and Linda place the recorder in the master bedroom and turn it on. The record button is pressed and the red recording light begins to glow.
> 11:26:25 secs: Someone or something turns off the recorder.
> 11.55 hrs: Tony and Michael return to the house.
> 12.02:41 secs: Someone or something activates the digital recorder.
> 12:02:51 secs: Jackie enters the room, picks up the recorder and deactivates it.

Whichever way you looked at it, it really seemed as if something or someone had deactivated the recorder, just as Jackie and Linda left the room, and then activated it again just before Jackie entered the room to retrieve it. This meant that instead of having one continuous recording over almost forty-five minutes, there were simply two extremely short recordings of the *beginning* and the *end* of that time period with no recording of the period in between. It was like skipping from the opening titles of a movie, to the credits without seeing anything in between the two.

On returning home from Middlesbrough, Michael telephoned Darren to tell him about Tony and Linda's experience. Darren picked up the receiver, and in the background Michael could hear music playing loudly.

'Just a minute, mate', said Darren, 'I need to turn the music down so I can hear you.'

As Darren walked away from the phone to turn the volume down on his music centre a little, Michael noticed that his friend was listening to a track by American rock legends, KISS. The track playing was none other than 'Unholy', from the band's 1992 *Revenge* album, the lyrics of which seemed to be chillingly appropriate. As Michael listened, a shiver ran down his spine.

When Darren returned to the phone, Michael asked him how long it had been since he had played that particular album. 'I'm not sure, maybe a few months. Why?'

'I think you'll figure that out for yourself when I tell you what I have to tell you.'

'I haven't said anything to you about this before, simply because I didn't have permission to. Now I have, so I can tell you about it.'

Michael went on to relate to Darren exactly what had happened to Linda. Darren was stunned to hear about what had happened to their mutual friend, but then said, 'Michael, I still don't see what that has to do with me listening to this CD.'

'It's the lyrics Darren. Listen to them again. I heard the first two lines before you turned the volume down. They're singing about an incubus, for Christ sake. I've got a horrible feeling that it may be an incubus that's targeting Linda.'

'Oh shit! How weird is that? I've just got that CD back this morning from a friend I lent it to quite some time ago. I started to play the damn thing just before the phone rang.'

The researchers don't want to read too much into some of the parallels and *seeming* 'coincidences' between the Middlesbrough case and others they have investigated. However, there is no doubt that they are there: the 'accompanying apparitions', other poltergeist-like phenomena, such as household objects disappearing... and then, to top it all, the fact that a song by one of the world's most popular rock bands, in which the lyrics discuss an actual incubus, was playing at exactly the same time that Michael rang Darren to tell him about a *possible* incubus case – or at least a case that showed symptoms of one.

Once again, it *seemed* that the entity, or whatever was at 'play' here, had demonstrated an uncanny ability to perfectly time its actions in a way that now left the researchers in no doubt whatsoever that, like the other cases, this one was also part of a much wider circle of malign influence. What else were they supposed to think? Later, Linda rang Michael, and for almost an hour talked about her feelings regarding what had happened. Both she and Tony were happy for Darren and Michael to spend a few nights in their home to see if they could determine exactly what was going on there. The researchers were certain that something was going on; the question was what? In the first edition of *Contagion*, this chapter ended by informing the reader that investigation of the case was continuing. Sadly, it never went forward, and Darren didn't get a chance to visit this alleged 'haunted house'. An incident occurred there, according to Tony, which left the family so terrified that they simply packed up, sold up, and left. We never did find out what it was, as they have refused to discuss it.

PART TWO
FORWARD THINKING: PROBING THE POLTERGEIST

16

STANDBY – THE POLTERGEIST POWER SOURCE?

Since 2008, the Green Campaign has stepped up its efforts to clean up the planet and protect the environment. In the UK, brown or green wheelie bins were introduced for garden waste, and recycling boxes were distributed nationwide to householders. September of that year saw the launch of a new TV advertising campaign, advising the British public to become 'greener', by, for example, turning off lights in the home when they didn't need to be on, thereby saving money and electricity, and reducing people's 'carbon footprint.'

Essentially, a carbon footprint is the measure of human activity that has a detrimental effect upon the environment. Greenhouse gasses that are produced from our everyday actions can be counted up in measurements. These units of carbon dioxide are measured up, and can determine just how much carbon dioxide is being expelled into the atmosphere from any given source, or indeed all of them. Once you know what your 'carbon footprint' is, you can take steps to reduce your carbon emissions, thus helping to prevent or at least slow down the global warming process.

This latest TV advert, is essentially no different from others. But there is one particular aspect of the campaign that is new on the 'keep things green' front, so to speak. When Darren saw this TV advertisement for the first time, bells began to ring, and he was suddenly struck with a rather intriguing thought. This particular advert mentioned the usual things such as dimming lights, half-filling kettles, saving water etc., but the aspect of it that made him sit up and pay attention was when it mentioned the detrimental effects of leaving electrical appliances on standby.

In recent years, theories have originated in regards to poltergeist activity, and the mechanics behind it. These new ideas include the idea that the poltergeist might use the dormant electrical energy that is so often stored in TVs and music systems when left on 'standby.' If electrical energy latent in appliances in standby-mode is utilised in this way by hungry poltergeists, turning the appliances off completely *may* indeed cut off one of their much-needed sources of energy or food. Darren and Michael found this to be a relevant factor in the South Shields case back in 2006. Many new electrical appliances *had* been brought into the Lock Street house when Marc moved in (e.g. TVs, DVD players and a music system for the master bedroom). They were left on 'standby', both day and night, when not in use. Upon the advice of Darren and Michael (after a recommendation from Stephen Swales, a university lecturer and a close colleague of the researchers), Marc and Marianne switched them off when they weren't in use. The poltergeist activity then ceased. Did this lack of electrical energy really help to bring the poltergeist infestation to an end? Or was it just a coincidence – a case of the phenomena having run their course?

At Lock Street, the poltergeist *seemed* to feed upon its victims fear (another theory as to how poltergeists persist in their endeavours), but, after being subjected to so much terror and alarm in their home, believe it or not, Marc and Marianne simply became accustomed to it and were victims no more. Over time, they literally became bored with it rather than frightened. Consequently, in Darren's view, the poltergeist lost an important 'food source': their fear. It now needed something else to feed upon, and it wasn't long before it discovered the latent electrical power in appliances that were in standby mode. This new/alternative food source sustained its ability to engage in destruction, but not for long. Once the householders at Lock Street began to turn off their appliances at night, the poltergeist simply couldn't feed at all. This is when the researchers believe they may have helped to bring its reign to an end, although this is, of course, conjectural.

Darren's point was that the people of Great Britain needed to take notice of this new advert by turning off lights in rooms that are not being used, turning off radios that are not being listened to, and, most importantly, not leaving one's appliances on standby (overnight or otherwise). Granted, we would have been reducing our carbon emission, which was/is of course a good thing, but one may also have been saving oneself from months of unnecessary trouble and torment at the hands of an uninvited, invisible intruder commonly known as a poltergeist.

In Darren's view, it would have been interesting to know whether reports of poltergeist cases were in depletion, after TV adverts started advising people to switch off electrical appliances that weren't in use. If the masses decided to 'unplug or switch off' rather than leave their electrical appliances 'on standby', maybe the incidences of genuine poltergeist cases will have indeed fallen. For this to have occurred it would have required a polt-count, and here lies the problem, as we shall soon see. Of course, poltergeist cases have been reported throughout the centuries, not just since electricity has been harnessed to power homes, workplaces, streetlights, etc. However, just because electricity as we know it wasn't understood and utilised by mankind until the early 1880s, it doesn't mean that electricity never actually *existed* prior to that.

One of the most natural forms of electricity is lightning, which has been discharging itself in the atmosphere since time immemorial, from cloud to cloud, or, more spectacularly, from cloud to ground. Lightning strikes carry an enormous amount of energy. The electricity that we have harnessed for ourselves, we call 'current' electricity, which is generated by the flow of electrical charge through a conductor across an electrical field flowing through man-made wires, ultimately creating power that we as a species, use to our own advantage. There are other types of natural electricity pervading the earth's atmosphere too, such as *static* electricity, which – for the record – was actually *thought* to have been discovered and used by the ancient Greeks around 600BC; this arises when two or more objects rub together, initiating a build-up of electric charge, causing 'sparks' or 'crackling', and acting like a magnet to material such as dust and hair.

It discharges when an excess charge is neutralised by a flow of electrons to or from the surroundings. It is not far-fetched to think, then, that if the poltergeist does indeed 'feed' or utilise electricity – man made, or indeed natural – then there has certainly been an abundant supply for it, dating as far back as the earliest known cases.

Having said that, it is evident that the poltergeist has the capacity to adapt to the modern world and utilise devices such as mobile phones and TV sets, as seen during the Lock Street investigation and other notable cases. In the 16th, 17th and early 18th centuries, when poltergeists were seen as 'imps' 'devils' 'ghosts' or 'spirits', if they needed electrical energy, they had to use natural sources. Since 'current' electricity started being pumped into homes and businesses in the early 1800s, has the poltergeist has been granted an easier meal? We don't know for sure. But, as already noted, the phenomena at Lock Street seemed to cease when electrical items were switched off.

This made us think that *possibly*, we had hit upon something which just happened to work 'in our case' – that is, of course if, as previously stated, the Lock Street Poltergeist didn't burn itself out naturally, which raises the question just *how and why* the activity burns itself out? And, if we did indeed cut off the poltergeist's 'food' or 'energy' supply, by asking Marc and Marianne to 'turn off' their electrical goods, then what was to stop the poltergeist from simply turning to the natural forms of electricity it *may* have once utilised, to continue its campaign of terror?

The idea of counting poltergeist cases post 2008, and comparing them with reported poltergeist cases in 2009, 2010, 2011 and so on, to see if there was a depletion in cases, Darren *thought*, wasn't a bad idea *per se*, so when he was compiling the updates for this work in 2020/2021, he decided to make a few enquiries – just to see if he could gather some information, and to see if this task *could* be worth undertaking. Of course, as previously stated in Chapter 12, 'there is no *official* code of practice and no governing body supervising ghost and poltergeist investigators; therefore it must be taken into consideration that many potential cases may have gone under the 'radar', and although investigated by one of the countless 'ghost hunting teams' out there these days – either poorly, or satisfactorily – depending on the quality and integrity of the researchers/investigators, there may be *no* official record of it. So in a sense, a *true* case count, really is out of the question, if indeed, anything could have been objectively drawn from it in the first place. Upon discussing this with Alan Murdie, (former head of the Spontaneous Cases Committee for the Society for Psychical Research) he advised Darren that it would be almost impossible to undertake such a task in an objective manner, because of the current level of understanding of the poltergeist phenomenon – or lack of it – and the fact there are no records, or no 'databases', of *all* the reported UK cases. Sadly, this is what Darren had already assumed to be the case.

In his fascinating and quite humorous new study of the poltergeist, *Blithe Spirits, An Imaginative History of the Poltergeist* by Fortean Times contributor and author S.D. Tucker, referring to the idea of counting the reported poltergeist cases post 2008, 2009, 2010 etc., states (p.160), 'Darren W. Ritson once proposed an experiment as comic as it was ingenious.' A comment to which the current updater of this work found particularly amusing yet was to some extent, irritated by it simply due to its obvious truth. In theory, it *was* potentially a good idea, but in practical terms, well; let us just say that it's back to the drawing board.

17

MY NAME IS LEGION, FOR WE ARE MANY

To set the scene for the exposition of Darren and Michael's hypothesis regarding the poltergeist phenomenon, it will first be necessary to provide the reader with an admittedly controversial theory that may well offend those of a religious disposition, specifically orthodox Christians. We don't wish to cause offence unnecessarily, but Darren and Michael are of the opinion that people in ancient times, and some who came later, *may* well have had a better understanding of the poltergeist enigma than we might imagine.

It is a truism to state that the population of 1st century AD Judea believed in the possession of people by evil entities. The New Testament is awash with incidents in which invisible, malign beings take over innocent victims and use them for their own wicked purposes. Jesus, as we know, made quite a name for himself by expelling such demons and freeing the victims from their clutches. A close examination of the poltergeist phenomenon throws up many parallels with the concept of spirit possession. They are similar, but not the same. Cases of supposed spirit possession usually involve radical changes in the personality of the possessed person. Those who play host to a poltergeist don't usually exhibit such changes, and may continue to behave perfectly normally. However, the two phenomena are similar in that they both involve a 'host' or 'focus' who, consciously or otherwise, has within him – or herself – a force or power that operates independently and has a great degree of independence. In both conditions, the attendant 'symptoms' are almost always negative, counter-productive and destructive. In Judaeo-Christian theology, demons are believed to be evil spirits who are subject to the whims of a master, commonly called *Satan* or the *Devil*. Muslims, it must be said, hold a somewhat different view. Further, some people believe that demons don't exist as sentient, autonomous entities, but are merely fragmentary aspects of a higher, satanic personality. Conversely, some Christians believe the same about angels: that they are not independent entities, but merely 'aspects of God.' A similar belief exists in ostensibly polytheistic societies or cultures, where many different 'deities' are believed to be simply one, great deity, presenting itself in different forms. Is there any evidence to suggest that this idea – that spiritual entities may be a part of a greater whole and not fully autonomous entities – affected the thinking of those who lived in Jesus' day? On the surface there is, and it can be found in one of the gospel accounts themselves.

In the Gospel of Luke, there is an account of a man who, it seems, was acting rather bizarrely. He had taken to wearing no clothes, and had forsaken his former abode, and began to reside in a local graveyard. Jesus happens to bump into the man, who was believed to be 'possessed by devils', and at this point the possessed individual speaks to him. However, it is clear from the outset that it is not the man as such who is doing the talking, but the entities, which allegedly possessed him:

'What have I got to do with you, Jesus, you Son of God Most High? I plead with you, don't torment me!' the devil says. Jesus, it seems, had attempted to carry out an impromptu exorcism and had commanded the evil spirits to come out of the man, something that they were clearly reluctant to do. In addition to living naked amongst the tombs, the man had also developed incredible superhuman strength. On several occasions he had been chained, but apparently shattered his bonds with ease. Desperate to rid their community of the possessed person, locals had driven him into the desert.

Just before the exorcism was complete, Jesus asked, 'What is your name?' This is intriguing, for although the man was said to be possessed by many devils, the son of Mary addressed them in the singular, as if he was talking to one personage only. The devil (or devils) replied, 'My name is Legion, for we are many.'

Jesus, as we know, then cast out the offending entities and sent them into a herd of swine, which then all raced over the edge of a nearby cliff into the water below. The fascinating thing about this account is that it alternates between the singular and the plural repeatedly. Was the man possessed by many demons, or just one? One interpretation would be to say that he was possessed both by one and by many at the same time. Let us imagine that evil spirits are not fully independent entities or spirits, but are essentially parts of a greater whole – an arch-spirit, if you will, and call him Satan, if you like – who merely presents himself to victims as a single individual or in a multiplicity of aspects, depending on how the mood takes him. If this is the case, then it is technically correct to speak of such an entity in both the singular and the plural, for it is truly both.

In cases of spirit possession, victims often manifest strikingly similar symptoms: levitation, use of foul language (often in Latin, Aramaic or some other defunct language), evacuation of huge amounts of excreta from the bowels, speaking in strange accents... all of which could reasonably be presented as evidence that the same guiding hand is behind each and every possession. Indeed, the cases of possession are often so similar that we may be confident enough to suggest that the same personality is at work, much as we may say the same about the serial killer who leaves a particular playing card on the bodies of his victims.

At this point, we can now ask what may metaphorically be deemed the $64,000 question; can we apply this same hypothesis to the poltergeist phenomenon? Could it be that there is, in reality, only one poltergeist – the arch-poltergeist, if you like – who, like demons, devils and deities, presents itself as one or many depending on how he/she/it feels? It is only a hypothesis, but it is one that Darren and Michael feel *may* well hold validity, both because of their personal experience, and the testimony from many other poltergeist incidents.

18

THE ENFIELD CASE, AND 'OUR' CASE PARALLELS

One of the strangest aspects of the poltergeist phenomenon, and one which impacts heavily upon one of the themes of this book, is the bizarre parallels that often occur between separate cases of poltergeist infestation. Some of these parallels will be obvious even to the amateur researcher: objects being moved without human intervention, disembodied footsteps, and loud rapping noises for example. However, there are other, more peculiar parallels, which, as previously stated, would seem to *imply* that the same entity is responsible for all of the phenomena regardless of *when* they took place, or *where* they were located.

Before going into detail regarding what conclusion Darren and Michael reached about this peculiarity, it is necessary to spell out exactly what sort of symptoms and signs they are referring to. Below is a chart, which draws attention to some – although certainly not all – of the parallels between the numerous cases that Darren and Michael have personally investigated or, in the case of Enfield, learned about. In the 'Location or Case' columns, the following key is used:

POLTERGEIST PARALLELS AND CONTAGION

En: Enfield. SS: South Shields. Ja: Jarrow. As: Ashington. Ne: Newcastle. Bly: Blyth. Go: Gosforth. Ho: Howdon. WB: West Boldon.

Location or Case

No.	Presenting Symptom of Poltergeistry	En	SS	Ja	As	Ne	Bly	Go	Ho	WB
1	Presentation of contagion or contagion-like phenomena	✓	✓	✓	✓	✓	✓	✓	✓	✓
2	Books flying off shelves	✓	✓	✓						✓
3	Knocking or rapping noises	✓	✓	✓	✓	✓				
4	Polt-fascination with plastic building blocks	✓	✓							
5	Phenomena involving glass marbles	✓	✓							
6	Drawers opening of their own accord	✓	✓							
7	Doors opening or closing of their own accord	✓	✓	✓		✓				
8	Objects passing through solid matter	✓	✓							
9	Sudden, icy breezes	✓	✓	✓			✓			
10	Stacking of objects	✓	✓						✓	✓
11	Phyical attacks upon witnesses	✓	✓	✓	✓					
12	Hearing voices	✓	✓	✓		✓				
13	Seeing apparitions	✓	✓	✓		✓			✓	
14	Appearance of shadows or shadow-like shapes	✓	✓	✓	✓	✓	✓			
15	Movement of, or interaction with, children's toys	✓	✓	✓					✓	
16	Movement of mobile phones from downstairs to upstairs		✓	✓			✓			
17	Involuntary movement or relocation of sleeping children	✓	✓							

THE ENFIELD CASE, AND 'OUR' CASE PARALLELS

No.	Presenting Symptom of Poltergeistry	En	SS	Ja	As	Ne	Bly	Go	Ho	WB
18	Movement of furniture	☐	☐	☐						
19	Polt-fascination with fish or fish tanks	☐	☐							
20	Intervention of clergy or other religious leaders	☐	☐	☐	☐					
21	Phenomena related to mineral water bottles		☐			☐				
22	'Shaking bed' or 'moving bed' phenomenon	☐	☐	☐	☐					
23	Aggressive use of projectiles	☐	☐	☐		☐				
24	Inexplicable power drainage from electrical equipment	☐	☐	☐			☐	☐		
25	Lithobolia, or 'stone-throwing' phenomena	☐	☐							
26	Possible masquerading of the poltergeist as a child	☐	☐	☐						
27	Fascination of the polt with technological or mechanical objects	☐	☐	☐		☐	☐	☐	☐	☐
28	Precise 'timing' of phenomena, indicating sentience on the part of the poltergeist	☐	☐	☐	☐	☐	☐			☐
29	Polt-fascination with 'red chairs'	☐	☐							
30	Witnessing the spontaneous materialisation of objects	☐	☐				☐			
31	Polt-related phenomena outside of 'ground zero', or the home of the witnesses	☐	☐	☐	☐	☐		☐	☐	☐
32	Inability of witnesses to open doors	☐	☐	☐						

POLTERGEIST PARALLELS AND CONTAGION

No.	Presenting Symptom of Poltergeistry	En	SS	Ja	As	Ne	Bly	Go	Ho	WB
33	'Fluorescent light' phenomenon (not 'orbs')	☐	☐			☐				
34	'Mischievous' movement of chairs as witnesses are sitting or attempting to sit down	☐	☐							
35	Throwing of/fascination with miniature or toy vehicles	☐	☐							
36	Spontaneous appearance of water pools	☐	☐							
37	Spontaneous appearance of urine		☐							
38	Movement of kitchen tables	☐	☐							
39	Poltergeists verifying their authenticity / existence to investigators	☐	☐							
40	Children subjected to trance-like states	☐	☐	☐						
41	'Burning sensations' felt before attacks		☐							
42	Pulling of bedclothes from bed	☐	☐	☐	☐					
43	Polt-fascination with footwear	☐	☐							
44	Soft toys thrown at witnesses whilst they lie in bed	☐	☐							
45	Polt-fascination with crayons, pencils, writing implements	☐	☐	☐						
46	Complete 'trashing' of rooms	☐	☐							
47	'Throwing' of knives	☐	☐							
48	Door-knocks by invisible entities	☐	☐							

THE ENFIELD CASE, AND 'OUR' CASE PARALLELS

No.	Presenting Symptom of Poltergeistry	En	SS	Ja	As	Ne	Bly	Go	Ho	WB
49	Leaving of written messages by poltergeists	☐	☐							
50	Spontaneous fire-starting	☐	☐							☐
51	Polt-fascination with wardrobes	☐	☐	☐	☐			☐		
52	Polt-fascination with refrigerators	☐	☐			☐				
53	Lavatory-related phenomena	☐	☐	☐					☐	
54	Coin or monetary-related phenomena	☐	☐			☐				
55	Witnesses being thrown or lifted out of bed	☐	☐							
56	'Doppelganger' phenomenon	☐	☐	☐						
57	Use of foul language by poltergeists	☐	☐							
58	Use of taunting euphemisms by poltergeists	☐	☐							
59	Threats to investigators by poltergeists	☐	☐							
60	Sexual undertones present			☐	☐					
61	Use of personal names by the poltergeist	☐		☐	☐		☐		☐	
62	Removing bath panels		☐	☐						
63	Spontaneous removal and replacement of documents from drawers			☐	☐	☐	☐			

Readers may note that there are *some* cases detailed earlier in the book that are *not* recorded in the above chart. Some of these cases also contain extraordinary parallels with cases detailed in the chart, but they were not investigated personally by Darren or Michael. Readers will also notice that by far the greatest number of parallels can be found between the Enfield and South Shields cases, but the temptation should be resisted to read too much into this. In both the Enfield and South Shields cases, a detailed case study was written up in book form, thus making it much easier for parallels to be spotted and noted.

Often, it is not the number of parallels that is the important thing, but rather the *quality* of them. As readers will see, there are occasions when a parallel can be drawn between only two cases, but it is so specific that any reasonable person would be forced to conclude that a link – whatever one may perceive it to be – is present. There are a number of quite startling parallels that need to be drawn to the reader's attention. In both the Enfield, and South Shields cases, the poltergeist seemed to have an unusual fascination with children's plastic building blocks. Darren and Michael are aware of other cases in which this same fascination was evident. In one US case, detailed earlier, a children's toy play mat was involved. Darren and Michael have already pointed out the precise, undeniable parallels present with the case they investigated at South Shields.

When Darren and Michael were compiling the first edition of this book, Darren contacted Guy Lyon Playfair, one of the two principal investigators of the Enfield Poltergeist case, and asked him whether either he or Maurice Grosse had experienced anything that could be classed as contagion-like phenomena. Guy contacted Darren and told him the following:

> Dear Darren;
> Maurice had all kinds of strange experiences, and of course I can't prove they were polt-related, but they did seem to escalate post-Enfield. The best one I remember, which Maurice told me about soon afterwards, was when his wife's ring went missing overnight from the bedside little china pot where she always kept it. Weeks of search of the whole house and grounds failed to find it. Reluctantly, Maurice wrote to his insurance company for a claim form. The next morning the ring was back in its pot. My own experience is: After listening to a rather silly BBC Radio 4 play, obviously based on the Enfield case, I heard a loud ping and found that one of the

tops of the knobs on my electric cooker had come off, travelled 2-3 feet and banged into a bottle on the floor. There was absolutely no conceivable way that could have been normal. The tops are quite hard to get off. The cooker was on, but on very low heat, and I have used it daily since 1975 (and still do). It has never malfunctioned in any way. Here, there was a clear connection to Enfield. The radio play was obviously based on the Enfield case – but set in South London and involving 2 teenage boys instead of girls and investigated by a woman. I listened to it without much interest, mainly to see if the author violated my copyright, which he took care not to do. When it was over, I thought to myself "what a waste of time", and soon afterwards there was this loud ping.

You're welcome to quote that.
YRS. GUY.

Playfair and Grosse (both now deceased) were recognised by many as two of the most knowledgeable researchers regarding the poltergeist phenomenon, and, if they experienced phenomena that they believed to be contagion-like, we must take their arguments seriously. Further instances of apparent contagion in the Enfield case, not mentioned in Playfair's email to Darren, will be mentioned in Chapter 21.

On 4 May 2008, Michael had a lengthy discussion with Darren about the whole matter of contagion and, afterwards, both Darren and Michael took a break from researching, so that Michael could take care of a personal project he had been working on. In 1918, his great-grandfather, Thomas Trewick, was serving with the British Army in France and was stationed in the town of Forceville. His battalion was moved to a nearby town, to stall a German advance, when, with two colleagues, he clambered down into what had been a German trench. Almost immediately, a shell landed inside the trench and all three men were killed.

Michael was particularly interested in his great-grandfather's war service, and had been working on a website dedicated to the man. At that point, he didn't know the exact date when Tom Trewick had been killed, although there was a story prevalent in the family that the tragedy had occurred on Armistice Day, 11 November 1918. Michael had an old, battered photograph of his great-grandfather and took it out of his file to examine. He flipped it over, and noticed for the first time that a small piece of paper had been glued over the back. Written on the reverse of the picture were the words, 'TOM TREWICK, KILLED 1918.' However, Michael could see that there was something else written underneath the piece of paper. For the next twenty minutes, Michael carefully scraped away at the now-brittle paper, until the writing underneath was exposed. It was, quite simply, the exact date on which Private Trewick had been killed. The date was 4 May – the very day that Michael was actually examining the photograph, and the very day that he had not only discussed the subject of poltergeist-contagion with Darren, but also had been writing about it with Darren in the manuscript of the first edition of this book.

The fact that the date was the very same as the one on which his great-grandfather was killed was extraordinary, but can this be connected robustly to the poltergeist phenomenon and classed as contagion? Directly, no. But Darren, Michael and other researchers have reported experiencing quite extraordinary 'coincidences' of this nature when dealing with poltergeist cases, and indeed with other aspects of the paranormal. There may be no direct connection in the same way that there was no direct connection between the Enfield case and Maurice Grosse's wife 'losing' her ring. However, the insistence of such phenomena in manifesting themselves, when investigations are ongoing, leaves one having to admit that there may indeed be such a connection.

In the South Shields, Ashington and Jarrow cases, the witnesses all reported feeling a 'sense of depression,' which overtook them when they felt the presence of the poltergeist. This is not uncommon and it is not a physically observable parallel, of course, but it is still worth mentioning. When Darren and Michael were originally working on the first edition of this book, Michael had occasion to ring their former agent, Natalie Lisbona. Just before the phone conversation, Natalie opened a cupboard in her kitchen and had a rather unnerving experience. Inside the cupboard was a packet of dried lentils. Without warning, the packet shot out of the cupboard and careened across the floor. What made the experience all the weirder was that, just before entering the kitchen, Natalie had been reviewing some footage that Darren and Michael had taken during their investigation into the South Shields poltergeist case.

Around the same time, Natalie also had another strange experience. Whilst lying in bed with her husband, the couple repeatedly heard the sound of someone placing a key in their front door and trying to open the lock. Every time they opened the door, there was no one there.

THE ENFIELD CASE, AND 'OUR' CASE PARALLELS

The mystery was never solved. Again, it seemed that the poltergeist phenomenon, whatever one thinks it to be, has an ability to transcend fixed geographical locations and 'infect' those who are involved with the case.

One of the most disturbing aspects of the poltergeist phenomenon – although, to be honest, it isn't a common one – is the presence of sexual undertones. This was certainly true at Ashington, and it was also true at Jarrow and Middlesbrough. During an interview with Mandy, Michael said:

> Mandy, you mentioned earlier on that you felt something touch you on the leg; again, that is something that is frightening, but have you ever felt any other of your body parts being touched – say, for example, something like fingers running through your hair?

Mandy replied:

> Erm... Just when I walked in from the kitchen one time, and I thought Derek touched my behind in a saucy but fun way, but he said it wasn't him.

To some, this incident may seem trivial, but, in reality, it speaks volumes about the essence or nature of the poltergeist. Whether such incidents are common or not, there can be no doubt that, at least on occasions, the poltergeist can display sexually provocative behaviour. Earlier in this book, Darren and Michael discussed the possibly related incubus/succubus phenomenon. However, as in all the cases they have investigated, the victim of such behaviour has been female, so the question must be asked: is the poltergeist essentially masculine in nature?

In 1982, a screenplay written by Frank De Felitta was turned into a movie. The film, *The Entity*, detailed the experiences of one Doris Bither (she was named Carla Moran for the movie), who claimed that she was repeatedly physically and sexually assaulted by a so-called demonic entity. The account was said to have been based on true life events, and was investigated by parapsychologist Barry E. Taff, Ph.D., whom we shall encounter later in this work in relation to another American poltergeist case that he discussed with Darren for this book. The sad truth, however, is that when people do claim to have genuinely experienced such encounters, they are usually doubted. Cynics, it seems, just don't possess the broadness of mind to grasp that these things really do happen.

Imagine that you are a woman at home alone. Then imagine that a demented psychopath is trying to break down your front door, and you strongly suspect that his sole intention is to rape you, and possibly kill you. You pick up the phone and call the police. What you want, of course, is for officers to respond immediately to protect you, and to apprehend the criminal. But supposing you don't actually get what you want. Suppose, for one terrible moment, the police refuse to respond to your call and tell you that, quite frankly, they don't believe your story.

'We don't get any rapes happening around here,' you are told.

Imagine your horror and disbelief at such a reaction. You know you are telling the truth, but the only people who can help you refuse to act, because they simply don't believe what you are telling them. What you thought was your worst nightmare has now just become even more terrifying.

It's a horrible thought, isn't it? And yet, all over the world, there are women who are genuinely afraid of being raped and brutalised, not *just* by flesh-and-blood males, but also by psychic entities with far more potential for doing harm. Very few are believed and, hence, they have nowhere to turn. Darren and Michael understand that there are troubled – or even mischievous – individuals out there, who are, for one reason or another, only too ready to lie and make up such stories. But they aren't all lying. Some are telling the truth. In a classic case of throwing the baby out with the bath water, some sceptics will often argue that if one such person is lying, then they all must be. Even if one takes the sexual element out of the equation, being attacked and/or terrorised by a poltergeist – whatever it may be – is a terrible thing.

Are such people lying? Sometimes, yes. Unfortunately, nowadays, too many people use the 'my house is haunted' excuse in an attempt to get re-housed when they are unhappy with their rented homes for whatever reason: noisy neighbours, bad surroundings or living conditions, or simply because they just want to move. Pleas for help from genuine victims of hauntings to be re-housed have worked in the past, so why not lie about a ghost or poltergeist and get re-housed hassle free? In genuine circumstances like the Maud Street case in Lemington, Newcastle-upon-Tyne, in 1974, the polt-victim was affected so badly that she had to be hospitalised. There was, as far as we know, no sexual aspect to this poltergeist infestation, but the victim was clearly traumatised.

When barefaced liars claim the same thing has happened to them, it is an insult to genuine victims of hauntings and poltergeist phenomena. Bogus claims are a serious headache for investigators. Time after time the so-called victims are proven to be untruthful, and when a genuine case *does* come along, no one will believe it. This happened after the South Shields poltergeist case in 2006. After the book that details the whole affair was released, some folk suggested that the family members in question were merely publicity-seeking liars who made it all up to be re-housed by their housing association. They were ignorant of the fact that Marc and Marianne were actually *buying* their house and not renting it; furthermore, they requested the anonymity in the book and they have since rebuffed all media attention and have done so to this day, over fifteen years after the events; indeed a recent 'review' of *The South Shields Poltergeist* book illustrates this point nicely. In it, the reviewer, simply known as A.S, states, 'this in itself lends credibility to the case, since, were they simply publicity-seekers after monetary gain, one wouldn't expect them to retreat into anonymity or still be within its cloak some fifteen years on.'

If those narrow-minded critics had actually read the book based upon the case properly, they would have been aware of most of these facts, and consequently not have embarrassed themselves. Our point is that not all claims of having a haunted house are false. Some people do live in fear of haunting phenomena and have nowhere to turn; if they live in rented accommodation, it is worse ten-fold, as they know that if they do ask to be moved, they may well be labelled liars – and it's just not on. The residents in Maud Street discovered this all too well.

19

TEXTUAL INNUENDOES

One of the things, which Darren and Michael noticed during their investigation at South Shields, was that the poltergeist displayed an impressive ability to utilise technology. This would demonstrate itself in relatively simple ways, such as the turning on and off of electrical appliances. It had a particular fondness for messing around with the TV, and, on numerous occasions, turned it on or off in the presence of both the witnesses and investigators. One slight variation on this party trick was to leave the TV on, but repeatedly change the channels. Its most impressive TV-related trick was to programme the attached digital satellite box to remind the couple when certain programmes were about to start. Inevitably, these would be documentaries or movies with a paranormal or horror theme.

However, the poltergeist also demonstrated a liking for mobile phones. Actually, it was more like an obsession. Within a short space of time, it mastered the art of using the mobile phone, and eventually was able to do things that appeared scientifically impossible. The poltergeist could make a mobile phone ring, and then stop it ringing. It then worked out – somehow – a way of making a mobile phone ring, even when it wasn't switched on. As its phone-related skills were honed, it began to send text messages – many of them of a vile and threatening nature.

On one occasion, the poltergeist sent a series of terrifying text messages to Marianne, one of the principal witnesses, whilst Michael was on the phone to her. The messages related to things that Marianne had said, just a split-second earlier in the conversation. It would have been physically impossible for a human being to compose even the briefest of text messages within such an incredibly short space of time, but the poltergeist managed it. A similar feat was executed by the poltergeist in the Rosenheim case in southern Bavaria, Germany, in 1967, that was investigated by parapsychologist, Hans Bender. The poltergeist somehow managed to rapidly ring the 'speaking clock' successively and many times more than any human could have.

As the reader will now be aware, one of the principal themes explored in this book is that of contagion: the possibility that, in some way, people may become infected by the poltergeist-presence and, in turn, experience poltergeist-related phenomena themselves. Another aspect of the poltergeist phenomenon that Darren and Michael have explored is the bizarre similarity between cases that are geographically – and often culturally – separated. Why would a poltergeist in Enfield, North London, display a fascination with children's toy building blocks, and a poltergeist three decades later at the opposite end of the country demonstrate exactly the same compulsion? Just why these poltergeist-parallels occur is something that we will explore later. However, for now, I simply wish to draw the reader's attention to an uncanny parallel between other cases – all of which repeated what the researchers had already discovered at South Shields: that the poltergeist just love telephones.

On Tuesday, April 29 2008, Darren and Michael were giving a lecture on the South Shields poltergeist case. Michael had arranged to meet Darren at Newcastle Central train station at 2pm, before they headed off for the venue of their talk. Michael – a stickler for punctuality – was well ahead of time and decided to browse through the magazine shelves at the W.H. Smith store inside the station. After a minute or two, his eyes fell upon the May edition of *Fortean Times*, one of the world's most respected magazines dealing with strange phenomena. He purchased a copy, and then sat himself at a table in one of the station's several open-air cafés, with a large coffee. Darren wouldn't be arriving for about another twenty minutes, so Michael decided to flick through the pages of the magazine to see if there were any stories of unusual interest.

And there was: on page 8, there was an article entitled, 'Cell Phone Stalkers Playing Mind Games'. The article dealt with a 'reign of terror' that three families had been forced to endure in the city of Fircrest, Pierce County, Washington State, beginning around the month of February, 2007. The case involved a variety of non-phone related phenomena, including horrendous banging noises on walls and screams seemingly uttered by disembodied voices. Inevitably, by the time the police arrived on the scene, the perpetrators had vanished. However, the worst aspects of the case were those that centred on mobile phones owned by the victims.

They would receive voice-mails spoken in guttural, chilling tones, which contained death threats. Worse, the callers obviously knew exactly what the victims were doing at any given time. The perpetrators would describe what they were wearing, what they were eating and, often, what they were actually doing within the confines of their homes.

A subsequent investigation showed that many (although not all) of the calls were seemingly coming from the phone of one of the victims, sixteen year-old Courtney Kuykendall. However, it was later proved that when many of the calls were made, Courtney wasn't using her phone, and that it had actually been switched off. Conversations made over the phone were occasionally recorded, and then sent to the victims as voice-mail messages. As the victims received their phone bills, they were horrified to find that they were enormous, sometimes approaching $1,000.

One of the victims was Taylor McKay, who went with her mother to meet with the principal of her school to discuss the situation. A police officer was present at the meeting. Both Taylor and her mother, Andrea, placed their cell-phones on the table in front of them. They were both switched off. Suddenly, Taylor's phone switched itself on and promptly sent a text message to her mother's phone. The victims tried all manner of things to rectify the situation, including changing their phone numbers. As soon as they did so, they would begin receiving more voice messages. On one occasion, Andrea McKay was slicing limes in the kitchen when she received a message from the perpetrators telling her that they actually preferred lemons.

There were two possible explanations for the enigma: the first was that the victims were the target of a highly sophisticated campaign of terror organised by malicious (but very human) perpetrators, who seemingly had the ability to hack into the websites of their service providers and effectively hijack their phones. Such a thing is possible, but to carry out such a campaign to that degree would need a sophisticated knowledge of phone and computer technology beyond that possessed by the vast majority of people. In any case, why would anyone want to go to such lengths, simply to make the lives of three ordinary families a misery? Furthermore, this explanation does not deal with how the perpetrators were able to monitor the exact movements and actions of the victims within their own homes. To do this, they would have needed to break into the families' dwellings and install covert surveillance equipment without being seen or apprehended. It just doesn't seem to make sense.

The second explanation was radically different, and involved the suggestion that the perpetrator may have been something far different: a poltergeist. Poltergeists are well known for creating banging noises and moving objects around, but those who took an interest in the case were astounded at the idea that a poltergeist could actually manipulate mobile phone technology to such a degree – and with such wanton vindictiveness. This didn't surprise Darren and Michael, because they'd seen it all before – at South Shields.

By Monday 28 August 2006, the incessant barrage of attacks had driven the family at Lock Street to distraction, and they decided to vacate the premises for the evening and stay with Marianne's mother. Michael asked Marianne to ring him later that evening and let him know if everyone was okay. Marianne did ring Michael, although she still sounded distressed. Marc, she said, had telephoned the landline of their home 'just to see what would happen', although he knew that no one was there. No one should have picked up the receiver, of course, because there wasn't supposed to *be* anyone there. But something *did* pick up the receiver, before immediately replacing it on the cradle. It was almost certainly the poltergeist.

Darren and Michael tried to reassure Marianne that things would turn out okay; she just needed to remain calm. Marianne said that it would be difficult, as during the day she'd received a series of nasty text messages from the entity, saying things like, 'tonight is the night you will die,' and, 'I'll come for you when you're asleep.' Marianne was searching desperately for reassurance, and said, 'Michael, please tell me that it hasn't come with me to my mum's! I couldn't stand it!'

Of course, this was a reassurance that couldn't be given, as poltergeists are, as previously discussed, usually person-centred and not always place-centred. It may very well have followed Marianne. This placed Michael on the horns of a dilemma – what should he do? Lie, and tell Marianne that the poltergeist couldn't or wouldn't have followed her, simply to make her feel better? Or should he tell her the brutal truth and frighten the living daylights out of her? Before he could even begin to consider the problem, the decision was taken out of his hands. Within the space of one second, the poltergeist sent Marianne another text message. It had obviously been listening to the conversation between her and Michael, for the message read, 'Please donwt gow now. I will just com with you bich!'

'Michael, I'm frightened to go to sleep!' said Marianne, understandably. Her words were followed by another text message which removed any residual doubt – not that there was any – that the poltergeist was listening in to the conversation with grim fascination: 'I cann get you when you awake and I'll come for you when you're asleep bich'.

This was only one incident of many in which the South Shields poltergeist used mobile phones – and sometimes landlines – to bring terror into the hearts of the people it had chosen to victimise. The messages it sent demonstrated that it, too, knew where the family members were, what they were doing and what they were thinking. What had happened at Fircrest, then, was nothing new. And yet the modus operandi utilised by the perpetrator in both cases was so similar that it left Darren and Michael in no doubt that the same guiding intelligence may very well have been behind both incidents.

When Darren arrived at the station to meet Michael, Michael showed him the article in *Fortean Times*. He was stunned. They discussed the ramifications of what they'd both read, and it was at this point that they finally realised something incredibly important about the nature of the poltergeist phenomenon.

20

CONTAGION: THE DESIRE TO SURVIVE

Earlier in this volume, a number of intriguing parallels were highlighted between several poltergeist cases that Darren and Michael had personally investigated, including those at South Shields, Jarrow and Ashington; and, to be honest, these strange similarities don't even begin to scratch the surface. During our research, we noted numerous parallels between the case at South Shields and that of Enfield. We also noted a range of parallels, which are so specific that it once again flags up the notion that the same, overriding presence could very well be behind most, or all poltergeist infestations.

Darren and Michael have discussed the concept of contagion throughout this volume, and also the fact that there are startling 'coincidences' that act as common denominators in many cases of poltergeist infestation. To try to understand what may precipitate the phenomenon of contagion, and ascertain just why so many bizarre parallels exist between certain cases, we need to look more closely at some of the terminology we employ as we struggle to come to grips with the poltergeist enigma. First of all, we need to look at the process of contagion itself. During the rest of this volume, the poltergeistry experienced at 'ground zero' will be referred to as the 'Primary Infestation'. The process of contagion will be described in stages:

1st Stage Contagion

This refers to instances of contagion that affect not the principal witnesses, but those who have had *direct* contact with them. For example, Darren and Michael had direct contact with the family at Lock Street for a protracted period of time. On one occasion, in Michael's study, a book was thrown from a shelf when he and Darren left the room. It landed on the floor with a thump. This is 1st Stage Contagion in action. In the experience of both Darren and Michael, 1st Stage Contagion always differs from the poltergeistry experienced in the Primary Infestation in at least one (but not necessarily all) of the following ways:

- 1st Stage Contagion does not last as long as Primary Infestation.
- The symptoms of 1st Stage Contagion are not as severe as those in the Primary Infestation.
- The events experienced during 1st Stage Contagion are fewer in number than those experienced in the Primary Infestation, and there may be longer periods of inactivity between them.

2nd Stage Contagion

This refers to instances of contagion that affect those who have only had *indirect* contact with the principal witnesses. On one occasion, the mobile phone of Michael's friend rang Michael's mobile phone in the early hours of the morning, without any human assistance. At that point, Michael's friend had had no contact with the family at Lock Street, and his only link to them was that he *knew* Michael, who in turn *knew* the principal witnesses. This is 2nd Stage Contagion in action. In the experience of Darren and Michael, 2nd Stage Contagion always differs from the poltergeistry experienced in 1st Stage Contagion in at least one (but not necessarily all) of the following ways:

- 2nd Stage Contagion does not last as long as 1st Stage Contagion.
- The symptoms of 2nd Stage Contagion are not as severe as those in 1st Stage Contagion.
- The events experienced during 2nd Stage Contagion are fewer in number than those experienced in 1st Stage Contagion, and there may be longer periods of inactivity between them.

3rd Stage Contagion

This refers to instances of contagion where the victims are distanced from the principal witnesses, by yet another link in the chain, and whose only contact with the principal witnesses is that they *know* someone who has been the victim of 2nd Stage Contagion. This form of contagion is extremely rare, and is usually restricted to a 'one-off' event or single display of poltergeistry, usually of a relatively minor nature. However, it is not just the terminology regarding the process of contagion that we need to get right, but also that which we use regarding the bizarre 'coincidences' that so often accompany poltergeist infestations. Enigmatic parallels between individual cases, weird 'coincidences' that inextricably link those associated with a case, and other manifestations of what we may call *synchronisation* also need to be broken down into precise types:

Coincidental Parallels

Coincidental Parallels are those which have no ostensible meaning or relevance and may, as their title suggests, simply be coincidences. To find an example of a Coincidental Parallel, we need look no further than the natural world. Ravens are black, and the gemstone known as jet is black. As far as we can determine, the similarity in colour between the Raven and the aforementioned gemstone is nothing more than a coincidence and has no 'meaning' whatsoever. There is no law of nature dictating that the gemstone known as jet and the Raven need to be the same colour. Life is teeming with Coincidental Parallels: oak leaves are green and broccoli is green. Snow is soft and marshmallow is soft. Escaping gas hisses and snarling cats hiss; the list is endless.

Significant Parallels

Significant Parallels are not coincidental, and exist because there is a demonstrable link between one 'subject' or set of circumstances and another. Again, we can look to the natural world for an example of a Significant Parallel. A human being born in Beijing will (genetically-linked deformities discounted) possess two arms. Similarly, a human being born in San Francisco will have two arms. There is a parallel or similarity here, but it is neither coincidental nor meaningless. The reason that both individuals have two arms is that they both belong to the human species, all members of which, under normal circumstances, have two arms. Human beings may differ in terms of gender, skin colour, height, religion and goodness knows how many other things, but they should always be born with two arms.

Person-Specific Parallels

Person-Specific Parallels are not found between separate individuals or artefacts. They are either a) similarities of action, but so specific and unique that they are almost certain to have been carried out by the same individual, or b) similarities of appearance, indicating that the persons or artefacts in question are actually one and the same. Imagine that a man attends a business meeting, and introduces himself as 'John Smith, CEO of the Delish Donut Company.' Later in the day, if someone attends another meeting and introduces himself as, 'John Smith, CEO of the Delish Donut Company', they are – conspiracy theories aside – highly likely to be one and the same person. This is an example of Person-Specific Action.

Person-Specific Appearance can be illustrated by an almost identical analogy. Imagine that the above-mentioned John Smith has an unusual birthmark on his forehead shaped, say, like a starfish. Let us also imagine that John Smith is short, thin, balding, and dressed in a green suit. His height, lack of hair and attire are not quite enough for us to say that we are working with an example of Person-Specific Appearance, for it is just possible that two men called John Smith, both of similar appearance, happen to be in the same city or town on the same day. However, when we factor in John Smith's unusual birthmark, we are presented with an extremely person-specific parallel. Both John Smiths are almost certainly one and the same. Both in appearance and action, they are essentially identical.

～

There is no doubt that poltergeist cases almost always display similarities. Indeed, it is these very similarities that enable us to state with some conviction that a poltergeist is at work. The question is, what kind of parallels do we actually see in poltergeist cases?

Without question there are *Coincidental Parallels*. A poltergeist case in London may be centred in a house with a tree in the garden. Another case may be centred in Oslo – also in a house, with a tree in the garden. The presence of a tree in the garden in two poltergeist-infested houses is almost certainly nothing more than a Coincidental Parallel and, unless additional factors indicate otherwise, should merit no further investigation. However, there are simply dozens of *Significant Parallels* that also present themselves in poltergeist cases, and these certainly *do* merit looking at. There are certain 'signatures' that indicate the presence of genuine poltergeist activity. No two cases are the same, and it is highly unlikely that all these signatures will be present in any two cases selected at random. Nevertheless, there will almost certainly be enough of these common denominators to enable the open-minded researcher to form a link.

Such Significant Parallels may include the translocation of household objects, mysterious bangs and whistles, the opening and shutting of doors without human assistance, strange odours, anomalous pools of water, the stacking of objects in geometrical patterns, and so on. Just as the presence of two relatively hairless arms indicates the presence of a human, the presence of one or more unique poltergeist symptoms may well indicate the presence of a poltergeist.

But what about *Person-Specific Parallels* – that testify to the 'omnipresent, singular polt' idea, which was proposed in chapter 17? Here we need to examine some of the 'signatures' or 'calling cards' that poltergeists leave behind; these are actions, which are so unique and specific that they point strongly to the idea that the same guiding intelligence is behind them. At Enfield, the poltergeist demonstrated a fascination with children's plastic building blocks. The poltergeist at South Shields did the same. At South Shields, the poltergeist repeatedly took mobile phones from the ground floor and placed them on the first floor. The poltergeist at Jarrow did the same. At Ashington, the poltergeist ran its fingers through the hair of its victim and stroked her thigh. The poltergeist at Middlesbrough did the same. In *four* cases, which the researchers have personally investigated, the poltergeist demonstrated a fascination with pulling the bedclothes off its victims during the night. In fact, Darren *was* one of its victims when he stayed over at Lock Street one night on the settee. After engaging in a battle of blanket tug-of-war with the Lock Street poltergeist, he eventually managed to get some sleep – only after it decided to let him.

In literally hundreds of cases, including those investigated by Darren and Michael, poltergeists have demonstrated an obsession with placing household objects in perfectly aligned geometric patterns. Perhaps one of the most startling parallels, however, is the way in which the South Shields, Newcastle and Watford/Frogmore poltergeist(s) took plastic bottles (a tall slender drinking glass in the Watford/Frogmore case) and balanced them bizarrely on edge at a 45-degree angle and even moving or spinning them without them falling over. To deny that there is something more than coincidence at work here would be rather foolhardy.

Darren and Michael believe that the incubus/succubus and the poltergeist could well be closely connected, and *may* even be two slightly different aspects of the same phenomenon. The researchers believe that the uncanny parallels between different cases is not coincidental, and may be indicative of the fact that the poltergeist is literally a hive-mind; a single, global entity which simultaneously comprises hundreds or possibly thousands of *aspects* or *sub-entities*. These 'aspects' would have a limited degree of independence, but basically be saturated with the overriding personality of the 'hive' or 'collective.' The poltergeist, just like the demon that Jesus exorcised, could be both one and many at the same time. This could explain why, on a global scale, poltergeists display the same characteristics and the same obscure idiosyncrasies; they are essentially of one mind.

When investigators grapple with a poltergeist, they are, on one level, dealing with a *single* poltergeist. However, it is also possible that they might be simultaneously dealing with every poltergeist that has ever been and currently is. Darren and Michael suggest that the 'hive-mind' or 'collective' concept may also help to explain the phenomenon of contagion. In the flesh-and-blood world, it is the disease that spreads whilst the carrier or host remains in the same place. With the poltergeist, it is somewhat different. As every aspect within the poltergeist 'hive-mind' carries within it the potential to exercise all the symptoms associated with poltergeistry, all that is necessary is for one personality to infect a victim. Other poltergeist-personalities within the 'hive mind' can then attach themselves to those who are directly or indirectly connected with the primary victims, although we don't as yet know why secondary infections like this always seem less virulent than the first. There are many, many things yet to be understood about this baffling enigma.

In the final analysis, all we can say with confidence is that the poltergeist phenomenon is a real one. The related phenomenon of contagion – as the next chapter will *also* sufficiently demonstrate – is also real. There is no doubt that the symptoms of poltergeist infestation can spread themselves outward like ripples on a pond, affecting others as well as the victims at the 'primary infestation' site. Like pond ripples, however, the ripples of poltergeist infestation weaken as they spread. Perhaps we should at least be thankful for this.

In Chapter 2, *Principles of Contagion*, the researchers discussed the difference between passive contagion and active contagion. We simply don't know enough about the nature of the poltergeist to determine how much contagion is passive and how much is active. However, in *The South Shields Poltergeist*, Darren and Michael argued strenuously that in the early stages of poltergeist infestation, the entity almost certainly has no sentience. It is unlikely to be conscious, possessing no self-awareness. However, they also argued that in the very later stages of a poltergeist's existence, it could actually separate from its 'host' and would, once acting independently, enjoy the self-awareness that it had previously been denied. This is an important point, because it may, at least theoretically, help us to differentiate between the aspects of passive and active contagion in the poltergeist's life cycle. If the poltergeist in its early stages of existence has no consciousness, then it cannot deliberately initiate the process of contagion. Therefore, any incidents of contagion in the early stages would be passive; that is, part of a natural process of contagion and not consciously enacted.

However, if the poltergeist is not truly a 'collective of independent entities', but actually a 'hive mind', or singular 'arch-poltergeist' that manifests itself in a multitude of different aspects – that is, as seemingly 'individual' poltergeists – then the concept of the poltergeist having no sentience or consciousness in its early stages is seriously open to doubt. An arch-poltergeist would obviously possess sentience, and this would almost certainly mean that its individual aspects were sentient from the outset, merely being extensions of the arch or 'parent' entity. If the above proposition is correct, then it would mean that the two types of contagion – active and passive – could only be present in a strictly limited set of scenarios. If the poltergeist does indeed possess the ability to actively and consciously infect others with its activity, then it is possible that active contagion is the only kind. However, it is also possible that both types of contagion, active and passive, work concurrently.

There may be an active form of contagion deliberately initiated by the entity, alongside a passive form, which infects people who find themselves interacting with the poltergeist in a certain set of circumstances that makes them vulnerable to it. There *is* a third scenario, however, although unlikely. There is little chance that the passive form of contagion could be present on its own without the active kind. This would infer that the arch-poltergeist or 'poltergeist collective' possessed no way of consciously targeting its victims and would have to rely purely on instances of passive contagion to achieve its ends. It would also imply that the poltergeist – individually or collectively – possessed so little intelligence that it was unable to manipulate circumstances in any way to bring its victims within the sphere of its influence. The likelihood is, then, that either both the active and passive forms of contagion exist concurrently, or the active form exists on its own.

Working on the presumption that at least some elements of poltergeist-related contagion are active – that is, deliberately and consciously generated by the poltergeist – the question arises as to just what its motivation might be in infecting others with its malign presence.

The almost universal common denominator in cases of poltergeist infestation is the inevitability that witnesses – particularly those at the 'primary infestation' site – become intensely frightened. It is no coincidence that there has long been a belief – and a well-grounded one – that the poltergeist actually feeds on fear or stress. We may not understand the scientific process involved, but Darren and Michael have been involved with far too many cases to dismiss the idea. Indeed, time after time, they have witnessed a correlation between the degree of fear being experienced by victims and the intensity of poltergeist-related phenomena. The worse the fear or stress, the more active the poltergeist becomes. Conversely, if the fear or stress experienced by victims begins to dissipate, poltergeist-related phenomena almost always become weaker and more sporadic. Even a cursory perusal of these facts flags up a blatantly obvious possibility.

If the poltergeist feeds on fear and stress, and spends much of its time acting in ways that are calculated to cause fear and stress in its victims, then there is a distinct possibility that the poltergeist deliberately precipitates stress and fear in its victims to enable it to feed. It is, we would venture, no different from the fisherman who baits his hook with a worm to enable him to catch the fish. Every intimidating poltergeist act is simply a metaphorical worm on the hook with which it can lure its victims into position.

The whole purpose behind *active* contagion – and the additional benefit of passive contagion – would then be patently obvious. The more victims the poltergeist is able to frighten, the more fear it has at its disposal to feed upon. Active contagion, then, may be stimulated by nothing less than the poltergeist's desire to survive.

21

HISTORIC CONTAGION

Throughout the course of this work, Darren and Michael have been looking at certain cases, mainly the ones that they have either investigated, or in some way assisted on or helped with, *pre* South Shields and *post* South Shields (with the exception of Enfield) and examining them for comparisons while exploring the 'contagion' aspect, at the same time, trying to make a little sense out of it all. The conclusions that we have ultimately arrived at, or at least the hypothesis that we put forward – it must be stated, is just that – a hypothesis. It is certainly not our final word on the subject because we readily admit we still have no idea whatsoever just what a poltergeist actually is. Our ideas and theories are nothing more than an attempt to kick-start reasoned discussion and thought, in relation to this aspect of the poltergeist phenomenon. To a certain degree, this has been accomplished.

Since the first publication of this book in 2014, the notion of the 'archpoltergeist – hive mind' has been welcomed by some, and discounted by others, so, essentially, the debate *has* commenced. Hopefully, the theme of this particular debate may continue until a satisfactory conclusion can be reached, ten, twenty, a hundred years, two hundred years down the line. Whether we are right or wrong it matters not.

Now, in the first 'edit' of this work, in regards to 'taking a poltergeist home' with you after spending time at an infested domicile, we had cited examples – as previously mentioned – that *had* been based upon *our* investigations and experiences. What Darren feels we *should* have done, in retrospect, is to cite more instances of contagion from other historic cases; after all, there are indeed many accounts of it, which sadly – and astonishingly – much to Darren's surprise, have seldom been discussed at all as an actual aspect of poltergeistry, but rather only mentioned in passing as an interesting note. Hopefully, this is now about to be rectified as Darren has been trawling the books and the archives, in his search for historic contagion examples – and he has not been disappointed. What follows is a selection of cases that have been deemed more than worthy for inclusion herein. All these examples, demonstrate at least in these respective cases, that at one point or another during the course of their life-cycle, one or more individuals, who were closely associated with the case, found that they suffered 'occasional symptoms' while away from what we have termed, 'ground zero' – the 'primary infested' site.

The Yorkshire Bed Shop, 1991

Noted SPR council member and parapsychologist Callum Cooper Ph.D., in his fascinating book *'Telephone Calls from the Dead'*, discusses a case that researcher Colin Davies had investigated in 1991, which had consisted of the usual array of poltergeist phenomena. This case write up first appeared in Volume 8 of the Association for the Scientific Study of Anomalous Phenomena's (ASSAP) journal, *Anomaly.*

It centred on a bed shop in Yorkshire, northern England, and, although Callum's intention was to discuss the 'telephone' aspect of the case, I did notice some documented occurrences that attracted my own attention, and aroused my interest; oddly, these were *also* telephone related, too. Objects in the shop would either mysteriously 'go missing', or they would be thrown around, as if by an unseen hand. Pens, notepads, and other stationary would simply fly around for no obvious reason.

Items that went missing would often turn up later and back in the spot where they had disappeared from in the first place – a common occurrence in poltergeist cases. This is a typical event, and is now known, or commonly referred to, as a JOTT *(Just One of Those Things)*; a term coined by the late Mary Rose Barrington (1926-2020); a distinguished SPR member, and very well-respected psychical researcher. They are discussed at length in her book, *JOTT* (2018). This particular occurrence is known as a 'comeback' JOTT, simply because after it had disappeared for a short while, it returned mysteriously to its original place. Interestingly, coins were seen to appear out of thin air, before being thrown, or dropped, to the ground – something that Darren and Michael, along with a host of other reliable witnesses, saw for themselves during the South Shields case in 2006. Of course, there is a lot more to this very interesting poltergeist case, but being solely interested in the contagion aspect of it, we shall delve into it no further, and simply concern ourselves with the details that are relevant to this study.

It is said, by Cooper, that Davies also witnessed some of the phenomena for himself, which is always good in cases like this, as it should add to the credibility to the case. But what caught Darren's eye was the fact that Davies was said to have experienced 'phenomena at his home', towards the end of the investigation. It is stated that he received almost *seventy* anomalous telephone calls. When he picked up the receiver, some of the calls were silent. With others, there were blips and beeps. He stated that, on other occasions, his answer machine recorded the shop owner saying, 'Hello, the bed shop, can I help you?' Oddly enough, it appears that at the same time, the shop was being called from Davies' phone, with messages being left there too. So it seems that *both* phones were calling each other, for which British Telecom (BT) could find no cause.

The poltergeist activity at the bed shop in Yorkshire eventually began to diminish – as is normally the case – and, before long, the shop owner, staff, and Colin Davies were free of this mischievous and unknown force that had somewhat consumed them for that brief period of time over 30 years ago. It had slowly released its firm 'psychic grip' that it once had upon them, and disappeared forever, leaving the scene as mysteriously as it came. A fascinating case, if the account is true, documented within the literature of spontaneous cases, and demonstrating for the first time, at least in *this* chapter, the ability of the poltergeist to be able to 'reach out' and 'infect'.

The Enfield Poltergeist, 1977-1979

I'd like to explore some more bewildering examples of contagion from the celebrated Enfield case in the late 1970s. Peggy Hodgson had a brother called John Burcombe, who lived at 272 Green Street, a few houses along from the Hodgson household, at number 284, whose home was the 'primary infestation' site. On 25 September 1977, Peggy decided to take herself and her children, including Janet (the apparent 'focus'), to John's house, after events had become too much, in the hope of a little respite from the relentless onslaught of poltergeist activity. However, it wasn't to be, for it is said that on that afternoon, John reported 'strange happenings' at *his* home, too. True, Janet was present during these events so, technically, we can't perhaps class these events at number 272 as 'contagion' – they may have occurred because the focal person was on the scene. However, it is stated that later on that day – although I'm not sure whether Janet was present then – more activity was documented at number 272.

For example, at this point, in 284, and inside 272, John had said that he had 'seen enough poltergeist activity to convert him from his scepticism.' A lamp, he said, 'slid across the table then fell to the floor'; he saw drawers opening and closing on their own, and his bedroom door refused to budge, after an 'unseen force' refused to let him pull it closed, whereas normally, he said, 'it swings closed on its own' (naturally, not paranormally). Guy Lyon Playfair states in his book on the case *This House is Haunted* that 'this was the first new development – the poltergeist could follow the family away from their house' – an interesting observation at that time, which raises the question: is this a *form* of contagion at work?

In their book *The Poltergeist Phenomenon*, (1996), John and Anne Spencer also note instances of possible poltergeist-contagion at Enfield. For example, after Maurice Grosse had visited another troubled house over the last three months of 1977 (at Holloway, in North London), where instances of poltergeist fire-starting had been encountered, he returned to Green Street, Enfield, only to begin to experience spontaneous outbreaks of fire there, too, as I shall soon discuss. Could the fires at Enfield, however, simply have been a natural 'progression' in the poltergeist's ever-growing repertoire, with no contagion occurring in this instance? Or, could this have been a case of contagion from that *other* case, which Maurice was simultaneously investigating? Another striking parallel between the Enfield and the Holloway disturbances that I noticed after rereading Playfair's book was that both poltergeists decided to remove a number of books from within the shelves of the respective homes, and then arrange them neatly around a pouffe.

And it doesn't end there. The poltergeist at Holloway set fire to a box of matches that was kept inside a drawer, scorching the box they were contained in but *not* actually igniting the matches themselves. This exact occurrence then repeated itself at Enfield, prompting Grosse to ask whether 'poltergeists [are] contagious like diseases'. If we look at the collective poltergeist theory, the 'one arch-polt' hypothesis, then the notion of this becomes that little bit more plausible, does it not? It seemed at the time, that *two* different poltergeists were operating independently, but what if they were actually working with one another, alongside each other, or even working together, as one? It could certainly go some way to explaining how the exact same fire at one location then repeated itself at another, and why it chose to arrange books around a pouffe in both instances.

The Spencers then go on to tell us that Maurice Grosse's car engine failed to operate properly at times during the Enfield's outbreak, which was subsequently commented on by 'the voice' that emanated from Janet: events that she wouldn't have known about by normal means. Grosse, it is said, also experienced unexplained footsteps upstairs in his house when he knew for certain that no one was there, and also heard a banging noise right next to him when he was in his garden, 'identical' to one he had heard at the Green Street house kitchen.

The Hodgson's next door neighbours – the Nottinghams – experienced some events when none of the Hodgson family was present. Playfair's book relates that on one occasion, Mr Nottingham's son poured himself a drink, only to discover that his glass was empty when he went to take a drink from it. Objects moved around the house on their own, and people reported a sensation of being touched, as if by invisible hands. A key also went missing for a few days, before turning up in an old van that belonged to the Nottinghams. It was as though the poltergeist had decided to 'move' next door. Having noticed strange things, friends of the Nottinghams stopped visiting the house, fearing that they'd take something home with them. One witness of an alleged contagion event flatly refused to make a statement about it, after hearing strange noises, out of fear that it would follow her back home to Leeds.

So, along with the other examples outlined earlier in these pages, it becomes clear that contagion at Enfield was a lot more apparent, and was experienced more than I had hitherto previously been aware. Playfair, in his preface to his book *This House is Haunted*, writes 'poltergeist activity is in fact what doctors call a syndrome, which means a group of symptoms that indicate a certain disease or an abnormal condition.' Interestingly enough, and quite relevant to our current study, Brian C Nisbet (a poltergeist investigator almost entirely forgotten these days, sadly) investigated two poltergeist outbreaks, in 1976 and in 1978, respectively, at a dwelling in West Croydon, UK. He made a fascinating observation:

On the assumption that a poltergeist outbreak is the symptom of some kind of illness then there is a similarity to some [other] well-known illnesses in which the symptoms manifest sometimes after the original infection, e.g., measles, in which there is an incubation period of seven to fourteen days unaccompanied by evident symptoms, or delayed shock, which takes some time to appear.

Essentially suggesting that what triggers the onset of poltergeist activity (the trauma that somehow brings it into its existence) may have occurred perhaps a week or two *prior* to its erupting. This is interesting, as a number of cases have indeed reported this very aspect leading some to think that the poltergeist may well indeed be virus-like; and it goes without saying that where there are active viruses, there will also be viral contagion.

The Hertfordshire Poltergeist, 1991-1996

Staying with *The Poltergeist Phenomenon* by John and Anne Spencer, another poltergeist case they assisted with, and co-investigated, was that of an unusually long, drawn-out case in Hertfordshire between 1991 and 1996. There were five years of intense paranormal activity, at the home of Elizabeth* and Jerry* (pseudonyms given by the Spencers), a normal, middle-aged married couple with, interestingly, no stereotypical teenage or pubescent poltergeist focus – very much like the Jarrow and South Shields case. At first, both Elizabeth and Jerry began to notice little things, odd things, occurring at their home, but they said nothing to each other, simply because they were both thinking that they were being silly. However, they were eventually forced to acknowledge to each other that something decidedly odd was taking place in their home.

Things escalated, day by day, into an intense and prolonged infestation, but, despite the poltergeist displaying and demonstrating most – if not all – of its typical characteristics, I'll focus my attention on the contagion aspects. For a full and detailed account of the Hertfordshire poltergeist case, I recommend the reader to consult John and Anne's book detailing the entire affair.

The first instance occurred early on, when strange telephone calls began at Jerry's place of work, which was an office. When the calls were answered, no one was there, echoing the telephone calls made in the aforementioned 'Yorkshire Bed Shop' case. Such calls and anomalies were also reported at Jerry's home. But that was the 'primary infestation' site, and therefore doesn't count as contagion. At Elizabeth's place of work, things of a paranormal nature seemed to be taking place as well, such as files and folders vanishing without a trace, only to turn up later in places where they really shouldn't have been. This is *another* form of Barrington's JOTT; on this occasion, the item, or items in question disappeared from their location and were found *elsewhere*, therefore the name given in this instance is, a 'walkabout' JOTT.

These first two examples, of course, were linked with Jerry and Elizabeth who, if you remember, were the principal witnesses in the 'primary infestation'. So, although the reports are interesting in themselves, we can't label them as instances of Stage One contagion. However, it is said that a family friend, who knew all about the poltergeist, agreed to look after Jerry and Elizabeth's car for a week. Quite why isn't clear, but maybe Jerry and Elizabeth were going on holiday. Anyway, the friend reportedly experienced odd activity at *his* home, although he was supposedly too frightened to discuss it in detail.

As a thank you for having looked after their car, Jerry and Elizabeth gave their friend a bottle containing an alcoholic beverage. But the friend was reportedly reluctant to take it, for fear of 'being infected' and suffering yet more poltergeist activity. He accepted the gift, out of courtesy, but put it in his garage rather than in the main part of his home.

Having seen and experienced contagion first-hand, and knowing full well that it *does* occur, I have no doubt that contagion experiences *were* experienced in this case. It is a shame, however, that we don't have more details regarding it. John and Anne Spencer (now retired from psychical research) were first-rate investigators, and very reliable in their work, and if *they* reported a case in which it was claimed that contagion occurred, then we can be sure that something odd did indeed happen.

The Cardiff Poltergeist, 1989-1991

A well-documented case of a poltergeist occurred in Cardiff, Wales, in the late 1980s and early 1990s at a small lawnmower workshop. It, too, featured the contagion phenomenon. The case was investigated and written up in the *Journal of the Society for Psychical Research* (JSPR) by the late Professor David Fontana (1934-2010) – a notable SPR member – who saw it through to its eventual cessation. The poltergeist, nicknamed 'Pete' by the staff, was incredibly 'responsive': when asked to perform a trick, or produce some phenomena, it almost always obliged.

For example, when it was suggested that those experiencing the phenomena should make notes of what was happening, a pen and paper materialised out of nowhere and dropped to the floor. Another example was when the investigators and witnesses asked for money or coins to be produced, whereupon old pennies dating from around 1912 seemingly appeared from nowhere and hit the floor with a clatter. Many other well-attested examples showed just how responsive 'Pete, the poltergeist' was. It seemed to centre on the owners of the property and business, John and Pat Matthews. Fred Cook and his wife, Gerry, who were related to John and Pat, also worked at the premises, and experienced a great deal of the phenomena; indeed, it was with the latter where the contagion aspect of this case lay.

By far one of the most impressive aspects of this case, it has to be said, was the 'stone throwing' game that was devised, in which all of those involved (including Fontana) would throw stones or small pebbles into a corner of the workshop when they knew for certain, that nobody was occupying that area, only to have the stones or pebbles tossed back toward them. Some of the stones and pebbles were actually 'marked' by the investigator, indicating it was the same pebbles that had been returned. A rapport had been built up with Pete, resulting in this game of 'pass the pebble'.

The first instances of contagion occurred when John and Pat began to receive anomalous telephone calls at their home (yet again, very much like Colin Davies did in Yorkshire, and very much like Jerry and Elizabeth in Hertfordshire), to which British Telecom (BT), as in the bed shop case, could also find no explanation. Then, following the subsidence of reported paranormal activity at the workshop, after the business relocated to other premises, the poltergeist seemingly 'attached' itself to Fred and Gerry and 'moved in with them', much to Fred's delight. Fred, it seemed, had an 'affinity' with Pete, and, according to John and Anne Spencer, 'closely associated himself to the phenomena', finding them 'very special.' Even when Fred and Gerry moved home, Pete seemingly went with them. Pictures, it is said, would be moved about on the wall of their house, and, in some instances, turned around altogether so that the picture itself was wall-facing and the back of the frame was room-facing. Money (yet again) would materialise in their home in the form of 'pound coins' and anything up to fifteen pounds a month would be counted.

Money or coins seem to be a common feature in poltergeist cases, as Darren can certainly attest. At South Shields, coins rained down upon the investigators, the home owners and their family and friends, materialising from out of nowhere. On one occasion, two distinguished guest observers whom Darren had invited up from the well-known research group called the Association for the Scientific Study of Anomalous Phenomena (ASSAP), experienced the very same phenomenon. By the end of one particular afternoon, after the poltergeist had finished its antics for the time being, a rather large pile of coins was piled up on the dining room table after we had gathered up its generous 'deposits'; we never did work out just *where* the money actually came from.

To a certain degree, the materialising money at Fred and Gerry's house was established and verified somewhat, when John Spencer, being on the phone to Fred at the time, actually heard a coin fall and clatter into Fred's kitchen sink! Heard and recorded by Spencer over the phone, but we have only Fred's actual 'word' that it *was* indeed Pete depositing the coin. However, based on all the documented evidence, there is little reason to doubt this particular event, although caution must always be exercised.

That said, then, surely we must consider that Fred was the focus of the Cardiff Poltergeist, and not John or Pat? After all, Fred was present at the workshop during most, if not all, of the activity; it then seemingly followed *him* home, and, in his own words, he found the phenomenon 'very special.' However, if Fred wasn't the poltergeist focus and merely an observer to its antics, then we do indeed have some very special documented instances of a poltergeist latching on to someone, and going home with them.

The Sauchie (Gartmorn Road) Poltergeist, 1986-1987

The little town of Sauchie, in Clackmannanshire in Central Scotland has been home to not one, but *three* poltergeist cases: the most well known, of course, occurring in 1960, featuring the eleven-year-old girl, Virginia Campbell. A second poltergeist outbreak occurred on Gartmorn Road in late 1986, which, interestingly, seemed to occupy not one house, but *three* adjacent houses. However, it was the *middle* house that was thought to have suffered the most disturbances. Sauchie poltergeist number three occurred in 1999 in a semi-detached council house that, oddly enough, was a stone's throw away from the 1960 poltergeist house of Virginia Campbell; in fact, it was on the same street, Park Crescent. One has to wonder just why the town of Sauchie itself is prone to such outbreaks of poltergeistry and alleged paranormal activity, with three cases in such close proximity between the years 1960 and 2000. In 2020, a good friend of mine, Malcolm Robinson, authored a book detailing his reinvestigation into the 1960 Virginia Campbell case: *The Sauchie Poltergeist,* which is a fascinating in-depth study into the affair.

Although the book centres on the 1960 case, it takes a look at the other, more recent, poltergeist cases that have been reported in Sauchie. It is one of these, the Gartmorn Road case from 1986 that I'll focus on. As I said, it was the 'middle' house of the three that suffered most of the poltergeist activity. This is quite telling, in my opinion, and suggests possible contagion. Unlike the 1960 Campbell case, this case was personally investigated by Robinson, along with Ron Halliday, and was subsequently written up (in 1987) in *Enigmas*, a newsletter of Strange Phenomena Investigations (SPI), a research group set up by Robinson in 1979. The account also featured in Halliday's book, *Evil Scotland*, and once again appeared in Robinson's book, *Paranormal Case Files of Great Britain: Volume One*. It is now featured as part of Geoff Holder's work, *Poltergeist over Scotland*. It is from Robinson's book that I draw my information regarding the case and, with permission from Malcolm, I have been allowed to reproduce certain extracts from within.

Robinson (P.53) commences his account by saying:

> ... Ron Halliday and I began our research into claims that three houses joined together in Gartmorn Road, Sauchie, were haunted. Early research showed that these houses, which were built around 1937, were, for the past six months, subject to strange footsteps, noises, bangs, smells, and all the usual phenomena associated with haunted buildings. Many of these noises, it must be said, were reported to have come from the loft. Interviews were conducted on audio tape with Cindy Hope* [author's note: Robinson's pseudonym], who told me that ever since she had first moved into the property, she just didn't feel at home, that there was something not quite right about it. Cindy's first experience was that of standing on a certain stair on the staircase, where she experienced strange sensations, dizziness being the main one. Cindy's eighteen year old daughter, Laura* [author's note: Robinson's pseudonym] had to sleep with the light on owing to constant bad dreams. Cindy's next door neighbour, Mrs Elaine Peters, also related similar events, but happening to her in her own home – again, with most of the noises coming from the loft area.

When the investigative team turned up on the scene, it was reported that 'much to our surprise, the two families that lived either side of Cindy's house, had had enough of the ghostly events that were happening in their homes; they abandoned their homes and joined up with Cindy.' When Cindy's neighbours came round to visit, Malcolm said, 'they were all sitting in the living room discussing all the weird events when suddenly the 'sound of thumping' came from upstairs. They all immediately got up out of their seats, stormed to the bottom of the stairs to confront whatever it was creating the disturbance only to see that no one was actually up there. Then, it is reported, that the 'unmistakable' sound of heavy footsteps came down the stairs towards them, and 'nobody, was there.'

Between Malcolm's first and second visit to Gartmorn Road, more strange occurrences were documented. Cold spots were reported to have been felt in the house, more strange noises were heard coming from the loft area, a kitchen drawer was said to have opened on its own and a knife and fork 'sailed' through mid-air without anyone touching them, subsequently falling to the floor with a clash. The Hope family dog also refused to go upstairs in the house, and if it was coerced in any way, it was said to get *really* aggressive and attempt to bite whoever it was encouraging the animal to go upstairs. One day, it was found locked in an 'upstairs room' from the *inside*, with the poor beast injuring its paws in a frantic attempt to escape.

Interestingly, a reported 'doppelgänger' of Cindy was observed walking down the stairs wearing a flowery gown, when in actual fact she was still in bed asleep at that particular time. Cindy's mother addressed the doppelgänger thinking it was Cindy, of course, and was bemused as to why Cindy had completely blanked her and walked into another room. It was only later on when she asked her daughter why she ignored her that this strange incident was identified; a most peculiar event involving someone's 'double'. The doppelgänger phenomenon was also reported in the Enfield case.

Another fascinating aspect of this case is that one of Cindy's neighbours, the aforementioned Mrs Elaine Peters, had an eleven-year-old son who claimed that he was being 'visited in the night' by a strange man and a woman; the woman was said to have been holding a small baby. The lady continually asked the boy, 'what is your name?' and asked him not to be afraid of them. During one of their visits to Mrs Peter's son in the night, it is said that the 'ghost' snatched the pillow beneath the head of the youngster and placed it at the bottom of the bed. An interesting parallel can be drawn here with the Virginia Campbell case of 1960, where *her* pillow was also 'interfered with' by the poltergeist, being seen to move round in a circular motion underneath Virginia's head. The most fascinating part of this account was when the apparitional woman admitted to the boy that they didn't like the dog that lived next door, and admitted that she had locked it in a room, for fear that it would bite them. Robinson's team later ascertained that Mrs Peters' son wasn't aware that the dog had been found locked inside a bedroom.

So, what do we make of all this? Certainly, there were classic poltergeist symptoms being displayed here, but what is intriguing most of all is that this case has the *potential* to be considered as a case where poltergeist-contagion has been experienced. Could it be that the middle house, where Cindy Hope and her daughter Laura lived, was in fact the site of the 'primary infestation', the 'ground zero', with the two houses on each side suffering due to the contagion phenomenon? The poltergeist focus in this case *may* well have been Laura, the eighteen-year-old daughter, and, because both sets of neighbouring individuals had close contact with the young girl, they were somehow 'vulnerable' to the poltergeist's ability to 'infect' them, resulting in activity being reported in their homes as well? We have seen this in other cases time and time again. During the Gartmorn Road investigations, the *possibility* of the poltergeist-contagion effect wasn't discussed or even considered. The Gartmorn Road poltergeist case has been classed as 'unique' (Holder, 2013), given that it involved three houses in a row. It may be unique, but the very fact that three adjoining properties were affected may reflect something that seems to be far from unique: the contagion phenomenon.

Buchlyvie Contagion, Scotland, 1994

The following case was also investigated by researcher and author Malcolm Robinson, along with Billy Devlin and Helen Walters, fellow members of Strange Phenomena Investigations (SPI). On this occasion, Robinson believes that he experienced an extraordinary one-off contagion event at his then-home in Alloa, Scotland.

The actual 'haunting' occurred for almost nine weeks at an old cottage in a village called Buchlyvie, in Stirlingshire, Scotland, between 29 September and 15 November 1994. Interestingly, the cottage had recently been quite extensively renovated. That could be relevant, because renovation work sometimes seems to precipitate ghostly manifestations. The activity was experienced and reported by a Mr and Mrs Matchett* (author's note: Robinson's pseudonyms) and three of their children, 17, 15 and 4 years old, respectively. A fourth sibling, aged 38, lived away from home.

It began when their fifteen-year-old daughter awoke one night to find a young boy standing at the foot of her bed; terrified, she refused to sleep in that bedroom again. Mr Matchett, believing the 'sighting' to be nothing more than a convincing dream, decided to sleep in the room, if only to make a point. His aim was to prove to his daughter that nothing at all was occurring of a paranormal nature; it appears he was wrong. He was awoken at 5:15am with a feeling that something was disturbing and moving the bed. He saw a boy, sitting on it, looking at him and smiling. He was astounded, and petrified in equal measure. Then something truly extraordinary happened. As Mr Matchett was contemplating a retreat from the bedroom, the boy, reportedly disappeared and then reappeared in the doorway of the room, as if the 'ghost' or whatever it was had read his thoughts and made a move to the door in order to prevent Mr Matchett from leaving.

With no other choice, he plucked up a little courage, and charged at the door in an attempt to escape the room, which necessitated running 'through' the ghost boy in the process. It was at this point that Robinson was called in to investigate. On 4 June 2020, I called him on the telephone and enquired about any other reported activity at that cottage. He went on to tell me that the usual array of poltergeist effects were indeed documented and witnessed by all those involved. Reported phenomena included knocking; the moving around of objects, doors opening and closing on their own, and a host of unexplained noises. It is Robinson's encounter with contagion that is particularly intriguing. This is what he said:

> A most peculiar thing happened after I returned from investigating the house at Buchlyvie. Like any investigation, upon completion, one finds oneself on a natural high; it is a feeling like no other. Your perception and concentration have been with you all night, staying at an alleged haunted house, and your senses are on high alert. This was certainly the case with me on that visit to the Matchett house. After the investigations of that night were complete, I was dropped off at my house in Sauchie, near Alloa, in central Scotland. It was the early hours of the morning and my wife and children had already gone to bed, so there I was, sitting in the living room in my favourite chair, reading a newspaper. The house was deathly quiet as I turned over each page, not really paying attention to the stories that my tired eyes were looking at. Suddenly, between four and six very loud rappings reverberated around the room, which seemed to come from directly behind my head. They were in quick succession and scared the living daylights out of me. Now, what makes this more interesting is the fact

that there was no house next door in that direction adjoined to my house. There was a gap roughly between nine and twelve feet outside in which a flight of stone stairs is situated; it led up through the estate – my house was on the end. So, I immediately knew that there couldn't have been anyone outside at that level banging on my wall. If memory serves me right, it was just after 02:00am and I quickly jumped up and rushed outside to see if anyone was there in the alleyway, and there was nobody out there. I looked around the nearby houses but all was still. I gingerly walked back indoors, slowly closing the back door, whilst having one last look around to see if I could see anyone, but it was all quiet. As a researcher, I am well aware that sometimes one can bring paranormal phenomena back after an investigation and I am convinced this was the case here, absolutely. Of course, it was only observed by me, and not taped or recorded, and, whilst it makes for a nice little after dinner discussion, it hardly serves as objective proof. But I do believe that that night I experienced a one-off contagion event due to my involvement at Buchlyvie.

Based on instances of documented contagion events in other cases, and assuming Malcolm is not mistaken in some way, then here we have yet another fascinating account of 'infection' by poltergeist. Another documented instance that can be added to the growing number of seemingly bona-fide contagion events that surround the poltergeist enigma.

The Battersea Poltergeist, Wycliffe Road, London, 1956-1968

From 1956 to 1968, the incredible tale of the Battersea poltergeist unfolded at 63 Wycliffe Road, Battersea, South London, at the home of Walter Hitchings (47), his wife Catherine (51), and their daughter Shirley (15), along with a relative of the family in his twenties, Mark*. This case – it must be specified – is the Battersea poltergeist of 1956 and *not* to be confused with the earlier Battersea poltergeist of Elland Road in 1928, which was investigated by Harry Price. If *this* account is to be believed then it has to be potentially one of the most remarkable cases of a 'communicative entity', call it what you will, on record. The amount of 'tapping', 'knocking' and eventual 'note-writing', which the poltergeist was reported to have carried out, told the story of a spirit of a young boy that claimed to have died during the French Revolution. Donald – the name given to the poltergeist by the Hitchings – claimed to be the son of Marie Antoinette, Louis XVII the Dauphin of France (Dauphin being the royal title to the heir apparent of the throne). He had escaped his imprisonment and fled to England in the latter part of the 18th Century; that was *his* claim, anyway.

What 'Donald' told the family and a psychical researcher (Harold Chibbett, 1900-1978) didn't always make sense or 'pan out', leaving those who heard his story confused and somewhat bewildered. No one knows for sure whether Donald was actually Louis XVII, but what cannot be disputed is the fact that 63 Wycliffe Road was the setting for poltergeist activity for so many years, with phenomena being witnessed by family, friends, TV personnel, newspaper reporters and neighbours. Moving furniture was observed, along with ornaments being thrown around, breakages, knocking and banging, doors opening and slamming closed on their own, objects 'apporting' from seemingly nowhere, and a lot of fire-starting. Many people visited the house as sceptics, and left convinced it was haunted.

Donald, it seems, was more than happy to convert the sceptical, cynical, and the sarcastic. On one occasion, when Shirley's (then) boyfriend was sitting in the family kitchen, scoffing and ridiculing Donald at the notion of his very existence, Donald responded by throwing a 'bowl of nuts' over his head from nowhere! After turning 'white as sheet' and being stunned into silence, he made his excuses and quickly vacated number 63, never to return. To get a full account of the case, based on Walter Hitchings' diary of events, the case notes and files of Harrold Chibbett, and from Shirley Hitchings, I would recommend reading *The Poltergeist Prince of London, the remarkable true story of the Battersea Poltergeist*, by Shirley Hitchings and James Clark. It really is fascinating and, by the time I'd finished reading it, I'd actually developed a liking for Donald.

During the course of the infestation it was noted that two individuals reported experiencing Donald away from number 63 at either their own homes, or elsewhere. On page 95 of the book, the authors state:

> Neither could Shirley have been responsible for some of the tapping sounds now being reported from locations other than no 63, according to the *South Western Star* (4th May 1956). Two unnamed visitors to the house were "followed by mysterious rappings" after they left. One man was described as an insurance agent and had probably visited following the fires of 30 April. The newspaper claimed he "heard strange knockings in his home" after his visit. The second visitor – Eric Davey – had been astonished to hear thuds coming up from under his feet when he hopped on a bus after a recent visit.

On July 9 1956, a further example of supposed contagion was reported by a friend of Mark (Shirley's brother) after visiting no. 63. In a signed statement given to lead investigator Harrold Chibbett on 15 July 1956, he reported:

> On arriving home from work on Monday July 9, I heard a series of taps – three in each case. I looked down the basement but there was nothing or no one to cause it. The same thing happened on Tuesday 10th and again on Wednesday 11th. On asking 'Donald' if it was him, the answer was YES.

Was this contagion at work perhaps, if indeed the accounts of these 'raps' away from no 63 are not misinterpretation or false in their claims, then quite possibly? Despite the fact that they are subjective accounts, I feel they do warrant inclusion in this work as part of this study into the phenomenon. The final word on this case – and indeed these contagion events – must, however, go to Hitchings and Clark when they correctly state; 'such incidences *might* (authors italics) only illustrate how some visitors became caught up in the story and mistakenly attributed quite natural happenings to Donald.'

Arun Bank, Pulborough, Sussex, Pre-1936

The following may have been a one-off contagion event. It certainly bears all the hallmarks of 'bringing something home with you'. The actual date of the occurrence isn't clear but, if genuine, it must have happened pre-1936, as it was written up in a book and published then: *Confessions of a Ghost Hunter* by Harry Price. The incident was also described, albeit briefly, in Price's book *Poltergeist over England*, first published in 1945.

Harry Price, as acting 'foreign research officer' for the American Society for Psychical Research (ASPR) travelled the length and breadth of Europe, investigating claims of the paranormal, but he stated that some of his 'major mysteries' were found in the country where he lived in the UK. One such event appears to have occurred in his own bedroom, and it is this strange occurrence we will look at. Having admitted that he was a 'sound sleeper' he was very much surprised to be woken in the early hours one January morning, by what sounded like the 'bare feet of a child', pattering all around his room – and even under his bed.

Rousing himself fully, to his 'full waking state', Price sat up in his bed in an attempt to listen. He was convinced that 'someone or something' was in his room. He concluded that no wild animal could have been responsible for the 'footfalls' nor could it have been his faithful dog that was asleep by the fire in the kitchen. He sat listening in bewilderment for ten minutes in a vain effort to work out what was happening. At any time during the disturbances, Price claimed, he could have picked out *where* this 'person' was in the room, the noises being so clear and distinct. At this point (03.45am), he was still in total darkness.

By his bedside he had an electric lamp, which he then decided to pick up. 'Choosing a moment when the sounds appeared nearest to me' he said, 'I suddenly flooded the room with light – and the pattering stopped instantaneously'. Upon getting out of bed the first thing Price did, was to look around his room and check *under* the bed, only to no avail. After moving 'every article of furniture', he found nothing. Exploring the house, he found nothing, stating that, 'no one was about and my retriever was sound asleep in his basket in the kitchen, the door of which was closed.' After returning to his bedroom he decided to get dressed rather than go back to sleep. Price ties up the section in his 'Confessions' book by stating, 'In my career as an investigator there have been few mysteries for which I couldn't find some sort of solution – but I must admit that the 'baby feet' in my bedroom puzzle me to this day.'

However, since it's unclear whether Price was actively involved in any investigation around that particular time, although it is highly likely he would have been, I can't be sure that this alleged incident qualifies as an episode of contagion. However, he *was* investigating Borley Rectory, 'the most haunted house in England' from 1929, until his death in 1948, so it may come as no surprise to think that he might have at least taken something home with him at some point in his career; perhaps this event was it?

This potential contagion event at Arun Bank is all conjecture of course, but what a fascinating example of an account of phenomena in your own home, when in actual fact your home is *not* even reputed to be haunted. Based on all the other examples in this work, is it not within the realms of possibility that the late Harry Price *maybe* experienced an isolated incident of poltergeist infection?

The Mayanup Poltergeist, Western Australia, 1955-1957

The following events reportedly occurred in the small town of Mayanup in Western Australia, and began in 1955. The case is written up in a book titled *Australian Poltergeist* (Healy and Cropper, 2014). In reinvestigating the case, the authors conducted interviews, obtaining first-hand witness testimony, and noted that some phenomena allegedly still occur, albeit mildly, in a 'less dramatic form'. They have also drawn on written reports that were prepared at the time by worthy and reliable sources. Healy and Cropper described (p.56) the case as being 'by far the most impressive in our files', also stating that 'very few other poltergeist events anywhere in the world are better documented.'

'Over the years,' Healy and Cropper said, 'the phenomena were witnessed by hundreds of people', but it all started on a property – a farm – named Keninup', which was owned by Bill Hack and his wife, Ethel. Healy and Cropper also tell us that she kept a detailed diary of events, which formed the basis of a book that would subsequently be written about the case by her daughter-in-law, Helen. *The Mystery of the Mayanup Poltergeist* is said to be the 'definitive account of the episode'.

Bill and Ethel Hack ran their farm at Mayanup with the assistance of a number of employees, some of whom were said to live on site. One employee, Gilbert Smith, along with his wife Jean and their five children, lived in a house on the farmstead, on top of a nearby hillock – five hundred meters from the main farm. It was here where the first instances of 'odd activity' were reported. On 17 May 1955, at around 'dusk' his Kangaroos suddenly, and for no known reason, became extremely agitated and started to holler and cry, reacting 'as if they were being savagely attacked'. They broke their chains and subsequently bolted. Later, Gilbert sought the help of Bill and Ethel, complaining that someone seemed to be pelting their galvanised iron shack with bricks and stones. He'd gone outside to see what was going on, but found no one around, and nothing to account for the bombardment. Later, during the family's evening meal, stones yet again hit the walls and roof and, once again, no explanation could be found. After a golfball came from nowhere and landed in their living quarters, Gilbert, then a thirty-six-year old well-built man, was clearly terrified.

Bill and Ethel agreed to help their most trusted employee, by conducting some all-night watches over the shack where the Smiths lived, in the hope of apprehending any culprits. This proved to be a fruitless exercise and only resulted in Bill and Ethel seeing some of the most extraordinary phenomena ever witnessed. It is said that Bill and his brother saw stones materialising out of thin air and falling on to the house. They reportedly fell in a most unusual fashion – very slow, and in odd trajectories. Inside the shack, they witnessed more stones being hurled about, and a piece of charcoal falling down from the ceiling.

This occurred almost every night for the next four months, until the following September, when the odd activity began to dwindle and then ceased altogether. During that time, many other witnesses claimed to have seen pretty much the same (and more), with all attempts to find fraud or outright vandalism yielding no results. Some of the stones, it is said, (p.60) were simply too big to have been hurled by hoaxers: one being 'a pumpkin sized rock', weighing almost 16 kilograms (35 pounds).

It was seen outside the Smiths' shack, descending slowly through the air, as if it were being lowered, before settling very gently on a water tank. They were all convinced that what they had witnessed were genuinely paranormal phenomena. It is interesting to note that despite the number of stones that were hurled around by the 'unseen hands', no reports of actual injury were documented, and there was no damage to any property. Healy and Cropper suggest that if fraudsters or vandals had been to blame, and if the stone-throwing had been perpetrated deliberately, by normal means, injury and damage would surely have occurred. The phenomena, Ethel noted, seemed to centre on Gilbert's wife, Jean, who had 'something of a volatile personality' with stones falling *only* when she was at home, according to Healy and Cropper. This, along with the fact that she was going through a tough time in her relationship with Gilbert, being pregnant with her seventh child and simultaneously having to deal with her dying father, makes her a prime candidate for being the poltergeist focus. Should the reader wish to learn more about Mayanup, I would recommend reading the full account of this truly extraordinary case in the aforementioned books for, in this section, one has only scratched the surface, to give a brief overview of what was happening, in a run up to what I would consider to be more relevant to this current work, and that is the Mayanup cases of bewildering contagion events.

Healy and Cropper state that 'on 19th June, one month after it began its activities at "Keninup", the polt extended its activities across the Boyup Brook–Kojonup Road to another large property, Lynford Hill.' This is interesting as the house was only six-hundred meters from the Smiths' home, but more interesting is the fact that the Krakouer family who lived there were relatives of Jean Smith, Molly Krakouer being her niece. Molly was married to Alf, and together they had seven children. They had lived and worked at Lynford Hill for a number of years and had, up to this point, never experienced anything of a paranormal nature. Healy and Cropper go on to tell us that:

POLTERGEIST PARALLELS AND CONTAGION

... the Krakouers became involved in the mysterious events right from the beginning: frequently visiting the polt-plagued dwelling and even staying overnight to provide comfort and support. Their acts of kindness, however, landed them in a weird world of trouble: the polt evidently took a shine to them, and followed them home.

'Stage One' contagion springs to mind.

As with the Smiths' poltergeist, the Lynford Hill occurrences mainly entailed stone throwing, although at the Smith's residence, a range of *other* poltergeist phenomena was documented, too, such as apports, where objects seemingly appear from nowhere, and, more interestingly, matter through matter penetration. It was witnessed and reported that hundreds of stones fell at the Krakouer house – again, with diligent attempts to find fraud or vandals meeting no success. Healy and Cropper then make a significant statement: they add that 'it is important to note that the polt didn't cease its activities at "Keninup" during that time; *stones fell simultaneously on both properties*' (Healy and Cropper's italics). This is significant in the respect that when one becomes a victim of poltergeist-contagion; the phenomena at the 'primary infestation site' always seem to remain ongoing and 'active'. The Smith's poltergeist had clearly initiated the contagion process.

Another interesting aspect of this case is in relation to the poltergeist focus. At Keninup, the focus was clearly Jean. However, it is reported that the poltergeist seemed to latch on to *another* focus, namely Alf and Molly's daughter – Audrey – who was fourteen years of age at the time. It seems that wherever she went inside the house, stones would fall about her, which Audrey thought was 'quite funny.' Switching focus? Contagion perhaps from the Smith poltergeist? Or another poltergeist entirely? Your guess is as good as mine, but, based on what we have gleaned from other historic cases, I'd put my money on 'poltergeist infection'.

Many more poltergeist events occurred at the Krakouer house, including, yet again, another example of a witness actually 'watching' a rather large stone materialising in mid-air – slowly – before falling onto the roof of the house. After an attempt at an exorcism of sorts, which was carried out by two Aboriginal shamans, who believed the activity was down to an evil spirit called the *Jannick*, the poltergeist departed the Smith and Krakouer dwellings, and was said to take up residence elsewhere – but *only* after the Krakouers and the Smiths packed up and left in an effort to flee it – the Smiths were first to depart the area in

1956, then the Krakouers the following year in 1957; they had simply had enough. However, it is reported that for many years after – and even to this day – the poltergeist has made its presence known by throwing a stone here, and a rock there, continuing to display its amazing ability and letting these families know that they can run, but they can't hide!

So, what happened *after* the poltergeist departed to pastures new? Well, that would be telling, but rest assured it was certainly not the end of the story. I think it is only fair, at this point, to suggest to the reader that they should purchase the books that detail this extraordinary case to find out more –as previously mentioned, it is only briefly told here. I have reported what I feel to be the best examples of contagion in this particular 'infestation', and hope the reader will agree that it is a truly outstanding case that highlights just how versatile the poltergeist can be; and, like the other examples recorded in this chapter, it also demonstrates how easily and effectively the poltergeist can reach out and infect others should it wish to do so. The last words I will leave to Healy and Cropper when they state: 'the polt (or polts) latched on to several different people, most of whom were extremely unhappy to have been chosen'.

The Case of Caressa, Australia, 1992-1997

Staying in Australia and keeping with the excellent work of Healy and Cropper, I shall now take a look at another fascinating poltergeist case that displays an example or two of contagion, albeit nowhere near as much as in the Mayanup case, or indeed other cases cited herein, but worth mentioning nonetheless. The case was originally investigated and documented by Ken Llewelyn, a former Royal Australian Air Force (RAAF) Reserve Wing Commander, who contacted Tony Healy and Paul Cropper in relation to another case entirely, that of the very famous Humpty Doo Poltergeist in 1998; Llewelyn had wanted to compare notes. During the discussions, mention was made of another case that was being looked into by Llewelyn: that of an Australian prostitute going by the name of Caressa. Strange events, centred on her, had been ongoing for a number of years, and Llewelyn had collated a dossier on them. His meticulous work was eventually published under the title *Caressa – From Call Girl to God's Child*, which Healy and Cropper endorse as being 'one of the best books about Australian poltergeists'.

For Caressa (real name Liz Fleming), the poltergeist began to make its presence known to her in 1992 when she began to work at a 'legal brothel', a place which, by all accounts, was *already* subject to events of paranormal activity, with poltergeist-like phenomena being frequently reported. That said, upon Caressa's arrival, the 'weirdness rating', as Healy and Cropper put it, was said have 'shot right through the roof, and it soon became clear to her employees and workmates that the polt(s) found her presence very stimulating.' Objects would fly around the brothel, with many of them falling at Caressa's feet, something that scared the other 'working girls' to a high degree, but, to Caressa, it all seemed to be water off a duck's back, as she found the episodes 'very entertaining'.

If there were any doubt that Caressa *was* indeed the focus of the poltergeist, then they were to be quickly removed after she relocated to another brothel, as the anomalous phenomena accompanied her. However, after a short while she was asked to leave. Caressa had taken to 'encouraging' the poltergeist by getting it to perform tricks on demand – which, as extraordinary as it sounds, is something that some *other* poltergeists that are said to have a 'rudimentary intelligence', have been reported to do; the Cardiff Poltergeist being a prime example, as we have previously seen.

After a while, the poltergeist began to demonstrate more examples of intelligence by leaving messages and scrawling writing – this is a classic poltergeist idiosyncrasy with instances coming from cases such as Borley Rectory, Wycliffe Road in Battersea, South Shields, Enfield, and in the Matthew Manning case. In Caressa's case the messages began when a red lipstick was left out on her dressing room table at the brothel after a medium, whom she had enlisted for help, suggested she try to communicate with it. After a while, the words 'I love you, Liz' appeared on her dressing table mirror. Alongside the message was a drawing of a heart with an arrow through it. More messages followed, but, to confuse matters, they all come from seemingly different entities.

The poltergeist wasn't just playful: like most poltergeist cases, they can be extremely vicious, nasty, and downright malevolent and the Caressa poltergeist was no different. Healy and Cropper state, (p.103) that 'loud rapping shook the walls, a large mattress hit Liz in the face, knocking her to the floor; vases of flowers were thrown around, narrowly missing people, and a male prostitute was pummelled and thrown against a wall by an invisible assailant', an all too familiar aspect of these terrifying encounters. Eventually, she began working from home, and the activity continued, with stones and potatoes being hurled around as well as other poltergeist peculiarities being reported.

In 1994, the medium that Caressa had employed for help then put her in touch with the aforementioned Ken Llewelyn, who took on the case.

At first, he was rather sceptical, but then he began to engage in discussions with many others who had also witnessed the wondrous activity. He became completely convinced when he experienced the poltergeist for himself. One of the most impressive feats was when one of Caressa's clients turned up at her house. As it transpired, he had unintentionally locked his car keys *inside* his car, whereupon Caressa asked the poltergeist to retrieve them. Out of the blue, and in an instant, they dropped out of nowhere onto the floor!

The contagion events of this case came when a friend of Caressa's, Tereza, experienced a few incidents of poltergeist activity *away* from Caressa, after expressing disapproval of what was going on. She'd reportedly experienced some mysterious 'electrical malfunctions' in her car, and also at home. During a telephone call [by Tereza] to Caressa, a vase was also said to have smashed into smithereens when nobody was anywhere near it. Make of this what you will. The case of Caressa was yet another truly extraordinary and well documented account of a poltergeist, being well researched and investigated. During his two and a half years of knowing Caressa (or Liz), Llewelyn never saw anything of an untoward nature that might have indicated any hoaxing or trickery.

Once again, I would recommend the dedicated researcher that has a desire to learn more about poltergeists to refer to Ken's book, or indeed consult the write up in Healy and Croppers thorough investigations into Australian poltergeists – you will not be disappointed.

The Olive Hill Poltergeist, Kentucky, USA, 1968

A very detailed account of a poltergeist haunting is reported in William Roll's book *The Poltergeist* (1972). It occurred in an area known as Olive Hill, Kentucky, in the USA, and it is yet another striking example of how the poltergeist (or 'demon', as it was referred to by Jehovah's Witnesses who experienced some of the activity) can reach out and infect others closely associated with those at the 'primary infestation' site.

Roger Callihan was the son of Tommy and Helen Callihan who lived near Henderson Branch, in the Kentucky Cumberland Mountains, along with four other siblings and a teenage girl, who was an adoptee of the family. However, despite 'many other unexplained occurrences in their small and neatly furnished home' this wasn't where the disturbances began. It actually commenced in the home of Tommy's mother and father, John and Ora Callihan, an elderly couple that lived close to them. In November of 1968, it was reported that strange noises were heard by the old couple along with unexplained breakages inside the house – one in particular was a glass pane that shattered in the frame of a picture of Jesus Christ, which was hanging on their wall. Over time, Mrs Callihan is reported to have 'filled two buckets with broken glass and porcelain', along with 'four crockery lamps' being smashed to pieces by the unseen force, along with certain items of their furniture being 'turned over.'

On 23 November, they fled the house and relocated in an area known as Zimmerman Hill, a short distance away. However, it wasn't long before they realised that whatever had caused their distress at Henderson Branch had begun to make its presence known in their new home. After only a week, Mrs Callihan claimed to see the ghost of a man, and identified him as the previous occupant of the home they'd just left. He'd died five years previously. Then, the following day, things in the house began moving around on their own, with Mrs Callihan assuming that this was being perpetrated by the ghost she'd seen the day before.

On 20 November 1968 – before the elderly couple fled to Zimmerman Hill – a front-page newspaper story by George Wolfford, in the *Ashland Daily Independent*, brought the matter to the attention of the public. The article was seen by an eager-eyed aficionado of psychical research, who cut it out of the paper and sent it to the Psychical Research Foundation (PRF) – an association in the USA that was founded in 1961 and dedicated to research and education in the field of parapsychology. The late William Roll was its long serving research director.

Roll contacted Wolfford on 10 December 1968. They discussed what had been occurring at Olive Hill. Roll was pleased to learn that the activity was 'ongoing'. The next day, John P. Stump, a psychology student at North Carolina University, and an associate of the PRF, was sent to look into the case. By the time that he'd arrived at Olive Hill, there had reportedly been over ninety events, many of them, according to Roll (p.150), 'involving coffee and side tables and even heavy pieces of furniture, such as the refrigerator and kitchen table.' In typical poltergeist fashion, and very much like in my own case at South Shields, days would go by where nothing at all out of the ordinary would occur, leading the families in question to wonder if it had finally departed the premises for good, then… and without warning, it would abruptly recommence with a renewed vigour and ferocity, much to the consternation of the families, and *always* just at the point where the overwhelming sense of relief was beginning to be felt; essentially lulling its victims into a false sense of security, and always timed and executed with absolute perfection. In fact, all had been quiet for a few days when John Stump arrived, but it wasn't long before he was to witness it for himself. On the Friday night and Saturday morning after his arrival, activity resumed, with over *fifty* events being recorded.

Roll states that 'in some cases, [Stump] was in a position to satisfy himself that there was no contrivance by any of those present and that known physical forces were not involved', including the movement of two bottles and a jar as they relocated themselves a distance of two feet from standing on the sink unit to being placed *inside* the sink. On another occasion, he watched in amazement as a chair flipped over and upside down with the closest person being three feet away – again, he could find no devices or any form of trickery by those present to account for the event, and was at a loss for how this could have happened. After witnessing many more poltergeist miracles, he phoned William Roll and suggested that he come and see the activity himself. Roll agreed.

On 14 December 1968, Roll arrived at Olive Hill to a rather packed out house, with no fewer than fourteen people crammed in there to see the poltergeist at work, with only one alleged incident being reported. However, as Roll and Stump were in another room when a kitchen cabinet was heard to fall over, they decided it couldn't be classed as an objective polt-occurrence, and, as a consequence, were not satisfied with it, although it *was* added to the notes and documented nonetheless. Tommy and Helen at this point wanted to return to their home, as their children needed to go to bed before going to school the following day. Roll and Stump took the opportunity to accompany them back to their home near Henderson Branch in order to glean more information in relation to the case. After leaving Zimmerman Hill, they arrived at Tommy and Helen's house at 7.30pm, and at about 10.00pm, the children were sent to their beds. Around 10.30pm, just as the interviews were about to commence, they were all disturbed by a loud crash coming from the bedrooms. When they hurried in to see what it was, they were astonished to find a glass bowl that had been standing on a shelf, now lying on the floor in the children's room. A hairbrush was also seen and reported to have been moving on its own prior to the bowl crashing to the floor.

Helen, by all accounts, was deeply upset by these incidents, because, up to this point, it seemed that the poltergeist (or demon, as Helen was more inclined to regard it, after her conversations with the Jehovah's

Witnesses) had only been operating in the house of her husband's parents', John and Ora. But *now*, it seemed to have 'changed its stamping ground'. In fact, though, a week or so earlier, they had been disturbed on two occasions by a knocking sound, for which they could find no explanation. Although it was a little odd, they thought nothing of it at that time. Roll then witnessed an event, which convinced him that the case was most definitely worthy of 'parapsychological interest'. At the beginning of his chapter on the case (p.148), he explains that on 16 December 1968:

> I was walking behind 12-year-old Roger Callihan as he entered the kitchen of his home. When he came to the sink, he turned toward me and at that moment the kitchen table, which was on his right, jumped in the air, rotated about 45 degrees, and came to rest on the back of the chairs that stood around it, with all four legs off the floor.

Roll went on to state that he just happened to be looking directly at the young man at that particular time, and was convinced he didn't go anywhere near the table or touch it in any way. Discovering no way of how the table could have moved in a normal way, he concluded that it must have been moved in an abnormal way, as 'no one else was in the kitchen'. 'The cups and plates, which had been left on the table', Roll says, 'crashed to the floor.' Interestingly, this was a contagion event.

Other events occurred that night at Tommy and Helen's home, including another incident with a huge and heavy table weighing around sixty pounds (almost thirty kilos) being moved about and played with as though it was a Butterfly caught on a summer breeze! Roll wanted to document the movement of this table, but was stopped in his tracks by Helen, who insisted 'No, this has got to stop!' Roll explains (p.155) that Helen came to the view that 'far from being helpful, John and I were actually in some way in league with the demon and had brought it from the grandparents' home to theirs.' On 17 December 1968, Roll and Stump abandoned the investigation at the behest of Helen, and left.

After the investigators left, the activity continued, therefore, someone else now had to be blamed, or maybe *something* else. In this case it was the clothes that belonged to Roger (of all things), and they were therefore gathered up – including the clothes he was wearing at the time – and burned on a fire! It appears an exorcism of sorts took place, where this information about Rogers's clothes being the source of the trouble came to light. After the actual ritual, as is usually the case, the poltergeist ignored the ceremony and continued as before. The family then fled in desperation and went to stay with relatives in Ohio, with no details forthcoming on whether or not the poltergeist tagged along; that said, upon their eventual return, all was quiet. The Olive Hill poltergeist had burned itself out, as they normally do, but not before displaying some rather bewildering demonstrations of what is now known and clearly recognised as *contagion*.

The Olive Hill affair was a truly astonishing case of a poltergeist that highlights a number of pitfalls, which those would-be investigators may be faced with when dealing with such extraordinary circumstances. What I noticed more than anything else, however, was the fact that Roll and Stump without question, put the family first *despite* it resulting in cutting their investigation short and terminating it before the poltergeist had a chance to burn itself out. They never argued, pleaded or requested a change of heart in order to continue the investigation to further the knowledge and understanding of the poltergeist phenomenon, no – they agreed, packed and left despite this golden opportunity to potentially remain involved with an active poltergeist; that, to me speaks volumes about the integrity of the investigators and highlights something that should be utilised on every investigation, ethics.

The Midwestern (Minnesota Poltergeist), USA, Late 1960's

In February 2021, I was contacted by Randy Liebeck, an American psychical researcher, who had read the first edition of this work and was intrigued by it. Having heard about a case or two in the USA in which contagion events had been experienced, he decided to contact me. He wrote:

> There was a poltergeist case in the late 1960s in the Midwestern USA that was detailed in D. Scott Rogo's book, *The Poltergeist Experience* (pp. 186-9) and where contagion phenomena were experienced. The family was experiencing typical poltergeist activity, including noises, electrical disturbances, mysterious pools of water, and items becoming waterlogged for no apparent reason. William Roll, under the auspices of the Psychical Research Foundation (PRF), sent out an experienced field investigator to the house [author's note: name of first investigator or place not reported, but Rogo places the events in Minnesota (p. 187) for an identification purpose]. The investigator had activity follow him back home – specifically, lights turning on and off and pools of water materializing in his house. According to D. Scott Rogo, the events so

frightened the investigator that he resigned from the PRF and left the field of parapsychology completely. Roll sent out a replacement investigator, a Dr. John Artley. The family had been keeping written notes, detailing the phenomena they experienced, and Artley took possession of the packet of notes to review them. Taking them home, he left them in his car. A couple of days later he found the packet open in the car, with the contents flung about, and the contents soaking wet. He later loaned the notes to a psychiatrist who was working to counsel the family, and the night the psychiatrist brought the notes home, his two children began complaining they couldn't sleep because of rapping and knocking sounds from the attic. The PRF conducted an experiment with the notes, placing the packet in a cage of gerbils, who immediately tried to cover it with wood shavings to bury it. They repeated the experiment with a rattlesnake, which immediately oriented toward the packet with an attack posture. As a control, they repeated both tests with a dummy packet, which the gerbils and snake ignored. Rogo doesn't give a lot more detail on the case, but I think it's fascinating because specific objects/material from the original house seemed to be the vector for the 'contagion', and the effects were experienced by credible scientific researchers.

The last comment Liebeck makes here regarding the 'material from the original house' being the vector (in this case the packet of notes) is rather interesting, because the same thoughts crossed my mind when I was researching the events at Pallister Street in Jarrow. If the reader can recall, Michael and I discussed the notion of letters and other such memorabilia from serial killers radiating evil, perhaps causing some, if not all, of the phenomena that were experienced there. However, the jury, as they say, is still out on that one. After a week or so, Liebeck emailed me again:

I chatted with Bryan Williams, research director at the PRF. Unfortunately, he has no knowledge of the case other than reading about it in Scott Rogo's book, and has never heard it being discussed by anyone at the PRF since he's worked there. They don't currently have any records going back that far, as all of the PRF's and William Roll's personal files were donated to the University of West Georgia's library special archives. While information about the case *might* be in those archives, without a specific location, case name, or even year to work with there is no practical way to search the archives. I also reached out to Loyd Auerbach to see if he knows anyone who worked with PRF back in the 1960s who is still alive and might remember the case. I'm still waiting to hear back from him, but the odds are that for something that happened so long ago, without it being written up in a journal or a book (in any detail), we won't be able to track down much more info about it.

It's really a shame, as, assuming that Rogo was accurately describing the case (which I suspect he was – his reputation as a researcher is highly regarded), it seems that the case was initially well-investigated by credible, credentialed parapsychologists at PRF and those investigators personally witnessed the phenomena, which followed them home *and* into the lab. The case seems to have profound implications for the study of poltergeists and seriously strains the limits of the traditional RSPK hypothesis. It seems really strange that the case was never written up in the PRF's journal or any of William Roll's (or any of the other PRF scientists') books. It almost seems like a 'cover-up' of something that didn't fit comfortably within the accepted parapsychological models. I now have a personal fascination with the case and am going to continue trying to track down more information on it. Maybe someday, after the Covid 19 crisis, I'll get down to Georgia and delve into the university library files. If I ever do get any more details I'll be sure to let you know.

This is an unfortunate case (and a good example) of how a poltergeist event can sadly be lost in the sands of time, due to a lack of documentation. Granted, as we have read, Liebeck *does* state that it is covered, only to a certain extent in D Scott Rogo's book, which I found online and purchased, in the hope it may have contained a little more detail than Randy had initially provided. Had it not been for Rogo's including the accounts of this case, and more interestingly, the alleged contagion events associated with it – however scant they may be – the complete account may well have been forgotten entirely. All we can say now at this stage, though, is that based on Rogo's fine reputation for reporting cases truthfully and diligently, it is very likely these events *did* occur, so unless any other information comes to light regarding them we can't take this any further.

The San Pedro/Weldon Poltergeist, USA, 1989-1990

For our final case study in this chapter we delve into what is possibly one of the most violent cases of a poltergeist ever recorded. In 1989, the San Pedro poltergeist was investigated by Dr. Barry E. Taff and his associate Barry Conrad. Taff is renowned for his work on violent poltergeists, but is probably most famous for his investigation into Doris Bither, a woman in her mid to late thirties living in Culver City, California in 1974. She claimed to have been repeatedly sexually assaulted by three male ghosts. She alleged that two of them held her down while a third actually raped her. The case became world famous when Hollywood portrayed the events of Taff's investigation on the big screen, in 'The Entity', starring Barbara Hershey and Ron Silver.

Randy Liebeck informed me about the contagion events of the San Pedro case while we were discussing the previously mentioned Midwestern case. He related that paranormal activity had followed Barry Conrad (and others) home after they were in contact with the poltergeist agent, and that Conrad had written a detailed and fascinating study of the case in his 2009 book *An Unknown Encounter*, and Barry Taff also had a chapter about the case in his book *Aliens Above, Ghosts Below*. In March 2021, I decided to contact Barry Taff, to see if he would tell me about his case, and, in particular, the contagion aspect in relation to it. I was quite surprised and also extremely delighted when he told me that he was more than happy to discuss his case with me for the update of this current volume. Furthermore, he told me that he would send me a complete copy of the relevant chapter from his book. He said 'it was the furthest thoughts from our minds that we would run into another case that, for most part, paralleled The Entity in almost every way.'

Taff received a telephone call in early 1989 from a woman named Susan Castenada, who claimed that her good friend, Jackie Hernandez, was being troubled by what she said were 'ghosts.' Jackie, at that time, however, was reluctant to allow investigators in, fearing they would label her as a crank; that, combined with the fact she was actually pregnant with her second child, made her think twice about outside help. It wasn't until the August of 1989 when Susan contacted Taff again to inform him that Jackie was now ready to talk about the events that were ongoing in her San Pedro home. A site visit was arranged for 8 August 1989. 'As we approached Jackie's little turn-of-the-century bungalow,' Taff stated, 'we had no way of knowing that this case would alter all our lives in ways we could never imagine.' Four individuals accompanied Taff on that first visit to San Pedro: Barry Conrad (a writer and cameraman who had been associated with Taff for quite some time), Jeff Wheatcraft (a skilled photographer, ardent sceptic and long-time friend of Conrad's), Beth Shatsky (a photo-journalist), and a colleague of hers, called Larry Brooks.

Upon entering the house, the five investigators were 'overwhelmed' by an intense putrid stench of what was described as 'decomposing organic matter' along with the 'strong sense of over-pressure'. It was like 'being at the bottom of a very deep pool.' Taff goes on by saying, 'interestingly, both of these sensations were present at the onset of The Entity investigation.' While taking their first tour of Jackie's house, they kept hearing a thumping noise, which they described as sounding like 'a two-hundred pound Rat running around in the attic'. Upon checking out the attic space, looking for what could have accounted for the noise, they found nothing. However, they would soon discover for themselves that 'something' was indeed lurking up there. Later, and from inside the dining room cupboards, a strange thick liquid with a sticky consistency was discovered and seen to seep down the walls. Samples of this gunge were collected and analysed, and it turned out to be male human blood plasma.

While all this was unfolding, Jackie told the investigators about what had been occurring in her house. She related that 'various pieces of furniture, lamps, children's toys, chairs, framed paintings, etc. were violently thrown about.' She also mentioned that 'cans of Pepsi were thrown about and were frequently hurled directly at her', and stated that 'electrical appliances behaved as if they had a mind of their own.' Jackie also reported seeing apparitions in her home, one being a 'gnarled old man' near the bathroom, and another being the figure of an old man sitting at her dining room table, which she stated she saw on a number of occasions. This sighting bears a striking similarity to an apparition seen during the Enfield poltergeist case where it, too, was seen sitting at the dining room table. Then, she informed Taff of the incident when she claimed to have almost lost her life to the poltergeist. One night, while sleeping on the living room floor with Susan, after deciding the bedrooms were far too active to get any good rest, a strange, dense cloud appeared over her and seemingly began to suffocate her. As Jackie began to choke and gasp for air, Susan awoke from her slumbers and was said to have 'observed the hovering cloud and pulled Jackie out from under it to safety'. Jackie, it seems, had good reason to call in some professional help.

Before packing up after the first visit to Jackie's home, it was suggested that Jeff Wheatcraft should venture into the attic space to take some photographs in the hope that he might be able to catch something on film. Although still quite sceptical, he readily agreed and took his camera out of his bag and made his way to the back of the house where the small loft hatch was located. He gingerly climbed up into the dark space through the small opening. It was only a few moments later when everyone heard a tremendous 'thump' before Wheatcraft made a rather sharp exit; upon his arrival back in the living room, trembling and shaking, he informed all present of what had occurred up there. He went on to tell his fellow investigators that an invisible force grabbed his camera while he was in the process of shooting, and it had been wrenched from his grip in a most violent manner.

Not wanting to leave his camera up in the attic after fleeing the scene, the intrepid investigators ventured up there to retrieve it. When they did eventually locate the camera, they found much to their surprise, that it was in two pieces on opposite sides of the attic, some sixteen feet apart. One part – the body of the camera – was tucked away in a box with the lens being placed upon the floor; both parts were undamaged. But how did the two pieces become detached? While searching the attic space in the hope of determining what may have been up there, Wheatcraft was then pushed by what seemed to be an invisible hand, which resulted in him needing immediate medical attention. Conrad was close by and watched in horror as Wheatcraft seemed to be launched into the darkness, with no natural reason to account for it. At this point, they decided to call it a night. By the time they had packed up and recuperated from their experiences, things had settled down.

A few weeks elapsed and, on 4 September 1989, Conrad, Wheatcraft and a photographer's assistant named Gary Boehm arrived at the house after being telephoned by Jackie, because the activity she was experiencing was becoming too much. Taff was unavailable due to family commitments. During this visit, Wheatcraft suffered yet another terrifying attack when he ventured into the attic. Taff writes in his book:

> Wheatcraft was walking towards the crawl space where Gary was about to descend, when suddenly he felt a restriction around his neck pulling him up and to his left. As the force tightened its grasp around Wheatcraft's neck, he let out a loud yell or moan that alerted Gary to his plight. Apparently, something had wrapped a plastic clothesline around Wheatcraft's neck, severely tightened it and pulled him over a large nail extending away from the rafter in the attic's ceiling. The force behind the attempted hanging threw Wheatcraft's glasses off, sent him into momentary shock and rendered him unconscious.

After that night, Wheatcraft never returned to the San Pedro house, but, as we shall soon see, the entity wasn't quite finished with him. He was to suffer yet another attack during the 'contagion events' that subsequently occurred at the apartment of Barry Conrad. These remarkable contagion events have to be seen to be believed. Fortunately, a lot of the activity at Conrad's home was recorded, and is available to see on a special DVD documentary made about the case by Conrad himself, who was, in fact, a TV producer and cameraman. It's now available on YouTube.

Several more months of poltergeist hell was endured by Jackie before she decided that enough was enough. She packed up her things, and moved away from San Pedro in the hope of fleeing this vicious entity for good. In October 1989 she relocated to Weldon, in Kern County, California, where she set up home in a small trailer park some 380 miles north of LA. Not long after her arrival, 'scratching' noises were heard coming from the shed behind the new abode, followed by the sighting of a ghost on a large TV screen that was being moved from the shed, into her home. The TV set was unplugged at the time, and three people can testify to seeing the apparitional 'head' appear in the top left of the screen. Jackie then contacted Taff yet again, and pleaded for more help. The poltergeist has followed her.

On 13 April 1990, Conrad and Wheatcraft travelled the 380 miles to visit Jackie in the hope they could help. What was Jeff thinking? Had he not had enough of the poltergeist already? No, he was under the impression that for some reason because the location had changed, he would now remain unharmed by the poltergeist; besides, he wanted to 'see it through' and help Jackie with her ongoing psychic disturbances. You have to give him credit for that. During an experiment at Jackie's new home, he was launched into the air yet again, only this time from a chair he was sitting down in, up against a wall yet again knocking him unconscious! Taff writes:

> The stunned group watched in horror as the event, lasting all of one second, resulted in Wheatcraft lying motionless on the floor like a broken ragdoll. Given the amount of force demonstrated, Conrad was actually concerned that Wheatcraft might be dead. Fortunately, he wasn't.

On occasions, in an attempt to get respite from the poltergeist, Jackie would return to San Pedro with her children to visit family and friends.

She would stay in a motel during her visits. But on one occasion, after returning to it after a night out, she was disturbed to find bright red writing all over her room. Words such as 'mad' and 'angry' were scrawled across the walls in marker pen. After reporting this to the motel owner, he asked Jackie to leave. In July 1990, realising she couldn't escape the poltergeist, and knowing her friends and family were all based in San Pedro, she moved back there and found herself a little house less than a mile from her original home. Poltergeist activity continued there, with objects and suchlike being continually thrown around for many months, much to Jackie's dismay.

It was at this point in the investigation where Taff says, 'the case took on a stranger turn.' Unexplained things happened in Barry Conrad's home in Studio City, which Jackie had visited on a number of occasions. Each time she departed, violent activity would erupt. For example, the large gas stove in Conrad's kitchen would often be found to be on, with its large blue flames burning furiously. On one occasion, a piece of paper and a pen were left on a worktop near this kitchen stove in an effort to communicate with the poltergeist. The investigators hoped that it might write messages for them as many poltergeists often do. It was left alone for a while, but, on their return to the kitchen, they found the piece of paper on fire and the gas stove alight. On one of the many other occasions when the stove turned on and ignited by itself, the researchers were actually being interviewed by a film crew from Fox TV about the poltergeist that they were currently experiencing, leaving yet more bewildered witnesses and adding more testimony to the poltergeist phenomenon.

Further events occurred; harrowingly, a box of live bullets that Conrad had stored away safely in his closet, crashed down upon the stove, whereupon the stove 'spontaneously erupted'. Had the investigators not been there to remove the bullets, goodness knows what may have happened. Furniture in Conrad's apartment began moving around on its own, a small bottle was seen moving slowly through the air, and Conrad's cordless telephone was found to be relocated, being placed precariously on top of a lampshade. Various items in the fridge were turned upside down, windows in his apartment exploded sending shards of glass everywhere, and a large pair of scissors was said to have started moving around the apartment, always ending up on Conrad's pillow on his bed. One time, the scissors actually began cutting into his pillow, inches away from his resting head while he was asleep.

Taff suggests that it may have been some sort of residual PK left over somehow from when Jackie's visited; however on other occasions and without visits from Jackie, Conrad suffered yet more contagion at his home, leaving the investigators perplexed as to how this could have happened. Taff, however, states quite categorically, 'I don't believe for one second that a ghost or discarnate intelligence followed Conrad back to his apartment to wreak havoc. It is far more likely that these occurrences were the result of some aspect of psychokinetic activity.' A theory of Taff's is very similar to what we have suggested earlier in this work: he states that PK:

> ... has a quasi-biological nature associated with it, sort of like when you have a bad cold or the flu. When you go over to a friend's house you unwittingly deposit a considerable amount of your airborne bacteria or virus into your friend's environment, and, even though you eventually leave, your friend can get ill from what you have left behind. As Conrad did have physical contact with Jackie, this might account for the paranormal contagion.

Taff refers to this as a 'psycho-virus', which in effect *is* poltergeist contagion. If true, this case has the most remarkable and intense examples of poltergeist-infection that I have ever heard about. If one were not aware of Jackie's plight, it would be easy to think that Conrad was the actual focus, given the amount of activity that occurred at his home. I shall, however, leave the closing words to Barry Taff as he discusses the contagion events in this remarkable case:

> These psychokinetic outbreaks resulted in frantic phone calls from Conrad to me at about 1 a.m. It's one thing to go out to someone else's home to investigate these strange occurrences, it's another to come back home, to a supposedly safe and secure environment, and discover that you have brought the phenomena home with you.

In the end, what I have aimed to achieve here, is to highlight *other* poltergeists cases that demonstrate instances of 'contagion at work', or at least to have shown to a certain degree, that 'contagion' does indeed occur. It is an aspect of the poltergeist that warrants further study. However, these examples may only be the tip of the iceberg, as, throughout history, many poltergeist cases have been reported and documented. One wonders just how many other cases have, hitherto, displayed acts of contagion but was barely even noticed, documented, or even ignored completely? Maybe, due to investigators focusing *solely* on the events at the 'primary infestation' site? SPR Council member John Fraser makes an observation in his recent book (2020), *Poltergeist, A new Investigation into Destructive Haunting*. On page 94, he writes:

> So when it comes to the poltergeist, it starts to seem that the syndrome could well turn out to be a tree with many roots. Some of the roots, such as JOTTs [one-off or occasional incidents, such as objects disappearing from a place and later being found there again], might not even be identified, with this particular root brushed aside as we try to rationalise "irrational" events in our busy and rather unspiritual modern lives. Other roots are simply ignored, as the language of differing cultures makes them seem beyond even an open-minded investigators' "boggle threshold." To understand the true nature of the "tree" it is first surely necessary to understand some of these roots far more deeply.

Could the act of poltergeist contagion, then – albeit passive or active – be considered as *another* of the tree's roots? A root that has been 'brushed aside', ignored, or should I use the term 'seldom discussed?' Yes, I feel it could be. My hope is that this work will encourage others to contemplate poltergeist contagion, in the hope that one day further studies will be made where more data can be gathered in order to build a bigger picture of this undeniable aspect of poltergeistry. Hopefully, over time, we'll better understand the extent and nature of contagion. I would like to think this work at least makes a start.

22

A UNIVERSAL POLTERGEIST?

Essentially, Darren and Michael are putting forward a *hypothesis* for discussion: that poltergeists may not be individual entities, living independently of each other, but rather, a 'hive-mind' or 'collective', which to all intents and purposes is one *arch-poltergeist*. Each aspect of the supreme poltergeist may just possibly enjoy a degree of 'independence', although it likely doesn't. Each individual poltergeist, we would suggest, may merely be a tentacle stretching out from the centre and carrying with it all the traits and characteristics of the parent body. The 'collective poltergeist' theory *may* also explain the number of astonishing coincidences and parallels found in a multitude of separate cases. Why? Because if there is in reality, only one universal poltergeist then the very same consciousness and personality must be the prime motivator in each instance.

This could explain why the South Shields poltergeist chose to balance a bottle of mineral water at a weird angle on a table, and the Newcastle poltergeist did exactly the same. Likewise, the South Shields poltergeist repeatedly took mobile phones from the ground floor of the house and placed them in a bedroom on the first floor. The Jarrow poltergeist did the same. Indeed, Darren and Michael are not the *first* researchers to point out such similarities between cases. In Alan Gauld and Tony

Cornell's book *Poltergeists*, mention is made (pp. 167-70) of two cases, one in Rerrick, Scotland, in 1695, known as 'the Ringcroft poltergeist', and the other in Naples, Italy, in 1696-97. The similarities and coincidences between the two cases led Gauld to state the following:

> It can, I think, hardly be denied that there are somewhat striking similarities between these two cases. It is almost as though the same demon, having completed his commission in Rerrick, and improved his skills in the process, then undertook a fresh assignment in Italy.

If – in my opinion – there is another suggestion that more than one poltergeist could be one and the same documented elsewhere, then surely this is it? Although Gauld does state there *are* a couple differences between the cases (no poltergeist outbreaks are ever *exactly* the same), it is hard not to come to the somewhat tantalising conclusion that these two poltergeists may very well have been simply one.

In their first book, *The South Shields Poltergeist*, Darren and Michael said they were at times puzzled by the fact that the personality behind the poltergeist seemed to mimic or parallel the personality of its host. On other occasions it would display character traits that were markedly different from those of the host. Their belief was that whenever the poltergeist took up residence in a human being, a fusion might have taken place between the poltergeist and human personality. Sometimes we might have been seeing the true poltergeist, and, at others, glimmers of the host's character shining through.

It must be pointed out, here, that Darren and Michael accept that these theories and ideas may not necessarily all gel together or blend consistently. There may be times when, in their offering of hypotheses, a number of statements seem to be inconsistent. There is a reason for this. They believe that their concept of an arch-poltergeist is a relatively new one, or at least has not been examined previously in any depth. We don't claim to have all the answers, or *any* of them for that matter. They simply wish to throw open to debate a series of crucially important questions regarding the poltergeist enigma, and to suggest, tentatively, some possible solutions. Their desire is that other investigators will go on to fine-tune these solutions, minimise or remove any inconsistencies and ultimately further our knowledge of a truly baffling and terrifying phenomenon. Having had first-hand experience in dealing with a truly vicious poltergeist at South Shields, and an abundance of others subsequently, which were not quite so bad, but still incredibly frightening to the witnesses, they feel they deserve the right to pose such questions.

Darren and Michael don't necessarily agree on all aspects of the very source of the poltergeist phenomenon, although they do agree to a large degree on the way the phenomenon presents itself. One question concerns the 'hive mind' concept. Whilst accepting that the presentation of the phenomenon sits well with the hive-mind notion, Michael now believes that there *may* be another explanation. As the final draft of the first edition of this manuscript was being prepared, Michael underwent a dramatic and radical change. Through an extraordinary set of circumstances, which intruded upon both his personal and professional lives, he was led to make a conversion to Islam. Islam is a spiritual path that is grossly misunderstood by those outside its provinces, but there is one doctrine that sits at the heart of the faith, which is hardly understood at all: a belief in what Muslims call the *Al Ghayb* or 'Unseen World.' This work, however, is not the arena in which to discuss this concept in any detail; however, the *Al Ghayb* – which Michael has now come to embrace – provides a *possible* alternative to the hive-mind theory.

The hive-mind theory was applied to the poltergeist phenomenon primarily for one reason: the uncanny number of parallels that seem to present themselves in cases all over the globe, leading us to conclude that poltergeists may simply be aspects of an arch-personality or 'super-polt.' However, in Islam it is generally believed that the majority of paranormal phenomena – if not all of them – are the handiwork of a race of spirit-beings known as the Jinn. The Jinn, in Islamic history and theology, are believed to be a race of creatures created by God after the angels but before human beings. The Jinn inhabit an alternative dimension and are usually not supposed to 'slip through' into the human world. However, as the large majority of Jinn are rebellious, mischievous and even malevolent, they disobey this command.

The leader of the Jinn is *Shaitan* – the Islamic equivalent of Satan. However, whereas in Christian theology, Satan is said to be a 'fallen angel', in Islam he is not an angel but one of the Jinn. Shaitan, Muslims believe, acts like a supreme commander over his army of Jinn, and issues them with detailed and precise instructions as to what he requires of them. All of the Jinn – with the exception of the minority of righteous ones, who still follow God – act in a nigh-identical manner to each other, not because they are part of a hive-mind, but because they obediently follow the operations manual of their malign leader. The instance, in which Jesus – or Issa, as Muslims call him – spoke in both the singular and the plural to the 'devils' that possessed a man, is also explicable within the confines of Islamic belief. Although Darren and Michael have discussed at length the *possibility* of the Jinn being an explanation for poltergeist phenomena as we know it, and indeed other forms of paranormal phenomena (e.g. UFOs and cryptids), Darren is somewhat reluctant to accept the idea, although he remains open-minded to the possibility. The thought occurs to Darren that the Jinn could simply be nothing more than the Islamic *interpretation* or perspective of a set of 'symptoms' and characteristics that currently defy all the known physical laws.

When Westerners experience these same symptoms, they are identified and labelled as a poltergeist; very much like John Fraser's suggestion (in his fascinating book, *Poltergeist! A New Investigation into Destructive Haunting*) that the Romanian and other European and Eastern European accounts of vampirism could in fact be poltergeists – albeit cloaked in Eastern European interpretations and perspectives based on their old folkloric and traditional beliefs.

So, what – if anything – can be learnt from all of this? What can be deduced or what observations can be made? Only more questions are ultimately raised; for example, as *most* cases that *seem* to feature instances of contagion are the 'prolonged infestations' that also just happen to be the incredibly *responsive* poltergeists (Cardiff, Hertfordshire, Battersea, South Shields, Enfield etc.), does the poltergeist need 'time' and a certain level of independence before it is able to reach out and infect? Indeed, why, in some cases, do poltergeists last far longer than others?

This, in turn, raises a further question. Bearing in mind, of course, that in this study we are looking at 'person-centred' cases and not 'place-centred' cases, are the *duration* of the infestation and the *intensity* of the phenomena, dependent on the 'mind-set' of the focal person? Each poltergeist focus differs in the respect of his or her stress 'trigger', the level of actual stress itself, and the person's coping mechanisms (or lack of them), so could this be why the duration and intensity of poltergeist phenomena differ from case to case? Can a poltergeist also 'switch' focus, creating the illusion of a contagion effect – creating mayhem at a new place before returning to its original focus at the 'primary infestation' site?

In relation to the Poona Poltergeist in India in 1927-1930, Alan Gauld states in *Poltergeists:* 'it is not clear whether we have one poltergeist case with *two* (authors' italics) agents or two poltergeist cases which happened to occur in the same family. I shall treat it as one case.' This is an interesting and 'telling' comment that *may* be indicative of poltergeists being able to switch from focus to focus; this, along with the account of the Mayanup case in Australia, where the poltergeist seemed to do the same, is interesting food for thought. There are so many questions, of course, with so much research, observation and study *yet* to be undertaken.

Hopefully, the fact that Darren and Michael admit to favouring different ideas about what's behind poltergeistry should make it clear that they are not united in pursuing a hidden agenda, and have no axe to grind. The poltergeist phenomenon remains one of the world's frightening and bewildering mysteries, and *nobody* yet has all the answers.

23

A FINAL THOUGHT

RSPK (recurrent spontaneous psychokinesis) is an inspired suggestion for a potential cause for poltergeist activity. The term was first coined by the American psychical researcher William G Roll in 1958 while writing a paper detailing an investigation he was carrying out at the time into the Seaford poltergeist on Long Island, New York, USA. RSPK, in a nutshell, is the alleged ability to manipulate inanimate objects subconsciously by utilising the mind to move them around, often in a violent and destructive manner; these objects could be anything as small as a coin, to something as big as household furniture; and anything in between. In line with this view, it is often assumed that focal persons are frustrated, troubled or suffering angst in some way, and, because they can't 'vent' their feelings in a normal way, they bottle them up, creating yet more frustration. Like a kettle letting off its steam, this pent up angst is then somehow released and externalised into the environment in the form of RSPK (what I have often called 'a psychic temper tantrum').

One thing I have noticed is that characteristics such as immorality, maliciousness, spite, being heartless, unkind, vindictive, aggressive, destructive and taking great pleasure in creating abject misery for others, whether consciously or unconsciously, are idiosyncrasies and traits, which both human beings and the poltergeist most certainly share. All people, every last one of us, regardless of how good we think we are, whether we like it or not, are more than capable of carrying out despicable deeds and acting in a conniving, selfish way; most of us choose not to, but it is there, lurking… within us. Whether we accept it or not, we all have a dark side and we all have terrible thoughts at times. Some people act upon their thoughts and cruel desires for no good reason other than to 'get at' or hurt someone else… does it all sound familiar?

Maybe this suggests in some way that the poltergeist does indeed come from within a person, after all? Could it be our way of expressing what is essentially the darker side of our true nature? It could explain why the poltergeist is almost always destructive. If poltergeist activity really is externalised RSPK, then the aforementioned negative traits could account for *why* poltergeist activity tends to be of a persecutory nature. Very rarely does a poltergeist do worthwhile things, although granted, on occasions, they have been known to do so. But that may be simply because there is also 'good' in everyone, and there is usually an exception or two to the rule, is there not? However, in most instances and for reasons unknown, their perplexing acts consist of general destruction and total chaos that instils fear, subsequently generating unrest within the family unit in which they materialise and erupt.

This is where it might get controversial. Humans, as a whole, are fundamentally bad if one is to be honest with oneself and look at things as they really are. To be good, we have to teach our children and instil in them right from wrong. We have to separate good from evil, while simultaneously we have to encourage and constantly tell ourselves and others to live worthwhile lives and be generally 'good' in nature. Please read the following carefully and consider this for a moment: Let's say, for example, that when a child is born, other than feeding, clothing, and sheltering him or her, the parents provide no guidance or discipline. How will that child grow and develop? We have all seen and have heard of what we call the 'terrible twos', where toddlers at around this age become more than a handful, shall we say, relentlessly throwing pretty impressive tantrums because they either 'want' or 'don't get' something, or maybe because they are encouraged to share something like a toy or a piece of chocolate. Young children find it very difficult to share if they are not taught how to, or even forced into it. Therefore, in my opinion, they must be all *naturally* greedy and selfish. That is, until it is taken out of them in the form or constant and relentless dictation

A FINAL THOUGHT

from their parents or guardians. In this respect, if children were left to their own devices, they would act as nature 'really' intended – in an uncivilised way! Of course, as mentioned, there's always 'the exception to the rule', and possibly there are some people who grow up in the aforementioned way and yet behave in a decent, moral and reasonable manner, but not many would, I expect.

This is one link/parallel between people and poltergeists that I feel is worth taking note of and I cannot think of a better example or, indeed, any other reason why a poltergeist may be linked with, or be generated by, a human being. Perhaps 'we' are that mischievous destructive force after all, consciously *and* subconsciously? Is the poltergeist really a manifestation of our true supressed nature? If that's one day proven to be the case, and if the RSPK theory becomes universally accepted, the poltergeist will ultimately be seen as a natural phenomenon rather than something supernatural or paranormal. Then, it stands to reason, our laws of physics will have to be revised.

Of course, those who favour the discarnate entity or 'noisy ghost' theory may fiercely dispute these ideas. On a personal level, I had always been very much undecided on the nature of the poltergeist until Michael and I investigated the case at South Shields. Seeing how things developed did make us lean slightly toward the 'discarnate entity' theory. I'm quite certain, however, that the South Shields poltergeist was unlikely to have been Satan's right hand man stationed on our plane, sent up from the depths of hell to wreak havoc and create pandemonium. So, if it was a responsive, intelligent and invisible entity, as the evidence clearly suggested, then the question must be asked: where else could it have come from?

After seeing aspects of Marc's personality emerging during the poltergeist's progression and development, the thought occurred that maybe a poltergeist personality could develop from within its focus, honing its skills before subsequently detaching itself – perhaps when the time was right – thus becoming fully independent with free rein. This was a thought first suggested by D. Scott Rogo and, to a certain degree, by Nandor Fodor many decades ago. Perhaps it may occur in every poltergeist case, or, at least, in the cases that last long enough for the entity to develop to its full potential? The South Shields poltergeist certainly illustrated that this could indeed be a distinct possibility. But then, of course, there is the arch-polt theory that is put forward in this book, drawing on the staggering number of striking coincidences and parallels between many, if not all poltergeist cases.

Rogo states (*The Poltergeist Experience*, p.88): 'those that believe the poltergeist is merely the projections of a frustrated adolescent are severely underestimating the poltergeist and its powers. It may be that there are different types of poltergeists, which we classify together merely because they share common characteristics.' This is indeed a thought-provoking suggestion, which could perhaps explain the differences between some cases, such as their different duration or intensity. It could also have a bearing on whether or not physical attack occurs, or perhaps whether or not there are outbreaks of fire. Could *one* arch-poltergeist still be responsible, then? Maybe. It's entirely possible that the postulated theoretical 'parent body' or 'hive mind' could be manifesting phenomena in a way that gives a false impression of 'multiple-type poltergeists'.

On page 231 of his book, Rogo seems to nail his flag to the mast, taking further what he suggested on page 88. He suggests there are two basic types of poltergeist'. 'Type one' is the 'adolescent poltergeist', where the activity is strictly limited to milder forms of basic PK in the vicinity of the alleged focus, such as the movement of objects and slamming of doors, suggesting that these poltergeists are 'devoid of sophisticated intelligence', with their behaviour being 'rather childish'. A 'type two' poltergeist (which he also refers to as an 'entity poltergeist') comes over as quite intelligent, by displaying 'some level of external will' such as communication and personal attacks.

However, could it not be that the type one poltergeist that Rogo refers to, when born to its existence, simply learns and develops before becoming a type two poltergeist, a bit like how a child grows and develops into an adult? The bottom line is we just don't know for certain what a poltergeist is, how many types there may be, or what causes them to happen; I personally think there is evidence to suggest it could be *any* of the above, even a combination maybe, or perhaps it is something we are yet to consider?

What I *can* say with conviction, however, is what the *true* poltergeist most certainly isn't: it isn't all false memory, influenced thinking, elaboration, or misattribution. Nor is the *true* poltergeist invented, exaggerated, or blatantly lied about; it is also not hallucination, wishful thinking, or monumental collaboration. Do these closed-minded claptrap spouting super-sceptics that exhibit a complete arrogance along with their blatant superiority complex, seriously entertain the notion that for centuries, the thousands of documented poltergeist outbreaks – every last one – from all over the world, have all been mistakenly attributed as being something of interest simply because those that reported them were all bare-faced liars or perhaps just too plain stupid to have known any better?

Guy Lyon Playfair and Maurice Grosse, the two main investigators of the Enfield poltergeist case, faced horrendous criticisms when they presented their own findings. Writing in the *Journal of the Society for Psychical Research* in 1988, they stated:

> Criticism of single items (of evidence) can be justified in some cases, and we have always welcomed normal explanations for any of the numerous phenomena reported at Enfield by ourselves or by others. The outright rejection of collective evidence, however, is inexcusable.

Playfair and Grosse went on to say, rather prophetically:

> ... we wish future investigators of such cases the best of luck, which they will need. They must be warned what to expect. They will find that whatever evidence of any kind they manage to record, they will be told it is either inadequate or suspect.

Personally, I find this an insult to any victim of the true poltergeist, and there are many. It is also an insult to those dedicated parapsychologists and seasoned researchers who – from the outset of organised psychical research, to this very day – have spent their entire lives giving up their time, and no doubt their money, too, trying honestly and passionately to demonstrate the reality of the phenomenon, or at least attempting to ascertain evidence to perhaps *support* the notion. D. Scott Rogo (1974), discussing the psychology behind people's reactions to poltergeist phenomena, stated:

> The majority of individuals who find themselves in psi situations have a different set of psychological reactions to them – they fear them, try to deny them, rationalise them, feel anxiety over them.

This could also be said to apply to *some* researchers who have set out to deliberately debunk the poltergeist phenomenon, despite being confronted with positive and compelling evidence of its authenticity. That said, we must bear in mind that there are some folk out there who will persistently argue the world is flat!

Early on in this book, it was stated that:

Darren and Michael have learned many lessons from their experience during the South Shields investigation. They have learned that human nature can, when plunged into the correct set of circumstances, be every bit as dark and untrustworthy as the poltergeist itself. They are now less trusting of those they meet in their professional lives and see the society they are part of in a far less favourable light.

We said this for a reason, and I personally still think it today: not only did we see the true, dark and malevolent nature of the poltergeist, whatever it is and wherever it comes from, we also witnessed, first-hand, the true dark and spiteful side of human nature during the course of the investigation, and after it; and, to be quite honest, there wasn't much difference between the two.

However, regarding the RSPK theory, the American parapsychologist and poltergeist researcher, L. Stafford Betty (1984) stated:

> Nowadays, we place less than complete confidence in this still very respectable hypothesis, for we are turning up many cases, which don't centre on adolescents, and, more importantly, some which centre on no identifiable living agent at all. As a result, the age-old discarnate entity hypothesis and the related deceased person hypothesis are today making something of a comeback.

So, whatever lies at the very heart of the enigma – RSPK, the spirit of an angry deceased person, a hive-mind collective, individual entity, or something else entirely – Darren W. Ritson and Michael J. Hallowell have no doubt or disagreement whatsoever about the important things: that the poltergeist phenomenon is real, and can spread like an insidious disease.

ABOUT THE AUTHOR

Darren W. Ritson was born in March 1972 in Newcastle-upon-Tyne (UK) and has been fascinated with the ghost and poltergeist phenomenon as far back as he can remember. His first 'real' attempts of collating and documenting accounts of alleged paranormal phenomena go way back to the early 1990s, when he regularly corresponded with UFO researcher and ghost hunter Malcolm Robinson. In later years, Darren corresponded with some of the literary greats within the paranormal field such as the late Peter Underwood, Guy Lyon Playfair, and Colin Wilson.

Darren has travelled across the UK, lecturing and speaking on the poltergeist phenomenon. He has been invited to carry out lectures to organisations such as the Society for Psychical Research (SPR) and the Ghost Club (both London-based). Further invites to lecture on the poltergeist phenomenon came from Professor Nick Neave at Northumbria University in Newcastle-upon-Tyne, where, for three years running, Darren talked to second-year psychology students as part of their parapsychology module; and the Scottish Society for Psychical Research, where he addressed over two hundred psychical researchers, parapsychologists, society members and students. His most recent invitation to lecture on the poltergeist phenomenon came in mid-2020, when he was invited to consider speaking at an upcoming conference of the SPR. Darren has been a member of the SPR since 2006.

He currently resides at Roker in Sunderland, after relocating there in 2018, and has a teenage daughter called Abbey. His other passions include: mountain climbing and fell-walking in the Lake District and Scotland; wildlife and landscape photography; and travel. He is a black belt in Judo and has trained on a number of occasions at the Kodokan International Judo Centre in Tokyo. During one of his trips to Japan, he achieved another of his many lifelong dreams and climbed Mt Fuji. Darren can be contacted on darren.ritson16@gmail.com

BIBLIOGRAPHY

Barrington, M. R. (2018). *JOTT, when things disappear... and come back or relocate – and why it really happens* (Anomalist Books).

Betty, L. S. (1984). The Kern City poltergeist: A case severely straining the living agent hypothesis, *JSPR*, Vol. 52, No. 798, p345-364.

Conrad, B. (2009). *An Unknown Encounter* (Rosedog Press).

Cooper, C. E. (2012). *Telephone Calls from the Dead* (Tricorn Books).

Fodor, N. (1958). *On the trail of the Poltergeist* (The Citadel Press, New York).

Fontana, D. (1991). A Responsive Poltergeist: a case from South Wales, JSPR, Vol 57, No 823, p385-403.

Fraser, J. (2020). *Poltergeist!: A New Investigation into Destructive Haunting* (Sixth Publishing).

Gauld, A. & Cornell, A. D. (1979). *Poltergeists* (Routledge & Keegan Paul; republished by White Crow Books, 2017).

Geller, U. & Playfair, G. L. (1986). *The Geller Effect* (Jonathan Cape).

Hack, H. (2000). *The Mystery of the Mayanup Poltergeist* (Hesperian Press).

Halliday, R. (2003). *Evil Scotland* (Fort Publishing).

Hallowell, M. J., & Ritson, D. W. (2008). *The South Shields Poltergeist: One Family's Fight against an Invisible Intruder* (The History Press).

Hallowell, M. J. & Ritson, D. W. (2011). *The Haunting of Willington Mill* (The History Press).

Healy, T. & Cropper, P. (2014). *Australian Poltergeist* (Strange Nation).

Hitchings, S. & Clark, J. (2013). *The Poltergeist Prince of London: The Remarkable True Story of the Battersea Poltergeist* (The History Press).

Holder, G. (2012). *What is a Poltergeist?* (David and Charles).

Holder, G. (2013), *Poltergeist over Scotland* (The History Press).

Llewelyn, K. (2002). *Caressa – From Call Girl to God's Child* (Sandstone Publishing, Leichardt NSW).

Murdie, A. (2010). Review of *The South Shields Poltergeist: One Family's Fight against an Invisible Intruder. JSPR*, Vol. 74.2, No. 899, p129-132.

Nisbet, B. C. (1979). A West Croydon poltergeist. *JSPR*, Vol. 50, No. 782, p229-237.

Owen, A. R. G. (1964). *Can We Explain the Poltergeist?* (New York, Garrett Publications).

Parsons, S. T. (2015). *Ghostology: The Art of the Ghost Hunter* (White Crow Books).

Parsons, S. T. (2018). *Guidance Notes for Investigators of Spontaneous Cases, Apparitions, Hauntings Poltergeists and Similar Phenomena*, New Edition (Society for Psychical Research).

Parsons, S. T. (2021). *Using Equipment: Guidance Notes for Investigators of Ghosts, Hauntings, Poltergeists and Similar Phenomena* (Society for Psychical Research).

Parsons, S. T. & Cooper, C. E. (eds) (2015). *Paracoustics: Sound & the Paranormal* (White Crow Books).

Playfair, G. L. (1980). *This House is Haunted: An investigation of the Enfield Poltergeist* (Souvenir Press).

Playfair, G. L. & Grosse, M. (1988). Enfield Revisited: The evaporation of positive evidence. *JSPR*, Vol. 55, No 813, p208-219.

Price, H. (1936). *Confessions of a Ghost Hunter* (Putnam, 1936).

Price, H. (1945). *Poltergeist over England* (Country Life Books; republished as *Poltergeist: Tales of the Supernatural*, by Bracken Books, 1993).

Ritson, D. W. (2020). *The South Shields Poltergeist: One Family's Fight against an Invisible Intruder* (The History Press).

Ritson, D. W., & Hallowell, M. J. (2014). *Contagion: In the Shadow of the South Shields Poltergeist* (Limbury Press).

Robinson, M. (2010). *Paranormal Case Files of Great Britain: Volume One* (Publish Nation).

Robinson, M. (2020). *The Sauchie Poltergeist, and other Scottish Ghostly Tales* (Publish Nation).

Rogo, D. S. (1974). Psychotherapy and the poltergeist, JSPR, Vol. 47, No. 761, p433-446.

Rogo, D. S. (1979). *The Poltergeist Experience* (Penguin Books).

Roll, W. G. (1972). *The Poltergeist* (Nelson Doubleday).

Smith, K. (1993). *Supernatural 2* (Pan Macmillan, Melbourne).

Spencer, J. & Spencer, A. (1996). *The Poltergeist Phenomenon: An investigation into Psychic Disturbance* (Headline).

Taff, B. (2011). *Aliens Above, Ghosts Below* (Lulu).

Tucker, S. D. (2020). *Blithe Spirits: An Imaginative History of the Poltergeist* (Amberley Publishing).

INDEX

A

Al Ghayb, 225
Alien Abduction Phenomenon, 43
Alone in the Dark Entertainment (AITDE), 19
Amazon Basin, 8
America, vi, 135,136
American Society for Psychical Research (ASPR), 202
Anthropomorphic figures, 49, 92, 112
Antibiotics, 12
Apparitions, xxiv, 62, 102, 107, 140,141, 144, 147, 162, 217
Arch-Poltergeist, xxvi, xxviii, 159, 185, 223,224, 232
Artley, Dr. John, 214
Arun Bank, Pulborough (Sussex), 202,203
Ashington, xviii, 124, 127, 162, 168,169, 179, 183
Ashland Daily Independent, 210
Association for the Scientific Study of Anomalous Phenomena, the; (ASSAP), 188, 195

Atchison, Texas case, 94,95
Atheism, 13
Auditory phenomena, 101
Auerbach, Loyd, 215
Avicenna, 12

B

Babylon, ancient, xix, 125
Bacteria, 11, 15, 221
Bartley, Drew, xiv, 113,114, 116
Barrington, Mary Rose, 188, 193
Battersea Poltergeist (1956), 200-201
BBC, 166
Beatles, the, 67
Bigfoot, 9
Bob Trollop's, 20
Borley Rectory, 203, 208
Bottle balance, 121
Bither, Doris, 169, 216
Betty, L. Stafford, 234
British Telecom, 189, 194
Buchlyvie Contagion, Scotland, 198
Burcombe, John, 189

C

Callihan, Tommy & Helen, 209, 211-212
Callihan, Roger, 209, 212
Campbell, Virginia, vii, 195, 197
Capitalism, 13
Carbon Footprint, 151
Cardiff Poltergeist, 193, 195, 208
Caressa (Liz Fleming), 207, 209
Christianity, xx, 58, 126, 157-158, 225
Chibbett, Harold, 201, 202
Church, Roman Catholic, xx, 126
Clark, James, 201, 202
Coincidences, poltergeist related, xxvii, 20, 24, 40, 76, 90, 95, 147, 168, 179, 224, 231
Conrad, Barry, 216, 219, 220
Contagion;
    active; 15-17, 185, 186, *passive*; xxvi, 15-17, 185, 186, stages of; 180-181
Cook, Fred & Gerry, 194
Cooper, Dr. Callum, 188, 189
Cornell, Anthony D., 224
Cottrell, Lesley., xiii
Covid 19, xv, 11, 12, 215
Cropper, Paul, 203, 209
Crystal Skulls, 135
Cynics, 2, 92, 98, 99, 169

D

Davies, Colin, 188, 189, 194
Demon Child TV programme, 92-94
Demons, xix, xx, 125, 126, 157, 159
Devil; 58, 154, 158
Discovery Channel, 92
Donald, (Battersea Poltergeist), 200-202
Dreams, 25, 41-42, 44, 48, 50, 68, 84, 101, 196, 199

E

Electrical phenomena, xvii, xviii, 9, 44, 53, 144, 151-155, 173, 209, 213, 217
Elemental spirits, xx, 129
Elves, xx, 129
Elland Road Poltergeist, 200
Enfield Poltergeist, 161-167, 189-191
Entity, the (movie), 169
Exorcism, xx, 126, 158, 206, 212

F

Fairies, xx, 129
Fircrest, Pierce County, Washington State case, 175, 177
Fleming, Alexander, 207
Fodor, Dr. Nandor, ix, 231
Fontana, Prof. David, 193, 194
Fortean Times, xxiv, xxix, 154, 174, 177
Fraser, John, viii, 222, 226
French Revolution, 200
Freud, Sigmund, xviii
Frogmore (Watford), 121, 183
Fungi, 11

G

Gartmorn Road (Scotland), 195, 198
Gauld, Dr. Alan, 223, 224, 226
Geometric patterns, 18
Ghost Club (Great Britain), 235
Ghosts, ii, viii, 7, 62, 99, 102, 104, 113, 154, 216
Gmelig-Meyling, Dono, xviii
Gnomes, xx, 129
Goblins, xx, xxi
God, gods, xxviii, 123, 158, 207, 225

INDEX

Gorner, (O' Conner) Gemma, xiv, 109, 114, 116
Greenhouse gas, 151
Green Street, North London, 189-191
Grosse, Maurice, vii, xviii, 91, 166,168, 190,191, 233

H

Hack, Helen, 204, 206
Hack, Ethel, 204, 206
Hack, Bill, 204, 206
Halliday, Ron, 196
Hallowell, Michael, viii, xiv, xv, xvii, xx, xxiii, xxix,1, 7, 234
Hallucination, 101, 139
Haunted Loom case, 71-76
Healy, Tony, 203,209
Hepatitis A, 15
Hernandez, Jackie, 216
Hertfordshire Poltergeist Case, 192-193
Hitchings, Shirley, 200,202
Hitchinson, Suzanne, 99
HIV virus, 3, 16
Hive-mind theory, 225
Hodgson, George B, 84-85
Hodgson, Peggy, 189
Hodgson, Janet, 189-191
Holder, Geoff, 78, 82, 196, 198
Holliday, (Rosie), xiv, 110-111, 116-120
Holloway Poltergeist (North London), 190
Hope, Cindy, 196, 198
Houran, James, xxx, 91
Humpty Doo Poltergeist, 207
Hypnopompic sleep state, 101
Hyslop, Professor James, xxi

I

Incubus, xii, xviii, xx, 123,127, 129, 131, 133, 135, 137, 147,148, 169, 184
India, 226
Islam, 225
Michael's conversion to, 225
Issa, 226

J

Jannick, the, 206
Jarrow Poltergeist, 223
Jehovah's Witnesses, 209
Jesus, 157,159, 184, 210, 226
Jinn, 225,226
JOTT, 188,189, 193, 222
Judaeo-Christian theology, 158
Judea, 157

K

Keninup (Australia), 204-206
Kentucky (Western Case USA), 92, 93, 95
Kentucky (Olive Hill Poltergeist), 209-213
Kiss (rock band), 147
Krakouer, Molly, 205,207
Krakouer, Alf, 205,207
Kuykendall, Courtney, 175

L

Legion, (collective noun for demons), xii, 157,159
Liebeck, Randy, x, xiii, 213,216
Lisbona, Natalie, 168
Little, Cindy, 91
Llewelyn, Ken, 207, 209
Louis XVII, 200,201
Luke, Gospel of, 158
Lynford Hill, 205, 206

M

Marc and Marianne (South Shields Poltergeist), 77, 80, 94, 152, 154, 171
Manning, Matthew, 208
Mayanup Poltergeist, 203, 204
Matthews, John & Pat, 194
Maud Street Poltergeist, 170-171
McCue, Dr. Peter A., x, xiii, xvi, xxiv, xxv, xxix, xxx
McDonald, Paul, xiv, 109
McKay, Andrea, 175
McKay, Taylor, 175
Mediums, 4, 20, 94, 103
Middlesbrough poltergeist case, 139-148
Mills, Liz, xiv, 111, 114-115
Milne, A. A., 89
Mobile phone, and anomalies, 1, 4, 13-14, 24, 53, 55-56, 76, 80-81, 162, 173, 175-177, 183, 223
Murdie, Alan, x, xiii, 91, 154

N

Naples, Italy, 224
Newcastle Keep, xiv, 109
New Dominion Pictures, 92
Nesbitt, Victoria, xiv, 71
New Testament, 157
Night terrors, 42
Nisbet, Brian C., xiv, 191
North East Ghost Research Team (NEGRT), 62, 81, 113
North Carolina University, 210

O

Offshore 44 (Pubic House), 20
Olfactory phenomena, 70
Olive Hill Poltergeist, 209-213
Olley, Darren, xiii, 89, 90, 93
Ouija Board, 51, 129, 131

P

Pallister Street, Jarrow, xiii, xiv, 23-24, 29, 32, 35, 36, 58-62, 70, 127, 214
Parallels, coincidental; significant; person specific; 181-182
Parapsychologist, vii, 91, 101, 215, 233, 235
Parsons, Steven T., ix, xiii, 102
Pete, the Poltergeist, 193-195
Physical attacks (scratches), 42, 43, 47, 50, 56, 142,-144
Pixies, 129
Playfair, Guy Lyon, vii, xiii, xviii, 63, 91, 166, 167, 190, 191, 233, 235
Pontefract (Poltergeist), xviii
Poona Poltergeist, 226
Possession, incidents of, 157, 159
Possession, symptoms of, 157, 159
Price, Harry, xiii, 63, 200, 202-203
Protozoa, 11
Psychical Research Foundation, 210, 213
Psycho-virus, 221
Puberty, relationship to poltergeist phenomenon, 52, 61, 127

Q

Quantum Physics, xxviii, xxix

R

Racism, 13
Rapping (anomalous), 31, 55, 161, 162, 199, 201, 202, 208, 214
Red House, The, 20
Roll, Dr. William G, vii, ix, xxv, xxx, 61, 209, 215, 229

Rook, Paul, xiv, 121
Rerrick Poltergeist (Ringcroft), 224
Risolino, Jo, xiv, 111
Rituals, 92, 94, 132
Ryhope case, 47
Ritson, Abbey May, 7, 34, 57, 88-89, 135, 235
Robert (South Shields Poltergeist), xvii, 14-15, 60, 63, 78-80, 88-89, 93-95
Robertson, Patricia, 103
Robinson, Malcolm, xiii, 195,196, 198,199, 235
Rogo, D. Scott, vii, 61, 213,215, 231,233
Roy, Prof. Archie, 103
Royal Australian Air Force (RAAF), 207
RSPK, 215, 229,231, 234
Rue des Noyers, xvii

S

Sallie's House case, 94
San Pedro Poltergeist (USA), xiii, 215-216, 219,
Satan, 158,159, 225, 231
Sauchie Poltergeist; Park Crescent (1960); Gartmorn Road (1986)
Seaford Poltergeist (New York), 229
Sceptics, 2, 44, 170, 201, 232
Serial killers, xxvi, xxvii, 64,65, 214
Sexually-related phenomena
Shadow man, 30, 113, 117
Shaitan, 225
Shaman, (Aboriginal), 206
Smith, Stuart and Lauren, xiv, 68, 174, 182
Smith, Gilbert, 204-205
Society for Psychical Research (SPR), Journal of, 91, 92, 193, 233, 235

Somnambulism (sleepwalking), 50
South Shields Poltergeist, ii, v, viii, xv, xvii, xxiii, xxvii,4, 7, 9, 13,14, 19,21, 40, 55, 76, 82, 84, 89,90, 92,95, 97, 121,123, 126, 168, 171, 174, 177, 185, 223,224, 231
Spencer, John & Anne, vii, 75, 190,195
Spontaneous combustion, 133, 165
Stacking phenomenon, 183
Stone Throwing (Lithobolia), 163, 194, 204-208
Strange Phenomena Investigations (SPI), 196, 198
Stump, John P., 210, 213
Succubus, xii, xix, 123, 125, 127, 129, 131, 133, 135, 137, 169, 184
Sumerians, ancient, xix, 125

T

Taff, Dr. Barry E., viii, xiii, 169, 216,221
Taylor, Steven, xiv, xviii, 19, 71, 123, 175
Telephone anomalies, 76, 136, 174, 188-189, 192, 194, 199, 220
Temperature anomalies, 73, 76, 116, 142, 143
Text messages, xxiv, 1, 173,174, 176
Trewick, Pte. Thomas, 167,168
Trigger objects, 114
Tucker, S. D., 154
TV-related phenomena, 53, 111, 153, 173

U

UFO, xxix, 44, 46, 226
Underwood, Peter, 63, 235
Universal Poltergeist, xii, 223, 225, 227
Unseen world, Islamic view of, 225

V

Vampirism (Eastern European), 226
Vipond, Fiona, 113-114
Voices, disembodied, 175

W

Watford Poltergeist, 121, 183
Wales, Cardiff Poltergeist, 193-195, 208, 226
Water-related phenomena, xviii, 78, 110, 116, 117, 119, 122, 163, 164, 183, 213, 223
Watson, Jayne, 34, 35, 83, 84
West Croydon Poltergeist, 191
Wheatcraft, Jeff, 216, 219
Wilson, Colin, xiii, xvi, xxi, 2, 63, 235
Winter, Mark, xiv, 62, 66, 113, 114
Written messages, anomalous, 165, 208, 220

Y

Yorkshire, Bed shop, 188, 192

Z

Zimmerman Hill (USA), 210-211

www.ingramcontent.com/pod-product-compliance
Lightning Source LLC
Chambersburg PA
CBHW032150080426
42735CB00008B/658